The Naked Parish Priest

The Naked Parish Priest

*What priests **really** think they're doing*

STEPHEN H. LOUDEN

and

LESLIE J. FRANCIS

continuum
LONDON • NEW YORK

Continuum

The Tower Building
11 York Road
London SE1 7NX

370 Lexington Avenue
New York
NY 10017-6503

www.continuumbooks.com

First published 2003 by Continuum

British Library Cataloguing-in-Publication Data
A catalogue record for this book is available from the British Library

ISBN 0-8264-6798-9

Typeset by Kenneth Burnley, Wirral, Cheshire
Printed and bound in Great Britain by MPG Books Ltd, Bodmin, Cornwall

Contents

Preface

This book has been written by two hands and shaped by two minds; each has made its distinctive contribution. The survey questionnaire at the heart of the book is the joint result of Monsignor Stephen H. Louden's lifelong commitment to the Catholic Church and his experience serving that Church as a priest, and of Professor Leslie J. Francis' long commitment to the scientific assessment of attitudes and values in the service of empirical theology. The findings from the survey are discussed in 22 tightly focused chapters covering issues like training for ministry, celibacy and priesthood, core doctrines of the Church, fallen priests, and clergy burnout. Stephen has provided the context for each of these issues and Leslie has interpreted the statistics. The collaboration has been enjoyable and fruitful.

We see this study as a major contribution from empirical theology to interpreting the health and potential of the Catholic priesthood in England and Wales today. Empirical theology (as established in the Catholic University of Nijmegen under the pioneering leadership of Professor Hans van der Ven, and as reinterpreted within the University of Wales by Leslie J. Francis and his colleagues) employs the techniques of the social sciences to address key issues raised by the agenda of practical theology. The issue raised by the present study concerns the nature and health of the priesthood.

Empirical theology has the capability of stripping bare the illusions and façade which the Church may wish to see and revealing the human reality within. This is no alien social scientific enterprise peering in at the Church from without. Empirical theology is able to hold up a mirror to the Church from within. Only a brave Church is willing and able to look into that mirror. Our conviction, however, is that the alternative to such bravery is foolishness.

When our questionnaire was distributed to all the Catholic priests serving in parochial ministry in England and Wales, it is rumoured that one diocesan bishop took the trouble to write to all his clergy instructing them not to participate. We can only anticipate a similar level of enthusiasm, encouragement, and support for the findings from our enquiry.

A project of this nature is both costly and time consuming to undertake. We wish to acknowledge with gratitude some financial support received at various states of the project from an anonymous Catholic benefactor and from the British Academy. Our gratitude is also extended to all those priests who took the trouble either to complete our detailed questionnaire or to write to us detailed accounts of why they were reluctant to do so. Without their active participation this study would clearly not have been possible. Finally we wish to thank colleagues at the Centre for Ministry Studies, University of Wales, Bangor, who have assisted us in shaping the manuscript: Diane Drayson, Michael Fearn, Mandy Robbins and Susan Thomas.

STEPHEN H. LOUDEN AND LESLIE J. FRANCIS
Centre for Ministry Studies, University of Wales, Bangor

September 2002

Introduction

Satan stood up against Israel, and incited David to take a census among the people of Israel (1 Chron. 21:1).

The purpose of this opening chapter is to provide the context for the *Catholic Parochial Clergy Survey* and the general background information against which the following chapters can be assessed. The following chapters provide the detailed findings from the survey. After introducing the survey, this opening chapter explores the following issues. First, a broad introduction is provided to earlier *research on Catholic clergy* on which the present study builds. Second, the 22 specific topics covered by the survey are described and discussed in a section styled *posing the questions*. Third, a section on *seeking the answers* discusses the design of the survey and the research methodology. Fourth, a section on *consulting the priests* discusses how the questionnaire was distributed and the response rate. Fifth, a section on *listening to the reaction* draws out both the critical and the supportive responses received from the priests consulted. Sixth, a section on *meeting the priests* provides a detailed demographic profile of those who responded to the survey. Seventh, a section on the *health of the clergy* examines some of the information provided by the priests about their general state of health. Finally, a section on *designing the book* discusses how the data are presented in the following chapters.

The Catholic Parochial Clergy Survey

During 1996 a detailed questionnaire, the *Catholic Parochial Clergy Survey*, was mailed to all Catholic priests serving in parish ministry in England and Wales. Not everybody within the Catholic Church approved of the idea. It is not known what opinions were held about the survey or expressed privately by individual diocesan bishops in England and Wales, but under the headline 'Clergy survey storm' it was reported by *The Universe* that 'a priest had come under fire for conducting an extensive survey on the views of Catholic clergy of England and Wales'. *The Universe* also reported that 'a group of priests in the Salford diocese said that they had decided not to send in their replies because the survey did not have the official backing of the Bishops' Conference' (*The Universe*, 7 July 1996).

Though initially considered, no approach was made to obtain the support of the Catholic diocesan bishops of England and Wales following advice from those

1

well-versed in the vagarious support by bishops of comparable research. The decision not to solicit episcopal support was not taken lightly, as their backing, if received, though not decisive, would have been advantageous. The decision not to approach the bishops was influenced by the two-edged nature of making such a request. However advantageous such support might have been as a strategy designed to boost the response rate, refusal of support would virtually have guaranteed the non-participation of priests from entire dioceses, especially if bishops were to have made public their disapproval or were to have privately advocated non-participation.

A recent apology from the bishop of Rome to the eminent researcher Galileo Galilei (1564–1642) for having, through the Holy Inquisition, forced him to recant his support of the Copernican system, was made after 360 years. The ordinary researcher is unable to operate within such a time scale. Hoge (1987) refers to the ambivalence of Catholic bishops to research, convinced on the one hand of possible advantages, but on the other hand, fearful of any findings that, if published, might embarrass the institution. This attitude was perfectly exemplified in a letter from a bishop's secretary, the burden of which, including the dismissive conclusion, reads as follows.

I was a little taken aback by the content of the questionnaire. The eventual results of such a survey are so potentially sensitive that I strongly feel it should only be carried out if officially sanctioned by the Bishops' Conference. After consulting with the General Secretariat in Westminster, I am returning the questionnaire uncompleted. Sorry. Please do not feel a need to trouble to reply. Yours etc.

It is unknown if there was any hostile intervention by the English and Welsh hierarchy with reference to the *Catholic Parochial Clergy Survey*. Nevertheless tacit episcopal disapproval, as well as imagined episcopal disapproval by priests, may have been responsible for the survey of Catholic priests receiving a much lower response rate than the response rate received by comparable surveys conducted during the same period among clergy of other denominations. Nonetheless, over two-fifths (42%) of the Catholic priests in England and Wales who received a copy of the survey completed it and returned it to us. This book tells the tale of that survey and reveals the major findings.

By comparison, one survey enjoying episcopal and diocesan support, conducted among parochial priests of a single English diocese, obtained 164 replies from 355 priests giving a response rate of 46% (Smith, 1996). A survey conducted by Knights and Murray (2002) among a sample of 1250 priests, to generate a report to the Catholic bishops on *Evangelisation in England and Wales*, received a response rate of 36%. A survey conducted among priests of the Dublin diocese, at the initiative of the Dublin diocesan priests' council, encouraged by the archbishop and funded by the diocese, obtained 323 replies from a total of 578 priests approached, giving a 56% response rate (Lane, 1997).

It is, of course, not unknown for the hierarchy to take a view and to adopt a position on unauthorized research into the Catholic Church. For example, the

Vatican Congregation for the clergy in 2001 sent a letter to nuncios in Austria, Germany, Switzerland, Poland and Croatia asking them to instruct bishops to make it clear to priests that they were not to participate in a questionnaire sent to 6000 priests and 300 seminarians by the Bureau for Church Social Research in Vienna. Significantly the article states that 2500 priests (42%) completed and returned the questionnaire (*The Tablet*, 14 July 2001, p. 1029). Evidence of such Vatican disapproval helps strengthen the impression, now frequently voiced, of an ingrained official culture within the Catholic Church that is anxious to preserve the Church's image at all costs. Whatever the latent cause of such a culture, it is manifested in structures that overvalue secrecy and image and may easily give the impression of a Church hostile to academic endeavour and debate.

The two authors bring different backgrounds, different skills and different perspectives to this book. The whole project began when they agreed to draw together these different strengths. Stephen H. Louden is a Catholic priest, ordained in 1968, who has served in both parochial and extra-parochial ministry, having spent ten years in parishes in the Liverpool diocese before serving for twenty years as a regular army chaplain from which he retired in 1997 as Principal Roman Catholic Chaplain and Vicar General for the Army. Leslie J. Francis is an Anglican priest, ordained in 1973, and a social psychologist, who has pioneered the development of empirical theology in England and Wales through quantitative studies of church life. He is currently Professor of Practical Theology in the University of Wales, Bangor. The study is well grounded, therefore, both in an understanding of the Catholic Church in England and Wales and in empirical research methodology.

Research on Catholic clergy

The present study builds on a long history of empirical research based on Catholic seminarians and clergy conducted in the United States of America. This long history demonstrates both the willingness of Catholic seminarians and priests to participate in such empirical enquiries, and the practical benefit that can be added to the Catholic Church from the findings of such research.

One specific strand within this long history of empirical research has made good use of instruments designed to examine the personal predisposition or personality profile of individuals who have responded to the call of a priestly celibate vocation or to a parallel vocation within a religious community. Some of the earliest and best known studies in this tradition employed the Minnesota Multiphasic Personality Inventory (see Hathaway and McKinley, 1967), including reports by Bier (1948, 1970, 1971), Murray and Connolly (1966), Jansen, Bonk and Garvey (1973), Keddy, Erdberg and Sammon (1990), and Plante, Manuel and Tandez (1996). A second instrument, the Sixteen Personality Factor Questionnaire (see Cattell, Eber and Tatsuoka, 1970) has been used among Catholic priests and seminarians, for example, by Lee (1971), Wilson (1974), Scordato (1975), Campagna and O'Toole (1981), and Plante, Manuel and Tandez (1996). A third instrument, the Myers-Briggs Type Indicator (see

Myers and McCaulley, 1985) has been used among Catholic priests, seminarians and religious by, for example, Cabral (1984), Holsworth (1984), and Bigelow, Fitzgerald, Busk, Girault and Avis (1988).

Other empirical studies have taken a different sociological or psychological perspective on Catholic clergy. For example, Fichter (1965, 1968) surveyed diocesan priests who were not yet pastors of parishes. Some of these priests, who had an average age of 36 years, were experiencing high stress. They complained about the lack of access to bishops, lack of free communication at all levels of the diocese, poor relations with pastors, and the menial tasks they were often given to perform. Young priests in parishes were unhappier than those in specialized diocesan posts. The most demoralized were full-time associates without special assignments outside the parish, especially those experiencing poor relations with their pastors.

Mills and Koval (1971) studied stress among Catholic priests and Protestant clergy. They found that, among both groups, younger clergy reported much greater stress than older clergy, with Catholic priests aged 30 or under reporting five times as much stress as their colleagues aged over 60. The main sources of stress reported by the priests were: lack of leadership from those in authority; disappointment regarding the position adopted by the Catholic Church on specific social or moral issues, like race and contraception; the slow pace of change following the Second Vatican Council; loneliness; and lack of support and encouragement from other priests.

Greeley's (1972) survey focused on issues like training, work, frustrations, and future plans. The data suggest that the greatest reason for leaving ministry was the desire to marry, which was partly a result of loneliness. A secondary reason was dissatisfaction with the way authority was handled by the leadership. Other important problems facing diocesan priests included the difficulty of really reaching people today, relationships with superiors and pastors, and celibacy. The main predictors of low morale were low work satisfaction, loneliness, and poor self-descriptions in comparison with other professionals.

Hall and Schneider (1973) studied the work lives of priests in the Archdiocese of Hartford. They found the lowest morale among young priests, largely because young priests had unchallenging jobs with too little autonomy and because pastors had excessive authority over them. Young associate pastors complained of getting inadequate feedback from pastors and of not being consulted in decisions affecting them.

Jeffries and Tygart (1974) compared the views of clergy from five different denominations on a range of social issues. Their first finding concerned the greater reluctance of Catholic priests to participate in the survey. There was a response rate of 36% from the Catholic clergy, compared with 52% from the Church of Christ clergy, 55% from the Methodist clergy, 55% from the Baptist clergy, and 67% from the Episcopal clergy.

Schoenherr and Greeley (1974) studied role commitment processes among a sample of 3045 priests. Their path analysis demonstrated that the cost of celibacy was the principal consideration in the commitment sequence. Priests who see marriage as a desirable opportunity forgone, who find that the cost of loneliness outweighs the satisfaction derived from the role, who are inner-directed, and who are relatively young, are more likely to exit from ministry.

Seidler (1979) used a national survey, with a 74% response rate, to examine the structural antecedents and consequences of diocesan resignation rates among priests during the period 1966–70. The data demonstrated that resignations were directly related to the following diocesan conditions: percentage of parishes run by religious clergy, the status of the diocese as 'province', proportion of Catholics in the population, proportion of diocesan priests engaged in full-time non-parish work, and estimated degree of priest passivity and disillusionment. Indirectly, traditional authority structures, ideological divisions, and the absence of social solidarity also increased the probability of resignations. Seidler also concluded that resignations appeared to have no immediate feedback effect on episcopal policies.

Gannon (1979) examined differences between secular and regular priests in respect of religious perspectives, professional attitudes, and the way they live. Some important differences emerged between the two groups. For example, 59% of regular clergy reported little problem with loneliness, compared with 52% of secular clergy; 78% of regular clergy reported feeling of personal fulfilment, compared with 70% of secular clergy; 55% of regular clergy reported work satisfaction, compared with 45% of secular clergy; 63% of regular clergy endorsed the value of celibacy, compared with 51% of secular clergy.

Another study conducted by Fichter and reported by the National Conference of Catholic Bishops (1985) studied emotional, behavioural and mental problems experienced by priests as indicators of stress. The data suggested that 40% had experienced such problems in the past year. In general, however, the health of priests was judged as no worse than the average health of men in the United States of America. In a further analysis of the same data, Fichter (1987) explored the relationship between 'lifestyle variables' and overall health, to test the hypothesis that good health depends on non-smoking, moderate drinking, physical exercise, adequate sleep, and control of body weight. The data demonstrated that priests who observe such health habits are more likely to be physically fit, and that priests who are physically fit are more likely to report emotional and mental balance, and are also more likely to watch their weight, get enough sleep and exercise, quit smoking and moderate their alcohol intake.

De Jong and Donovan (1988) examined the relationships between age and three aspects of religion among a sample of 1027 diocesan priests. The three aspects of religion were the basis of belief, attitude toward religious experience, and frequency of religious practices. The data demonstrated that older priests were more certain of their belief and more likely to base their belief on logic and less likely to base their belief on experience, in comparison with younger priests. The younger the priest, the more he tended to experience God through people and events. Younger priests engaged in interpersonal religious practices more than older priests, while older priests engaged in solitary religious practices more than younger priests.

Hoge, Shields and Verdieck (1988) and Verdieck, Shields and Hoge (1988) drew together data from two surveys, conducted in 1970 and 1985, to analyse changing age distribution and theological attitudes of Catholic priests. The data suggested three main areas of change during this period. Overall the theological attitudes of the priests became significantly more liberal during this fifteen-year period. The overall level of morale among the priests rose between 1970 and 1985. The youngest priests in the 1985 study were more conservative than the youngest priests in the 1970 study. The cost of celibacy as measured by desire to marry, although weaker in 1985 than in 1970, remained the principal consideration in determining whether a priest would withdraw or continue in active ministerial priesthood. These data were subsequently reanalysed by Young and Schoenherr (1992). Based on the simultaneous operation of the cohort and ageing effects, as well as the growing conservatism of younger priests, Young and Schoenherr concluded that an increasingly conservative clergy is to be expected.

Hoge, Shields and Soroka (1993) assessed stress levels among a nationwide sample of 515 diocesan priests. The priests scored slightly lower in stress than the average of other occupational groups. Younger priests and priests serving as assistant pastors reported the highest levels of stress. The organizational stressors experienced most frequently were inadequate feedback on ministry tasks, inadequate rewards, and unfairness. The stressors contributing most to the intense stress were overwork, over-responsibility for other people, and time pressure. Priests reported more stress if diocesan communications were not open and if the Ordinary was perceived as not taking an interest in them.

Hoge, Shields and Griffin (1995) drew together data from three surveys, conducted in 1970, 1985, and 1993, to analyse changes in satisfaction, morale, theological and ecclesiological attitudes, and professionalization of Catholic priests. Overall morale and happiness were higher in 1985 and 1993 than in 1970. Problems of overwork and of meeting the rising expectations of laity rose over time. Self-identity as professionals gradually increased. In 1993 young priests were very conservative on institutional church issues.

Harper and Schulte-Murray (1998) examined differences between the perceptions and responses of priests working in two contiguous dioceses, with the intention of exploring the relationship between these differences and the wider 'culture' of the two dioceses. Leadership in one diocese was epitomized as 'tight' and 'closed', although not heavy-handed or authoritarian. Leadership in the other diocese was epitomized as looser and more permissive. Clergy serving under a more permissive leadership style were themselves more inclined to espouse liberal attitudes toward issues like contraception and sex outside marriage.

Swenson (1998) explored the relationship between celibacy and 'spiritual life' among samples of 1294 evangelical ministers (most of whom were married) and 80 Catholic priests. Spiritual life was assessed by four constructs in this study: meditation, frequency of prayer, amount of time spent in prayer, and parochial commitment. Priests were shown to score higher on the two measures of prayer, but there were no significant differences regarding the measures of meditation and parochial commitment. The data remain, however, contaminated by wider differences in church tradition alongside the issue of celibacy.

Smith (2000) examined the experiences of 402 Irish-born and Irish seminary-educated priests who live and work in dioceses in the United States of America. The priests were asked about their seminary preparation, the influence of American culture on their lives, how they view their ethnicity, how satisfied they are with priesthood, what problems they face as priests, their ecclesiological and theological concerns, and their views of the impact of the Second Vatican Council on the Catholic Church. Two-fifths of the priests (39%) considered that the impact of the Second Vatican Council had not gone far enough, half (51%) considered that the impact had gone far enough, and 10% considered that it had gone too far.

Other studies in this tradition include reports by Fichter (1961), Stewart (1969), Struzzo (1970), Hemrick and Hoge (1985, 1991), and Wittberg (1993).

Research in England and Wales

A foundation study for research into clergy in England was provided by Ranson, Bryman and Hinings' (1977) survey of Anglican clergy, Methodist ministers and Catholic priests, conducted between 1971 and 1973, and published in their book, *Clergy, Ministers and Priests*. The Catholic component of the survey was based on 'the whole population of full-time working priests from three unnamed dioceses: a large mainly urban diocese, a medium-sized mainly urban diocese, and a small mixed rural and urban diocese. For the two larger dioceses all members of the hierarchy were included, from rural deans up, but a 50% sample was taken of parish clergy. Members of religious orders not in full-time parish work were not included. A total of 876 questionnaires were despatched and 412 were returned, making a response rate of 47%. The questionnaire included the following areas: definition of role, ecumenical perception and operation, organizational perception, participation in decision-making, professional beliefs, and reform attitudes.

Some of the key findings from Ranson, Bryman and Hinings' comparative study are worth highlighting. Already in the early 1970s the Catholic Church was becoming conscious of an ageing priesthood and of difficulties in recruiting young people into ministry. Thus 49% of Catholic priests were aged 50 or over, compared with 43% of Anglican clergymen; 58% of Catholic priests had been in ordained ministry for at least twenty years, compared with 40% of Anglican clergymen.

Given the opportunity to rank order the various roles that they performed in their ministry, Catholic priests put celebrant in the first position, compared with the priority given to pastor by both Anglican clergy and Methodist ministers. In decreasing order of priority the roles were ranked as follows by Catholic priests: celebrant, pastor, preacher, counsellor, leader, administrator, and official or representative.

On the subject of ecumenism, 52% of the Catholic priests were in favour of clergy from different denominations preaching in each other's churches, 55% had preached in a non-Catholic church and 40% had invited a non-Catholic to preach in their church. Between a quarter and a third of the Catholic priests (29%) were in favour of joint theological colleges, compared with 72% of the Anglican clergymen and 92% of the Methodist ministers. Half of the Catholic priests (50%) participated in a local clergy fraternal, 31% in a local council of churches, and 12% in a Council of Christian Churches.

On the subject of reform, 70% of the Catholic priests maintained that their Church needed more than a little reform, compared with 91% of Anglican clergymen and 90% of Methodist ministers. Examining specific areas of reform, the following prioritization emerged where reform was considered to be either most important or quite important: training (94%), place of the laity (90%), liturgy (77%), bishops (66%), parochial system (63%) and celibacy (39%).

On the subject of organizational context, the Catholic priests saw themselves as operating within a bureaucratic climate. They felt that there was a clear hierarchy, procedures existed to routinize tasks, rules were enforced and job autonomy was low. All of these features provided quite a contrast with the views of Anglican clergymen and Methodist ministers.

In 1985, Bryman (1989) attempted a replication of the original study conducted between 1971 and 1973. Reduced resources limited the research potential to just one Anglican diocese, one Catholic diocese, and one Methodist district. Bryman (1989, p. 33) explains why this re-study was eventually undertaken only among the Anglicans and Methodists.

> Unfortunately, it became apparent at an early juncture that access to the Roman Catholic diocese was unlikely to be forthcoming (since the author's correspondence was not answered).

An ideal opportunity to map changing perspectives among priests between 1973 and 1985 was thus lost.

Posing the questions

After an exhaustive review of the international literature and conversations with Catholic priests in England and Wales, we identified 22 topics that were to become the focus for the survey.

Topic 1 is concerned with how priests evaluate the training provided by their seminary for *public ministry*. Public ministry, broadly conceived, embraces aspects of the priests' role like conducting the liturgy, public speaking, and preaching. It also includes those wider points of intersection with the public world like handling the changes that have taken place in the Catholic Church and dealing with interfaith dialogue.

Topic 2 is concerned with how priests evaluate the training provided by their seminary for *pastoral ministry*. Pastoral ministry, broadly conceived, embraces meeting people where they are, making home calls, visiting the sick and dealing with individuals at major turning points in their lives. Given the importance in Catholic teaching attributed to marriage and family life, particular attention needs to be given to the major pastoral areas of pre-marriage instruction and marriage counselling, areas that a male celibate priesthood may find particularly alien to their own immediate experience.

Topic 3 is concerned with how priests evaluate the training provided by their seminary for *work with people*. Different skills are needed for relating to different sectors of society. Work with people, broadly conceived, embraces specific skills for working with children and for working with teenagers, specific skills for working with women and for working with men, and specific skills for working with the elderly and for working with the bereaved.

Topic 4 is concerned with how priests evaluate the training provided by their seminary for *the priestly life*. The priestly life, broadly conceived, and as lived out in England and Wales today, embraces such features as living on limited means, often living alone and looking after oneself, living as a single man, coming to terms with a life of celibacy, accepting one's sexuality, making a creative use of leisure time away from parish commitments, and developing a spiritual life.

Topic 5 is concerned with the *theology of priesthood* espoused by priests in the Catholic Church. Broadly conceived, theology of priesthood embraces those theologically motivated practices that give shape to the priestly way of life, including the daily mass and the daily office.

Topic 6 is concerned with how priests respond to the practicalities and realities of *experiencing priesthood* in the Catholic parish. The experience of priesthood, broadly conceived, includes making sense of living in the presbytery on the small clerical stipend, dealing with the expectations and demands of parishioners and of society as a whole, and establishing a balance between the demands of the office and the needs for recreation.

Topic 7 is concerned with how priests evaluate and respond to those outward signs of priesthood that help to set the priest apart from other men. This consideration of the outward trappings of *dress and deference*, broadly conceived, embraces the notion of distinctive clerical dress, use of the clerical collar, and attachment to deferential forms of address, like the title 'Father'.

Topic 8 is concerned with how priests *relate to the laity* in their parishes. Consideration of the relationship between priests and laity involves both discussion of the nature of the Church and evaluation of how comfortable and confident priests are about their ability to work with lay people.

Topic 9 is concerned with how priests understand the relationship between *celibacy and priesthood*. Consideration of this issue involves discussing their understanding of chastity and celibacy. It raises issues about their understanding regarding whether married men can be validly ordained and about their reaction to the reordination of married former Anglican clergymen who turned to the Catholic Church after the Church of England decided to ordain women as priests.

Topic 10 is concerned with exploring the contentious area of *fallen priests*. It includes the attitude of priests toward colleagues who have fallen from the standards that the Catholic Church expects of them and that society at large expects of them. Attention needs to be given to the case of priests who practise homosexuality, who have sex with a married woman, who have sex with an unmarried woman, and who become alcoholics. Special attention also needs to be given to the high profile issue of priest paedophiles and priest ephebophiles.

Topic 11 is concerned with doctrinal orthodoxy and the extent to which priests remain committed to the doctrinal teachings of the Catholic Church. These wider perspectives can be tested against specific beliefs concerning *Jesus* and *Mary*, ranging from core Christological statements to the doctrine of the assumption of Mary.

Topic 12 is concerned with the moral teaching of the Catholic Church and the extent to which priests remain committed to moral orthodoxy on issues concerned with *marriage, sex* and *death*. These wider principles can be tested against teaching concerned specifically with abortion, euthanasia, artificial contraception and annulment.

Topic 13 is concerned with the priests' theological beliefs about the divine nature of the *Catholic Church* and about the special character of the *blessed sacrament* within the Catholic Church. Special consideration also needs to be given to the priests' understanding of the hierarchical structure of the Catholic Church.

Topic 14 is concerned with the priests' attitude toward *Rome and the Vatican*. Particular attention needs to be given to the priests' perceptions of the balance of power between the central structures in Rome and the local dioceses and parishes. Opportunity also needs to be given to assess the strength of the desire among priests to return to a pre-Vatican II Church.

Topic 15 is concerned with exploring the priests' attitude toward *Catholic institutions*. Particular attention needs to be given among Catholic institutions to Opus Dei, Catholic schools, the Catholic press and bishops.

Topic 16 is concerned with the priests' views on *ecumenism and intercommunion*. Particular attention needs to be given to their views on the place of papal supremacy for any church unity scheme, their views on the validity of Anglican orders, their attitude toward Catholics communicating in non-Catholic churches, and their attitude toward non-Catholics being permitted to communicate at mass.

Topic 17 is concerned with the priests' attitude toward *changes in the Catholic Church*. Particular attention needs to be given to the climate of change initiated by the Second Vatican Council, to the growth of feminism in the Catholic Church and to the decline in the number of Catholics drawn to the sacrament of reconciliation.

Topic 18 is concerned with examining the priests' attitude toward the *ordination of women*. Attention needs to be given to their understanding regarding whether women can be validly ordained to the orders of deacon, priest or bishop.

Topic 19 turns attention to the concept of *emotional exhaustion* as the first of three central defining characteristics of professional burnout. Attention needs to be given to the extent to which clergy in the Catholic Church may be subject to or experience emotional exhaustion as a consequence of their work in ministry.

Topic 20 focuses on the concept of *depersonalization* as the second of three central defining characteristics of professional burnout. Attention needs to be given to the extent to which clergy in the Catholic Church may be subject to or experience depersonalization as a consequence of their work in ministry.

Topic 21 focuses on the concept of *reduced personal accomplishment* as the third of three central defining characteristics of professional burnout. Attention needs to be given to the extent to which clergy in the Catholic Church may be subject to or experience reduced levels of personal accomplishment as a consequence of their work in ministry.

Topic 22 is concerned with the extent to which the priests who participated in the survey continue to see for themselves *a future in priesthood*. This topic needs to examine how many priests remain happy with their original intention to become ordained and, if they could have their time all over again, whether they would still choose to be a priest. It also needs to examine how many priests currently engaged in parish work long to leave ministry.

Seeking the answers

Having identified the key areas to be explored by the survey, a questionnaire was designed to operationalize these issues. The major debate in questionnaire design concerns the comparative merits of 'open ended' and 'closed' questions. The former provide rich data for qualitative analysis, while the later provide rich data for quantitative analysis. Given the clear focus of the questions being posed and the large number of priests being approached for responses, the main weight in the study was placed on the organization of quantitative data. Nonetheless, plenty of opportunity was also provided for the priests to expand on their answers in a qualitative manner if they so wished.

For the quantitative aspect of the survey the scaling method originally proposed by Likert (1932) was adopted. According to this method each question is formulated as a short, sharp statement embodying just one main idea. Respondents are then invited to scale their level of agreement or disagreement with each statement. A number of different possibilities exist for scaling the response. In the present study we opted for a five-point scale that recognizes the legitimacy of allowing respondents a middle or neutral category. The five points of the response scale were anchored by the following descriptions: agree strongly, agree, not certain, disagree and disagree strongly. All told there were 133 items of this nature in the questionnaire. Each item was formulated and then discussed in a small focus group to assess its validity and lack of ambiguity.

In addition to these Likert-type items the questionnaire also included a series of multiple-choice questions seeking information about the priest's background, a personality inventory and an inventory concerned with various forms of religious experience and expression. These parts of the questionnaire go beyond the focus of the present book, although some of the findings are available elsewhere. For example, we have published studies on the personality profile of parochial secular priests (Louden and Francis, 1999), the personality profile of regular priests engaged in parochial ministry (Francis and Louden, 2001), the assessment of mystical orientation among Catholic priests (Francis and Louden, 2000), the psychological correlates of attraction to the charismatic movement among

Catholic priests (Louden and Francis, 2001), the psychological dynamics of the clerical persona among Catholic priests in comparison with male and female Anglican priests (Francis, Louden, Robbins and Rutledge, 2000), and burnout among Catholic parochial clergy in England and Wales (Francis, Louden and Rutledge, 2003).

Consulting the priests

Having designed the questionnaire, the next major task was to assemble the distribution list. The aim was to post a copy of the questionnaire to all secular and regular Catholic priests engaged in parochial ministry in England or in Wales. This distribution list was constructed from a combination of the address database kindly provided by the Catholic Agency for Overseas Development (CAFOD) with the names and addresses of priests from the Catholic Directory of England and Wales (1995). Directories and address lists can never be entirely up-to-date due to subsequent clergy postings, resignations, retirements and deaths. As it is general practice in presbyteries that mail addressed to former priests of the parish is invariably redirected, the possibility of a small mismatch of priests and places was not regarded as a serious problem.

Each name and address was entered on a computer database and given its own number. The questionnaire carried the same number. The purpose of the number was explained in an accompanying letter as to identify those who had responded so that a gentle reminder might be sent to those who had not responded. Priests were assured that the number would be removed from the questionnaire as soon as it was received and that no attempt would be made to identify individual respondents. Priests were also given the option to remove the number before returning the questionnaire if they so preferred, but with the inevitable consequence that they would receive further reminder letters. This device had been used in a number of previous studies among clergy of other denominations.

This numbering system seems, however, to have caused greater offence among Catholic priests than among clergy of other denominations. It was widely interpreted, both by those refusing and those completing the questionnaire, as subverting all assurances of confidentiality and anonymity. One priest commented gently that 'Speaking with other priests, I found we were all mildly amused by your disclaimer about anonymity, yet including a serial number for non-returns.' Another priest commented more strongly that 'Offence has been taken at the numbering of the documents.'

The Catholic Church seems to love secrecy. Priests seem much affected by an ethos of taciturnity concerning themselves and their work. If an organization behaves as if it is hiding something, it ought to come as no surprise when even benevolent outsiders express suspicion not only that the organization appears to have something to hide, but that such secrecy is concealment of something disreputable.

In May 1996 the questionnaire, together with a freepost reply envelope and explanatory letter, was sent by post to 3581 priests serving in parochial appointments. Those who had not replied were sent a second copy of the questionnaire in November 1996, followed by a third in February 1997. The arrival of the third questionnaire was obliquely acknowledged in one instance by an unsigned note, 'Please do not send me any more of your offensive and intrusive questionnaires. This is the third time I have received junk mail from you.'

Of the 3581 questionnaires posted, just 63 were returned as undeliverable because the priests had left parish ministry, were in retirement, were extremely old, were deceased, or had otherwise vanished. This left 3518, which we must assume were safely delivered by the postal service to the rightful recipient. A total of 1482 questionnaires were finally returned, thoroughly completed and useful for analysis, making a response rate of 42.1%.

This response rate was in many ways disappointing when compared with the response rate received to comparable surveys conducted among clergy of other denominations by related projects. For example, Jones' survey conducted among 672 Anglican clergy in Wales received a response rate of 82% (Jones and Francis, 1997). Thomas' survey conducted among 375 Anglican clergy in Wales received a response rate of 64% (Francis and Thomas, 1996a, 1996b, 1997). Rutledge's survey conducted among 1476 Anglican clergymen in England received a response rate of 73% (Francis and Rutledge, 2000). Robbins' survey conducted among 1698 Anglican clergywomen in England, Ireland, Scotland and Wales received a response rate of 73% (Francis and Robbins, 1999; Robbins, 1998, 2001). Musson's survey conducted among 583 Anglican clergymen and 404 Anglican clergywomen in England received a response rate of 60% among the men and 64% among the women (Musson, 2001, 2002; Musson and Francis, 2002). Turton's survey conducted among 1967 Anglican clergymen in England received a response rate of 65% (Turton and Francis, 2002; Francis and Turton, 2002). Francis' survey conducted among all clergy ordained into the Anglican Church in England, Ireland, Scotland and Wales during that year achieved response rates of 62% in 1992, 68% in 1993, 62% in 1994, 72% in 1995 and 62% in 1996 (Francis, Jones, Jackson and Robbins, 2001; Jones and Francis, 2002). Haley's survey conducted among 1809 Methodist ministers throughout England, Wales, Scotland, the Shetland Islands, the Channel Islands and the Isle of Man received a response rate of 74% (Robbins, Francis, Haley and Kay, 2001). Kay's survey conducted among Pentecostal pastors received a response rate of 64% and 367 useable questionnaires from Elim pastors, and a response rate of 57% and 401 useable questionnaires from Assembly of God pastors (Kay, 2000).

The lower response rate received from Catholic clergy in the present family of studies mirrors the experience of a study conducted between 1970 and 1973 and reported by Ranson, Bryman and Hinings (1977). Their survey received a 78% response rate among 721 Anglican clergy, and a 93% response rate among 275 Methodist ministers. Among their sample of 876 Catholic priests, however, the response rate fell to 47%. This can only lead us to surmise that surveys of this nature may be perceived much more negatively by Catholic priests than by clergy, ministers and pastors serving in other denominations.

Listening to the reaction

The survey drew a great number of comments from the recipients. In all, 535 separate letters, notes and comments written on the questionnaire itself were received, amounting to over twenty thousand words. One refusal was couched in the advice to 'Kindly consult a competent taxidermist.' Other reactions ranged from the aggressively dismissive epithet 'Junk mail' used by a few refusing to take part in the survey to others which showed undisguised annoyance. One priest wrote:

> I cannot wish you any success but hope that you can find some more worthwhile employment.

Another priest wrote:

> I cannot believe that any findings based on this questionnaire would help anyone, least of all myself.

Yet another priest wrote:

> It seems to me that such a survey is pointless and can have little practical use.

These responses, typical of very many such others, serve to exemplify the adage that in general most adults are loath to complete tests, which they regard as ridiculous and time-wasting. However, that most of us could not derive useful information, for instance, from blood samples taken routinely from hospital patients would not lead many of us to conclude that no one else could do so, and declare the practice to be pointless. Perhaps it should not be too surprising that a few official representatives of an essentially dogmatic organization should manifest an inappropriate dogmatism outside the field of their professional competence.

Slightly more surprising were the many responses reflecting a prevalent attitude that because the bishops had not given their authority, the priests themselves could not take part. Such notable deference to real or imagined episcopal disapproval of the survey is quite marked. A comment typical of many others that were sent states:

> If we had the official blessing of the diocese, I would be very happy to complete the survey.

Another priest in similar vein declares:

> My attitude might have been different if your survey had received the blessing of the bishops of England and Wales, but as you admit in your letter, you have received no explicit approval for this project.

One religious priest, favoured it would seem by an enviably sheltered existence, continues:

> I shall not be returning your questionnaire, which I dislike more than any other communication I have ever received from a member of the Catholic Church. I notice – in fact we noticed – that you give no authority for asking these questions.

Criticisms were made and anxieties expressed over the content, purpose, structure and wording of the questionnaire. Many criticisms referred to perceived ambiguities, complexities, inconsistencies and limitations connected with the wording of forced-choice questions. One priest's anxiety arose from a perceived hidden agenda.

> I think there is a conservative and right wing bias in this survey and questionnaire. It disturbs me and makes me unhappy about the priesthood.

Another priest wrote, without further explanation, that he was 'aware of a hidden but benign radical agenda'.

Counterbalancing the reproachful comments were a roughly equal number of affirmative observations commending the enterprise and expressing the hope that the findings might be made public. Significantly, the article about the survey in *The Universe*, on 7 July 1996, which reported that 'a group of priests in the Salford diocese said that they had decided not to send in their replies because the survey did not have the official backing of the Bishops' Conference', also quoted two individual priests who voiced opposing views. One priest, who 'preferred not to be named', said, 'The general feeling is that the priests were ill-informed and did not know who had commissioned it.' The other priest from the Birmingham diocese, who significantly also asked to remain anonymous, said, 'I believe it has been well-received in the diocese and the priests here don't share the same concern as those in Salford.'

One letter in particular saw potential value in what was attempted.

> Please accept my sincere thanks and congratulations that you have undertaken this task ... I am sure that your work will be of great value to the bishops, religious superiors and those concerned with pastoral planning ...
> I hope that it will not be put under wraps of confidentiality by the authorities.

That traditional priestly culture of dependency shown in the final wording of this letter is continued in the use of the verb 'allowed' by another priest when he writes that:

> I hope you will be allowed to publish your results.

One priest showed awareness of what was being attempted in the survey.

> I think it is excellent that some in-depth statistical and attitudinal information is being sought. The future development and planning in all dioceses needs this if it is objectively going to rejuvenate the Catholic Church.

Another on the same theme wrote that:

> We need to be putting in place, now, support stratagems that will help people in the future.

The strong and general impression of encouragement in many letters and comments is exemplified in the following.

> Thank you for taking this crucial survey on – I hope it receives much publicity.

Meeting the priests

The questionnaire included enough demographic and background questions to provide a useful profile of priests currently involved in parochial ministry, based on the assumption that those who responded to the questionnaire were basically representative of the total population of parochial priests. Unfortunately it is not possible to test this assumption because there are no readily available sources in the public domain against which the profile of the respondents can be assessed. Comparable surveys conducted among Anglican clergy in England and Wales have at least been able to check the age profile of respondents against the age profile of the clergy as a whole, since the Anglican handbook, *Crockford's Clerical Directory*, includes the year of birth against each named entry (see Francis and Lankshear, 1994). *The Catholic Directory of England and Wales* does not provide data on the age of the clergy. In this sense the profile provided by the present survey may be breaking new ground.

In this section data are provided on the priests' age, years in the priesthood, canonical status, living arrangements, workload, social class background, level of university education, financial security and satisfaction in ministry.

Age

The overall age profile of the parochial Catholic clergy tends to be high, partly through difficulties involved in recruiting young men into the priesthood and partly through retaining priests in active parochial ministry well beyond the normal retirement age required in most secular professions and, indeed, in many other Christian denominations. Thus, one in four of the priests currently engaged in active parochial ministry are aged 65 and over. Just over another one in four (28%) are aged between 55 and 64. Looked at from another perspective, 2% of the priests are in their twenties, 13% in their thirties, 20% in their forties, 25% in their fifties, 26% in their sixties, 12% in their seventies and 2% in their eighties.

Years in priesthood

A second clue concerning recruitment patterns to the priesthood is provided by an analysis of the number of years in priesthood already experienced by those engaged in parochial ministry. Well over half of the priests (56%) had been ordained at least 25 years ago. Looked at in greater detail, 18% had been priests for up to 10 years, 16% for between 10 and 19 years, 22% for between 20 and 29 years, 25% for between 30 and 39 years, 15% for between 40 and 49 years and 4% for 50 years or more.

Canonical status

In the Catholic Church parishes are served both by diocesan priests (secular clergy) and by priest members of religious communities (regular clergy). Generally certain parishes are sponsored by specific religious orders. One in five of the respondents (20%) identified themselves as regular priests and four in five as secular priests (80%). Since regular priests, being members of a religious community, are less likely than secular priests to be living and working alone, it is likely that these statistics indicate that well under 20% of the *parishes* are served by regular clergy. All told 50 different religious orders were identified among the respondents, including 43 Benedictines, 18 Oblates of Mary, 17 Franciscans, 17 Jesuits, 14 Salesians and 14 Rosminians.

Living arrangements

Historically presbyteries were generally built to house several priests who were able to share a common life and a common ministry. Today half of the priests (50%) are living alone, leaving 35% living with one or two priest colleagues and 15% living with three or more priest colleagues. Comparatively few priests turned to a pet for companionship. Just 11% lived with a dog and 6% with a cat.

Workload

In light both of declining vocations and financial stringency, clergy of all denominations are being expected to take on wider responsibilities. Where one church was staffed formerly by several clergy, it may now be staffed by only one. Where each church was assigned its own clergy, several churches may now be staffed by the same minister. The present data demonstrate that two-thirds of the Catholic priests (66%) remain responsible for just one church or mass centre. One in four of the priests (24%), however, now have responsibility for two churches or mass centres, 8% have responsibility for three and 2% have responsibility for four or more.

Social class background

In order to provide an assessment of social class of origin the priests were asked to describe their father's occupation when they were 18 years old. These data were then classified according to the Registrar General's five-fold classification system, subdividing class three into the two subcomponents of manual and non-manual (Office of Population, Censuses and Surveys, 1980). Although this system has now been much revised for subsequent censuses, it was chosen as being more properly representative of the generation it was being used to classify. According to this system, class one embraces professional and higher administrative occupations, including, for example, architects, clergy, doctors, lawyers, managers and university teachers. Class two embraces intermediate professionals and administrative occupations, including, for example, actors, authors, farm owners and managers, musicians, senior police officers and teachers. Class three embraces non-manual skilled occupations, including, for example, clerical workers, estate agents, draftsmen, police officers and shop assistants. Class three also embraces manual skilled occupations, including, for example, bricklayers, butchers, carpenters, decorators, electricians and foremen. Class four embraces partly skilled occupations, including, for example, bar-staff, caretakers, farmers, fishermen, and postmen and postwomen. Class five embraces unskilled occupations, including, for example, cleaners, labourers, porters, refuse collectors and window cleaners.

In their earlier comparison of the social backgrounds of Catholic priests, Anglican clergymen and Methodist ministers, Ranson, Bryman and Hinings (1977, p. 154) demonstrated that 'parents of priests showed a much more heterogeneous picture of social class than was the case for Anglicans and Methodists'. That study also observed that Catholic priests were the only group with a substantial element from manual backgrounds. The findings from the present survey confirm that picture of the Catholic priesthood. Just 6% of the priests had fathers in social class one occupations, 20% in social class two occupations, 33% in social class three non-manual occupations, 35% in social class three manual occupations and 6% in social class four occupations. Only one priest identified his father as working in a social class five occupation.

University occupation

One historical consequence of the Reformation in England and Wales had been that, on the restoration of the Catholic hierarchy in 1850, diocesan seminaries were not affiliated to the universities, so that even six years of seminary training did not lead to an academic degree. Ranson, Bryman and Hinings' (1977) study reported that few Catholic priests proceeded to university, but they also found among those who did that a greater proportion of priests had studied to a higher level than either Anglicans or Methodists. They noted that the theologically gifted were financially supported at home and in continental universities or seminaries.

Today the picture is beginning to change. Nearly one in four of the priests (24%) possessed a university degree in a subject other than theology, with 9% being at master's level and 1% at doctoral level. At the same time, one in ten priests (9%) possessed a university degree in theology, with 7% being at master's level and 2% at doctoral level.

Financial security

Low stipend and tied housing neither encourages nor enables priests to establish their personal financial security. The survey included four questions to gauge the financial health of the priests. The findings show that over a quarter of the priests (28%) had no savings of their own, and three-quarters (76%) had no pension scheme of their own. Just 8% owned their own house. In spite of this broad lack of financial provision, only a small minority of priests (7%) had built up personal debts.

Satisfaction in ministry

The present survey was clearly based on those priests who were currently engaged in parochial ministry. Other priests ordained at the same time as these priests will already have exited from ministry, and done so for a variety of reasons. This survey, therefore, is concerned with those who have persisted in ministry. Two final questions in the demographic part of the questionnaire tested the security of this persistence in ministry. The first question asked, 'Have you since ordination ever considered leaving the priesthood?' Two-thirds of the priests (68%) had never considered doing so, but the thought had occurred once or twice to 25%, and more often to the remaining 7%. The second question asked, 'Have you since ordination ever considered finding secular employment?' Three-quarters of the priests (78%) had never considered doing so, but the other 22% had, with 7% of them following up possibilities and 4% actually making an application.

Health of the clergy

Following a model employed in a number of other studies among clergy (Francis, 2002), the priests were invited to assess their mental, physical and spiritual health on a five-point scale: excellent, good, middling, poor and very poor. Only a small proportion of priests chose to categorize themselves below middling. Thus, 2% described their mental health as poor or very poor; 6% described their physical health as poor or very poor; and 8% described their spiritual health as poor or very poor. Given the overall age profile of the Catholic clergy, these figures show a group of men who have a very robust view of themselves.

The next step in the survey, however, tried to penetrate behind this robust view by asking specific questions about a variety of health indicators. While the Catholic clergy are not inclined publicly to complain about their health, many of them recognize within themselves conditions that are not altogether healthy. Nearly one in three of the priests (30%) noted that they suffered from depression; one in five of the priests (20%) suffered from stomach complaints; 17% suffered from acute anxiety; 14% suffered from insomnia; 7% suffered from angina, asthma, diabetes, frequent headaches or migraines; 6% suffered from chronic indigestion, or suicidal thoughts; 4% suffered from psoriasis; and 4% had suffered a nervous breakdown.

Another important health-related indicator concerns the use of alcohol. Given the opportunity to describe their drinking habits on a five-point scale (abstainer, non-drinker, light drinker, moderate drinker and heavy drinker), just 4% of the priests described themselves as heavy drinkers and 36% as moderate drinkers. Two-fifths of the priests (42%) described themselves as light drinkers, 8% as non-drinkers, and 10% as abstainers. It is recognized, however, that self-reported drinking behaviour can be a very unreliable indicator.

Approached from a different perspective, 53% of the priests claimed never to drink beer, lager, stout or cider in an average week, while only 6% claimed to drink more than 7 pints a week. A small minority of the priests (2%) claimed to drink between 14 and 45 pints in an average week. Turning attention to spirits, 44% of the priests claimed never to drink spirits in an average week, while only 12% claimed to drink more than 7 glasses a week. A small minority of the priests (2%) claimed to drink between 14 and 80 glasses in a week. Regarding wine, 31% of the priests claimed never to drink wine in an average week, while only 12% claimed to drink more than 7 glasses a week. A small minority of priests (5%) claimed to drink between 14 and 50 glasses in a week. Regarding fortified wines, 85% of priests claimed never to drink sherry, port or liqueur in an average week, while only 1% claimed to drink more than 7 glasses a week. Less than 1% of the priests claimed to drink between 14 and 40 glasses in a week.

Many Catholic clergy, it is assumed, were once notable devotees of tobacco smoking, the rather coy admission being that, together with alcohol, tobacco was one of the few 'vices' permitted to them. Given the opportunity to describe their smoking habits on a five-point scale (abstainer, non-smoker, light smoker, moderate smoker and heavy smoker), just 6% of the priests described themselves as heavy smokers and 10% as moderate smokers. Half of the priests (48%) described themselves as non-smokers, 30% as abstainers, and 6% as light smokers. Looked at from another perspective, one in ten priests (10%) claimed to smoke at least 16 cigarettes a day, while 2% claimed to smoke more than 30 cigarettes a day.

One final indicator of health concerns regular engagement in physical activity. Given the age profile of the clergy, the level of physical activity in which they engage seems reasonable. The most frequently cited activity is walking, which was listed by nearly two-thirds of the priests (63%). Then, in descending order of frequency, the following activities were listed: golf (17%), swimming (17%), running or jogging (6%), badminton (3%), tennis (2%), and soccer (2%).

Designing the book

Our book has been designed around the 22 topics covered by the survey. Each topic has been given a chapter of its own, each chapter has been designed in a standard way, and the two authors have shared the writing in a methodical fashion.

Stephen has begun each chapter by contributing two formative sections. The first section, which we have styled *context*, highlights why we regard the topic of the chapter to be of importance within our overall study. Here Stephen has drawn on his personal experience of the Catholic priesthood in England and Wales, the international research literature, and the important clues and insights which accrue from the religious press and the national religious landscape. In the second section, which we have styled *listening to the priests*, Stephen has drawn extensively on the qualitative data generated by our survey and brought these data into dialogue with the main themes raised in his first section.

Following these two opening sections Leslie introduces the quantitative data in four steps. The first step, which we have called *shaping the questions*, spells out how the broad themes identified by the chapter were translated into tightly focused questions for the survey. The second step, which we have called *interpreting the statistics*, examines the responses of 1482 priests to each of the statements relevant to the section. This information is also presented in a simple table displaying the responses of the priests under three headings: yes, ?, no, which may be found in the Appendix. The 'yes' category combines the two responses in the questionnaire defined as 'agree strongly' and 'agree'. The '?' category expresses the response in the questionnaire defined as 'not certain'. The 'no' category combines the two responses in the questionnaire defined as 'disagree strongly' and 'disagree'.

The third step, which we have called *regular and secular*, compares the responses of these two categories of Catholic priests. While the majority of parochial ministry is conducted by secular clergy, a number of parishes remain staffed by priests attached to religious orders. This section, therefore, tests the extent to which these two groups of priests hold views in common and the extent to which they may inhabit somewhat different worldviews. The comparison is based on replies from 1176 secular priests and from 304 regular priests. The remaining two respondents failed to identify their canonical status. The tables for this section, which again may be found in the Appendix, present the proportions of priests within each of the two groups who have checked the 'agree strongly' or the 'agree' response to each statement. Then the final two columns in each table check the statistical significance of the differences in the responses of the two groups. The chi-square test has been used for this purpose. If the differences between the two groups are so small that they could have occurred by mere chance this is indicated by the letters 'NS' which means 'not significant'. If the differences between the two groups are statistically significant, the probability level has been expressed in terms of the three standard levels of .05, .01 and .001. The probability level of .05, for example, indicates the differences between the three groups could have arisen by chance less than five times in a hundred, while the level of .001 reduces the probability of chance to less than once in a thousand. Using a statistical test of this nature safeguards us against the mistake of looking at figures and thinking there may be a difference when in fact there is none.

The fourth step, which we have called *generational differences*, compares the responses of three different age groups of priests: the 338 priests who were under 45 years of age, the 552 priests who were aged between 45 and 59, and the 588 priests who were 60 or over. The remaining four respondents failed to reveal their ages. The assumption being made in this section is that these three cohorts will reflect not only age differences but also very different experiences of the Catholic

Church. For example, while by no means all of those aged 60 and over will have trained for the priesthood as young men, this cohort will reflect the experiences of a substantial proportion of priests who trained in a pre-Vatican II church. This section also employs the chi-square test in the same way as the section on the differences between regular priests and secular priests.

CHAPTER ONE

Training for Public Ministry

Each week the villagers gathered to hear one of their leaders extol the virtues and benefits of playing the violin. He spoke with great eloquence of the joy which ensues, of the healing effects, and of the new strength given to those who play the violin. He also upbraided those who could not play. Each week the people came, and each week they listened and each week they went home feeling guilty that they could not play the violin, or if they could play, could only scratch out a feeble tune. The eloquent speaker did not offer to show them how, he just talked about it. Then one day, to their dismay, the villagers found out that the eloquent speaker did not know how to play the violin either (Jud, Mills and Burch, 1970, p. 130).

This chapter is concerned with the seminary training received by Catholic priests to equip them for *public ministry*. Public ministry, broadly conceived, is considered to embrace the obvious aspects of the priests' public role like conducting the liturgy, public speaking and preaching. It also includes those wider points of intersection with the public world like handling changes in the Church and dealing with interfaith dialogue.

Context

The parable about the violin, once familiar to priests ordained thirty or more years ago, rang very true as an expression of pre–1960s seminary training and of an increasingly questioned and questioning parish ministry. Such a separation between precept and practice, or between seminary training and public ministry, can be seen as a virtual guarantee of psychological conflict.

Prior to the upheaval in the Catholic Church that accompanied the Second Vatican Council (1962–5), very many of those bishops and priests responsible for major seminary education shared a remarkably old-fashioned, outdated image of what they were doing and for what kind of Church they were training seminarians. The point is well illustrated by a televised interview between Malcolm Muggeridge and the then Cardinal Archbishop of Westminster, John Carmel Heenan (1963–75). When asked to summarize the Catholic Church in one word, Cardinal Heenan answered 'authority'.

The ideal-typical style of the Catholic priest took the form of authoritarian paternalism (Drewett, 1966). This style was almost expected of him by his almost invariably less well-educated parishioners, and it had been the image of the role with which the vast majority of those ordained had grown up. Such a leadership style was encouraged by the priest's own understanding of the distinctive character of his role as a man set apart, as an agent of the divine, ordained to celebrate what Catholics referred to as the holy sacrifice of the mass, to forgive sins and to teach and to lead his people. He was the shepherd and the sheep did not answer back. In Liverpool in particular the great strength of those in the priesthood before the Second Vatican Council (1962–5), it was said, had lain in their amazing ability to share the life of their parishioners while, at the same time, maintaining a spiritual aloofness that added a compelling force to their leadership (Brothers, 1963). Others might say that religious infantilism suited the character and corresponded with the theology of the era prior to the Second Vatican Council.

Training for public ministry is training for a particular role. Religion provides a system of meaning and offers explanation of the unknown, with a system of beliefs to guide and direct behaviour. The rituals and ceremonies of religion are intended to provide a structure for focusing on and bringing order to natural events. In this way religion, which concentrates on the spiritual realm, provides a link with the everyday world through the public role of the priest. This is achieved within the Catholic sacramental system, particularly at important moments connected with birth, maturity, marriage, reconciliation, illness and death, by the priest in his roles as celebrant, counsellor, intermediary, interpreter and witness. This is achieved on a day-to-day basis uniquely by the priest's celebration of the eucharist at mass (Goldner, Ference and Ritti, 1973).

The defining function of the priest's role, the ritual function of leading public worship and celebrating the sacraments, is given at least notional pre-eminence, though it might in practice take up comparatively little of the priest's time. A universal complaint among younger clergy reported by Jud, Mills and Burch (1970) was that they had learned to be ministers after they left the seminary. Catholic seminary training prior to the 1960s resulted in the seminarian developing an idealistic portrait of what his role was to be. Before the advent of practical pastoral placements, seminary training as likely as not provided a purely academic model of ministry.

An almost total lack of practical pastoral experience, once a major cause of apprehension in the newly ordained priests, has no longer been true since the 1960s. Today each diocesan seminary has its own approach to pastoral training. With smaller numbers and depending on the work experience of seminarians, the pastoral training programme can be tailored better to suit the needs of the individual. At Ushaw, the seminary which trains priests for dioceses in the North of England, from year one to year five seminarians spend half a day per week in a succession of pastoral roles, visiting people in their homes, children in primary and secondary schools, patients in hospital and prisoners in jail. Continuous assessment by on-site supervisors, parish priests, teachers, hospital chaplains and by the seminarians themselves assists the pastoral directors in honing individual skills as well as softening hard edges. In their fourth year seminarians spend a whole term in a parish, and following ordination to the diaconate each weekend is spent in a parish. In this way the seminarian is provided with role practice which puts him in touch with his prospective clientele.

In addition to the aspects of public ministry clearly visible within the context of the Catholic Church through conducting liturgy, preaching and public speaking, the priest must also be prepared for a second form of public ministry in the sense of representing the face of the Catholic community in the local area.

It is little wonder that priests felt ill-prepared for interfaith dialogue, if the first author's own experience in seminary was anything to go by. As late as the 1960s the otherwise estimable moral theology professor invariably hyphenated any reference to the Archbishop of Canterbury as that 'doubtfully baptised layman'. In a phrase, not only the ministry, but also the very Christianity of all non-Catholic Christians and their clergy was held up to ridicule.

Seminary preparation for change in the Catholic Church has meant different things for priests ordained in successive decades. No priest ordained before the 1960s, nor any after for that matter, had foreseen the unprecedented changes following the Second Vatican Council, which overthrew so much of what had been looked upon as unchanging Catholic thought and practice in the Catholic Church they were trained to serve. Though many priests clearly welcomed the changes, a number were overwhelmed by them. The Catholic priestly culture is by definition conservative. The culture of seminary training is also conservative, for it is in this context that norms, values, attitudes and beliefs are handed on. This may be so in any large organization, but in the Catholic Church the underlying culture is represented as complying with a sacred tradition and even with a tradition divinely mandated. It is unsurprising, therefore, in such an organization that the notion of change should lie uneasily, especially with those newly joining its ruling élite. The term 'loyal opposition' has a long tradition as an oxymoron in the Catholic Church.

Listening to the priests

Increasing numbers of those who profess themselves to be Catholic appear detached from the central beliefs, religious practices and day-to-day concerns of the Catholic Church. For example, as statistics from successive editions of the *Catholic Directory of England and Wales* show, less than one-third of Catholics regularly attend Sunday mass.

This is the context for which new generations of priests are being trained and in which they will be required to work in order to revitalize Catholic belief and practice. They can no longer rely on automatic goodwill toward themselves as priests, nor take for granted a level of religious literacy among the growing number of nominal Catholics who have had little contact with Catholic school or parish. Notwithstanding the difficulty of the task, one regular priest wrote as follows:

> One wonders whether the questions relating to seminary training betray unreal expectations of seminaries alone. Yes, formation is needed in all these areas, but we do not only rely on the seminaries. They in so many instances merely support and affirm what happens in a much wider sphere of personal formation (priest aged between 65 and 69).

Such might well have been the experience for some regular priests during their training, but it is a far cry from a commonly expressed experience of secular priests. One went so far as to imply that the seminary did nothing in assisting his ministerial skills.

> On seminary training, all my answers are negative. Yet it was a very happy time for me and for all of us (priest aged between 65 and 69).

The deep level of misgivings appearing to underlie one priest's criticism of seminary training prior to the 1960s will certainly evoke a strong resonance in the memory of many priests trained at that time. Although it is not something easy to admit, priests were undeniably educated into harsh ecclesiastical attitudes, with various escape-clauses serving to assuage the tenderminded attitudes of some of the priests themselves.

> The pre-Vatican II seminary training was slave-training. (Mine was quite liberal.) Dogma – *de fide* – heretic – moral – mortal sin – hell – canon law – suspension – excommunication – a spiritual terrorism (priest aged between 75 and 79).

Addressed in more general and milder terms, seminary training is once more faulted in the following comment, but the discovery, much later, of collaborative ministry is prized.

> Seminary experience [was] enjoyed but much of it [was] irrelevant to the life of a priest . . . Ministry has been a joy but often difficult as [it is] reassessed over and again. I value enormously the growth of collaborative ministry – for real 'co-operation' not 'delegation' (priest aged between 70 and 74).

In spite of very considerable changes in seminary training over the past forty years, one priest's comment expresses the opinion of many of his colleagues regarding the unimpressive qualities of the present day seminary product, though it is unclear whether the fault should lie at the door of the personality of the candidate or the quality of his training.

> In my own experience 'young priests' are ill-equipped and inexperienced in a 'street-wise' sense, on graduation from seminary and in their initial appointments in parish life. As a late vocation I believe there are numerous advantages and benefits not experienced by younger priests (priest aged between 50 and 54).

Shaping the questions

Against this background, the *Catholic Parochial Clergy Survey* developed two main themes concerned with the preparation or training priests perceived themselves as having received for public ministry. The first theme focused on the public role assumed in leadership in the Catholic Church. How well do priests feel that their seminary training prepared them for conducting the liturgy? How well do priests feel that their seminary training prepared them for preaching? How well do priests feel that their seminary training prepared them for public speaking more generally?

The second theme focused on two key issues of public ministry in which the leadership of the local parish priest may be quite crucial for the character and identity of the local congregation. These issues concern change within the Catholic Church and relationships with other faith groups outside the Catholic Church. How well do priests feel that their seminary training prepared them for changes in the Catholic Church? How well do priests feel that their seminary training prepared them for interfaith dialogue?

Interpreting the statistics

Table 1.1 demonstrates that more priests are appreciative than critical of the way they were prepared for public ministry by their seminary. According to their view, seminaries made a better job of preparing them for conducting the liturgy than for preaching, and really failed to equip them for participating in interfaith dialogue.

Two out of every three priests considered that they had been well prepared for conducting the liturgy. Indeed, three times as many priests felt confident that their seminary training prepared them well for conducting the liturgy (66%), compared with those who felt that their seminary training failed to prepare them well for this area of ministry (22%).

The preparation provided by the seminary for the ministries of public speaking and of preaching is also rated quite favourably. Over twice as many priests felt confident that their seminary training prepared them well for public speaking (59%), compared with those who felt inadequately prepared for public speaking (26%). Similarly, over twice as many priests felt confident that their seminary training prepared them well for preaching (57%), compared with those who felt inadequately prepared for preaching (26%).

On the other hand, these statistics leave little room for complacency. A third (34%) of the priests could not affirm that seminary had prepared them well for conducting liturgy, 41% could not affirm that seminary had prepared them well for public speaking and 43% could not affirm that seminary had prepared them well for preaching.

Conducting the liturgy, public speaking and preaching are all established and traditional roles in the Catholic Church and around three-fifths of the priests felt that seminaries were performing well in these areas. Seminaries are rated less highly for their ability to prepare priests for handling changes in the Church. The proportion dropped to 49% who felt that their seminary training prepared them for changes in the Church.

The final question in this section clearly shows that interfaith dialogue has not been high on the agenda of seminaries. One in four (25%) of the priests agreed that their seminary training had prepared them well for interfaith dialogue, compared with 56% who disagreed that this was the case. Lack of adequate preparation in this area may make ministry particularly problematic for those priests assigned to parishes in strongly multifaith areas.

Regular and secular

Table 1.2 demonstrates that there are no significant differences in the perceptions of seminary training for public ministry between secular priests and regular priests. This suggests that the seminary training for public ministry by the two systems has been perceived in similar ways by the seminarians trained in these systems. For example, 63% of the regular priests and 67% of the secular priests considered their seminary training had prepared them well for conducting the liturgy. Around three-fifths of the regular priests (57%) and the secular priests (59%) considered that their seminary training had prepared them well for public speaking. Around three-fifths of the regular priests (57%) and the secular priests (57%) considered that their seminary training had prepared them well for preaching. Around half of the regular priests (52%) and the secular priests (48%) considered that their seminary training had prepared them well for changes in the Church. Around a quarter of the regular priests (26%) and the secular priests (25%) considered that their seminary training had prepared them well for inter-faith dialogue.

Generational differences

Table 1.3 reveals important shifts in the perceptions of seminary training for aspects of public ministry across different generations of priests. Generally speaking the younger priests rated their seminary training for the public aspects of ministry more highly than the older priests. All five issues included in this section of the survey deserve comment.

First, training in liturgy is consistently rated in the highest place by all three generations of priests. Moreover, there is no significant difference in the proportions of priests across the three generations who felt that their seminary training prepared them well for conducting the liturgy. This suggests that the performance of seminaries has not changed significantly in this area. Training in liturgy was high on the seminary agenda and it has remained so.

Second, across the three generations the proportion of priests who felt that their seminary training has prepared them well for public speaking has consistently increased. While 51% of those aged 60 and over considered that their seminary training prepared them well for public speaking, the proportions rose to 60% among the 45–59-year-olds, and to 69% among those under the age of 45.

Third, an improvement has also occurred in the evaluation of training for preaching. Here improvement was slightly less pronounced and later to start. While 54% of those aged 60 and over and 55% of the 45–59 year olds considered that their seminary training prepared them well for preaching, the proportion rose to 66% among those under the age of 45.

Fourth, it is the priests aged 60 and over who felt least prepared by their seminary training for changes in the Church. Those trained in the aftermath of the Second Vatican Council perceived themselves to have been better prepared for changes in the Church. While only a third (33%) of those aged 60 and over considered that their seminary training prepared them well for changes in the Church, the proportion rose to 59% among the 45–59-year-olds, and remained at this level (59%) among those under the age of 45.

Fifth, the attention given by seminaries to interfaith dialogue appears to have gained importance across the generations. While only 15% of those aged 60 and over considered that their seminary training prepared them well for interfaith dialogue, the proportions rose to 27% among the 45–59-year-olds, and to 37% among those under the age of 45.

CHAPTER TWO

Training for Pastoral Ministry

The dropout rate in the seminary system is staggering but they still prefer the present system. There is a whole other agenda at work here: many seminary profs and administrators want to be bishops. In fact they're often appointed to the seminary system so that they can be positioned to be bishops. The present Pope leans toward conservative seminary profs. That was his background. It affects all their actions (Lynch, 1993, p. 192).

This chapter is concerned with the training received by Catholic priests to equip them for *pastoral ministry*. Pastoral ministry, broadly conceived, is considered to embrace meeting with people where they are, making home calls, visiting the sick, and dealing with individuals at major turning points in their lives. Given the importance in Catholic teaching attributed to marriage and family life, particular attention is given to the major areas of pre-marriage instruction and marriage counselling, areas which a male celibate priesthood may find particularly alien to their own immediate experiences.

Context

Although Lynch's observation represents a viewpoint from the United States of America, its applicability to the seminary in Britain will be clear. What was so idiosyncratic about the pastoral training of so many priests in seminaries before the Second Vatican Council was the collective dearth of pastoral experience among the seminary teachers or 'profs' as they were almost universally known. The following catches one of the more bizarre yet fairly typical moods of that self-complacent seminary world.

A moral theology examination once asked us to state the number of sins committed by an Irish labourer working on a Sunday on a building site for an Anglican church, and to give our views on the validity of an absolution given by a curate to a nun who made her confession to him while they were both swimming in the local bathing pool. Regurgitation of received instruction was the criterion of success and those students who distinguished themselves in such examinations were gravely warned against contracting spiritual pride (McLaughlin, 1998, p. 34).

So many priests presently ministering in England and Wales, and certainly the hundreds of priests who have now retired, began their priesthood before anyone had the vision to question, still less the authority to change, a regime in which a newly ordained curate, with no pastoral experience whatsoever, was expected over a weekend to transform himself from ill-considered seminarian into effective priest. The move into pastoral ministry was from a semi-monastic training regime. After reveille at 6.00 am, meditation in the chapel from 6.30 to 7.00 was followed by mass at 7.00. Before lunch at 1.00 pm there was a 'visit' to the blessed sacrament with set prayers. From 5.00 to 5.15 five decades of the rosary were recited and from 6.45 to 7.00 spiritual reading was obligatory. Night prayers in the chapel at 9.15 heralded the start of the great silence invariably known by its Latin name of *magnum silentium* which lasted until after the grace at the start of breakfast the following morning.

> Even odder than this enforcement of a monastic regime on men who were going to live in and minister to a secular world in which they would have to organise and take responsibility for their own lives was the fact that few of us found it odd. Most of us, I suspect, enjoyed the regularity and security of the routine which provided immunity from the real problems and created the illusion that we were daily coming closer to God (McLaughlin, 1998, pp. 36–7).

The ignorance of life shown by many young priests must have been obvious to their parishioners. Priests thought they knew what was expected of them in a given pastoral situation and with varying degrees of success carried out the function. The temptation to become functionaries was very strong, especially in that area of pastoral ministry that involved the sacraments. The priest can appear particularly efficient, for instance, in a hospital setting where staff have been instructed to send for the priest in a near death emergency involving a Catholic patient. Because he always attended and gave the last rites, the priest's presence was a predictable fact in such a hospital event. The Catholic procedures dovetailed well with hospital procedures.

> Particularly in emergencies when little time is available sacramental rituals have an objectivity and 'professionalism' that can be more effective than improvised care and counsel . . . In situations that are totally new and bewildering, rituals can supply boundaries and signposts, so reducing the sense of chaotic novelty (Wilkinson, 1978, p. 133).

It appears significant that in those areas of pastoral ministry apart from the sacramental, such as hospital and house visiting, pre-marriage instruction and marriage counselling, Catholic priests discovered the difficulty shared by so many of their non-Catholic ministerial colleagues. Those more elderly priests still ministering were the final victims of a centuries old seminary regime that, in the interests of preserving those training for the priesthood from the blandishments of the outside world, denied them practical pastoral training as part of their priestly education.

The older generation of Catholic priests were as aware as many who were to follow them at the seminaries, of the boast of Catholic priests that they knew their people because of the practice of regular house-to-house visiting. It was a practice that helped create a bond between priests and people. In parochial schools the children grew accustomed to seeing the priest frequently and he became a familiar figure. Though criticism was heard of the brevity and superficiality of house visits, as well as their link with collecting money, they served as reinforcement to the faith of the committed and as reminder to the so-called 'lapsed' of the continued expectation of their return to churchgoing.

Hospital visiting can be seen as an extension of house-to-house visiting. It is based upon the evangelical practice commended in Matthew: 'I was sick and you visited me' (Matthew 25:36). Success depended more upon the personality of the priest than upon educational precept or training. In spite of increasing evidence to the contrary, there is a strong abiding clerical culture that would argue that 'these things cannot be taught', militating against a policy of consistent training and review of particular pastoral ministries.

With little justification there was a lot of intellectual arrogance among Catholic clergy. Not only did they see themselves as authoritative representatives of the one true Church, but also they believed they were led by an infallible Pope and had the correct answer to just about every theological question that could be asked. Or had they? In the 1940s and 1950s more thoughtful and perceptive priests thought they could see the inevitability of change. It could be asserted even in the 1970s with considerable justification that 'some priests appear to share the feeling that it is humiliating and undignified for the Church to admit that it had or has anything to learn from anyone' (Hebblethwaite, 1975, p. 18). Rumours grew that the Catholic Church was in the process of reconsidering its position on birth control. On 29 July 1967 the encyclical entitled *Humanae Vitae* (Of Human Life) was published, expressing among other things the sanctity of marital love, urging the need to nurture life in marriage and restating a belief in human dignity. Rejecting the findings of a majority report of the commission which had been called by Pope Paul VI, *Humanae Vitae* unambiguously reiterated and upheld the Catholic Church's ban on artificial birth control. Its tone, however, was more diffident, stating that 'the spirit . . . illuminates the hearts of the faithful and invites their consent'.

Humanae Vitae was not without its strong supporters, but the division between the hierarchy and the laity on birth control grew rather than diminished. Evidence indicates that the teaching is largely ignored by Catholic couples at the beginning of the twenty-first century. Fox (1995, p. 80) states that less than a decade after the encyclical's promulgation, polls indicated more than eight out of ten adult Catholics in the United States of America simply disregarded it, adding that that was not all. It was, he wrote, eroding Catholic confidence in the institution.

Generations of young priests at ordination with a head full of moral theology and Canon Law concerning the sixth and ninth commandments were unwise enough to have been convinced that their time in the seminary had equipped them to speak knowledgeably about marriage. Generations of married couples had been made aware, but were conditioned by deference, not to tell those generations of priests that priests on the whole did not really know what they were talking about. Generations of priests had been engaged in personifying variations on the violin parable. The publication of *Humanae Vitae* and the experience of subsequent history has brought home to Catholic priests the need for a much more realistic appraisal of their personal competence in the field of pre-marriage instruction and marriage counselling. The breakdown of so many marriages in the last quarter of the twentieth century, misfortunes to which Catholic marriages have been equally prone, has urged further caution upon celibate priests if ever they had thought of themselves as experts on marriage, with or without pastoral training.

The majority of priests working in England and Wales have been enveloped all of their lives in a Catholic ethos in which the Catholic Church has provided their sustaining framework. Among younger priests and many younger Catholics, such a taken-for-grantedness about the place of Catholicism is less sharply defined than it is to those who grew up in the church before the 1960s. The pastoral challenge facing priests today appears to be one of attempting to restore to their context in a pluralist world Catholic doctrines, images and symbols for believers of all ages, thereby presenting a coherent vision and practice that fosters authentic flourishing of the human spirit (Schuth, 1999).

Listening to the priests

It is readily recognized that adequate training makes ministry less problematic and provides priests with a more realistic perspective. This point is made by one priest who wrote as follows.

I think sometimes we can be over pessimistic about our lives and work and if not careful, can become too whingeing. I know there are problems but these have to be faced in any walk of life. If there is sufficient pastoral training in seminaries most priests should have some idea of what they are to face (priest aged between 40 and 44).

Inevitably, when priests are asked to review their own seminary training, they take issue with shortcomings which have now possibly changed in the interim, but which were problematic at the time. Candidates for ministry to the world of the parish were trained as if the world did not exist, being denied access even to radio and newspapers.

Not to be 'of' the world, yes, that was fine [but] we were being trained not to be 'in' the world. We had to persuade the seminary authority to let us have daily newspapers. Happiness could come again if bishops and priests kept to preaching the word and did pastoral work (priest aged between 60 and 64).

Not only had a particular form of seminary training become close to being counter-productive, but also a glut of vocations appeared to have reduced wise concern for optimum placement.

I was ordained in 1960. Training was monastic and intellectual (philosophy and theology). Little sensitivity was shown in appointments, why sent, what the place was like, what I had to offer. One seemed like a pawn on a board. There is so much spiritual power to be unlocked if we become a people of faith, hope and charity. We still have to become a post-Vatican II Church (priest aged between 55 and 59).

Whether it is called in-service training, sabbatical, or time-out, the benefit of such an interlude can help enormously in supplying some of the pastoral and other training which was unavailable in the seminary. One priest wrote about the opportunities given to him to expand the experience of seminary training.

I had the benefit of a year out for personal growth, counselling skills, etc. I believe it was one of the best years of my life helping me to cope now with living on my own, responding to the pressures and demands of parish ministry, growing in celibacy, etc. I would like such benefits to be more readily available ... I believe we need to be more realistic in our own expectations of ourselves, in order not only to survive but to thrive as diocesan priests (priest aged between 40 and 44).

Shaping the questions

Against this background, the *Catholic Parochial Clergy Survey* developed two main themes concerned with the preparation or training priests perceived themselves as having received for pastoral ministry. The first theme focused on the pastoral ministry of visiting. How well do priests feel that their seminary training prepared them for pastoral visiting in general? How well do priests feel that their seminary training prepared them for hospital visiting in particular? How well do priests feel that their seminary training prepared them for ministry to the sick, whether in hospital or at home?

The second theme took the context of the sacrament of marriage as a key test of readiness for pastoral ministry. Priests come face-to-face with the practical needs of parishioners when couples come seeking the sacrament of marriage and when the married come seeking help and advice with their marriage relationship. How well do priests feel that their seminary training prepared them for providing pre-marriage instruction? How well do priests feel that their seminary training prepared them for marriage counselling?

Interpreting the statistics

Table 2.1 demonstrates that overall the priests felt much less well prepared by their seminaries for pastoral ministry than for public ministry as discussed in chapter 1. While fewer than half felt properly prepared for any area of pastoral ministry, only a handful felt prepared for the ministry of marriage counselling.

The area of pastoral ministry for which seminary training was rated most highly was that of ministry to the sick. Nonetheless, fewer than half of the priests

(46%) felt that their seminary training had prepared them well for ministry to the sick, while 39% were clear that they had not been well prepared for this key area of their pastoral work.

Closely following ministry to the sick came pastoral visiting. Just over two-fifths of the priests (43%) felt that their seminary training had prepared them well for pastoral visiting. Once again, two-fifths (40%) felt that they had not been well prepared for this area of their pastoral work.

These figures show that slightly more priests felt that their seminary training had prepared them well for ministry to the sick than rejected this view (46% compared with 39%). Similarly, slightly more priests felt that their seminary training had prepared them well for pastoral visiting than rejected this view (43% compared with 40%). In the case of hospital visiting, however, the situation is reversed. Slightly more priests felt that their seminary training had *not* prepared them well for hospital visiting than felt that they had been well prepared for this aspect of pastoral ministry (45% compared with 37%).

The value of seminary training for preparing priests to deal with marriage-related issues was rated very low. In this area, marriage counselling fared even less well than pre-marriage instruction. Only one in five of the priests (22%) felt that their seminary training prepared them well for pre-marriage instruction. The proportion fell to one in seven of the priests (14%) who felt that their seminary training prepared them well for marriage counselling.

Looked at from the opposite perspective, three-fifths of the priests (59%) clearly felt unprepared by their seminary for the ministry of pre-marriage instruction, while two-thirds of the priests (66%) clearly felt unprepared by their seminary for the ministry of marriage counselling.

Regular and secular

Table 2.2 demonstrates that there are significant differences in the perceptions of regular priests and secular priests regarding the adequacy of their seminary training to equip them for aspects of pastoral ministry. In some areas the regular priests felt even less well prepared than the secular priests.

Regular priests felt less well prepared than secular priests for ministry to the sick, for pastoral visiting, and for hospital visiting. While 48% of the secular priests felt well prepared by their seminary training for ministry to the sick, the proportion fell to 39% among the regular clergy. While 45% of the secular priests felt well prepared by their seminary training for pastoral visiting, the proportion fell to 37% among the regular priests. While 39% of the secular priests felt well prepared by their seminary training for hospital visiting, the proportion fell to 27% among the regular priests. The data suggest that regular priests may be less well prepared by their seminary for pastoral ministry in comparison with secular priests.

At the same time, regular priests and secular priests felt equally badly prepared by their seminaries for undertaking pre-marriage instruction and for undertaking marriage counselling. Thus, just over one in every five of the regular priests (22%) and of the secular priests (22%) considered that their seminary training had prepared them well for pre-marriage instruction. Around one in every six of the regular priests (16%) and of the secular priests (14%) considered that their seminary training had prepared them well for marriage counselling.

Generational differences

Table 2.3 demonstrates that priorities in seminary training for pastoral ministry have changed across the generations. In some areas of pastoral ministry, younger priests felt better equipped by their seminaries than was the case among their older colleagues. In other areas of pastoral ministry, younger priests felt less well equipped by their seminaries than was the case among their older colleagues. In yet other areas of pastoral ministry, no significant differences emerged between the generations. These three areas will be discussed in turn.

First, younger priests felt better prepared than their older colleagues in respect of hospital visiting and in respect of pastoral visiting. Thus, 47% of the priests under the age of 45 considered that their seminary training had prepared them well for hospital visiting, compared with 37% of those between 45 and 59, and with 30% of those aged 60 and over. Similarly, 50% of the priests under the age of 45 considered that their seminary training had prepared them well for pastoral visiting, compared with 39% of those between 45 and 59, and with 43% of those aged 60 and over. Seminaries may be gaining confidence in equipping priests for pastoral ministry beyond the walls of their churches, but there still seems considerable room for further improvement.

Second, younger priests felt less well prepared than their older colleagues in respect of ministry to the sick and in respect of pre-marriage instruction. Thus, 41% of the priests under the age of 45 and 41% of those between 45 and 59 considered that their seminary training had prepared them well for ministry to the sick, compared with 53% of those aged 60 and over. Similarly, 19% of the priests under the age of 45 and 20% of those between 45 and 59 considered that their seminary training had prepared them well for pre-marriage instruction, compared with 25% of those aged 60 and over. Seminaries may be losing confidence in equipping priests for certain aspects of sacramentally based pastoral ministry. When traditional strategies in such areas of pastoral ministry have lost credibility, priests may appear even less confident in such pastoral situations.

Third, no significant difference emerges between the generations of priests in respect of their perception of the adequacy of their seminary training to equip them for marriage counselling. Even among the youngest cohort of priests, 83% did not feel confident to say that their seminary training prepared them well for the pastoral ministry of marriage counselling. Seminaries may still need to reconsider how best to equip priests for this aspect of their pastoral work.

CHAPTER THREE

Training for Work with People

Sister Brunhilde was coaching a Krebsbach on his catechism one morning in Our Lady lunchroom and suddenly asked a question out of order. 'Why did God make you?' she said sharply, as if it were an accusation. The boy opened his mouth, wavered, then looked at a spot on the linoleum and put his breakfast there. He ran to the lavatory and Sister, after a moment's thought, strolled down the hall to the fifth grade classroom. 'Who wants to be a nurse when she grows up?' she asked. Six girls raised their hands and she picked Betty Diener. 'Nurses help sick people in many different ways', she told Betty as they walked to the lunchroom. 'They have many different jobs to do. Now here is one of them. The mop is in the kitchen. Be sure to use plenty of Pine-Sol' (Keillor, 1986, p. 14).

This chapter is concerned with the seminary training received by Catholic priests to equip them for *work with people*. Different skills are needed for relating to different sectors of society. Work with people, broadly conceived, is considered to embrace specific skills for working with children or for working with teenagers, specific skills for working with women or for working with men, and specific skills for working with the elderly or for working with the bereaved.

Context

Not many priests could have matched Sister Brunhilde's genius for what Keillor (1986, p. 14) describes as making children 'realize themselves as finer persons than they were allowed to be at home'. Nevertheless, a remarkable opportunity is given to priests to engage with children through infant, primary and secondary education in Catholic schools. The level of training given to seminarians to enable them to maximize such an opportunity to influence children and teenagers, at all stages of their education, was until all too recently non-existent, and even now appears to leave too much to chance or natural inclination.

Recent correspondence in the religious press, relating to this hit-and-miss nature of the contribution of the seminaries to a key area of priestly formation, stressed the overall failure of seminaries to exploit the expertise now present among seminarians themselves. The higher average age of those now applying to seminaries has meant that a greater proportion of seminarians coming from professional secular occupations, particularly in the field of education, possess levels of expertise not hitherto as accessible to the academic staff within the seminary.

For instance, one correspondent with the experience of ten years as a primary school headteacher bemoaned the fact that such a potential resource was never made use of in the seminary (*The Tablet*, 26 August 2000, p. 1133).

It was largely as a consequence of the Council of Trent (1545–63) that seminary training as we know it arose. The aim was to provide a well-trained, and more or less uniform clergy with similar ideals and ideas. The environment in which seminarians were trained virtually separated them from family and friends. This all-male ambience had at its core the objective of 'preserving their vocation', and most priests of the older school will have stories of the identification of 'women as temptress' that led one eminent moral theologian to marvel that seminarians and priests 'were not more disturbed than they were' (Häring, 1996, p. 80). A man as enlightened in his own day as any in England, Father John Carmel Heenan, wrote in 1950 of the advisability of priests to relate socially only with priests, and in the same book referred to women as 'sources of temptation'.

The eleven o'clock presbytery rule, obliging priests to return before the curfew hour, was predicated upon the curiously mistaken presumption that sexual impropriety was most likely to coincide with what is commonly known as bedtime. It was an unspoken assumption as unwarranted as it was expected, derived predictably from a delightfully ignorant, celibate source. Exhortations to treat all woman as you would your mother, your sister or Our Lady, and the warning never to find yourself alone in a room with a woman, were scarcely a sound basis on which to build a psychologically healthy attitude to relating with women, but were often all the training seminarians were given on the matter. Apocryphal stories based on the textbook recommendation, 'Women, see under "occasion of sin"', come closer to the truth than many would care to admit.

It might reasonably be assumed that seminarians trained in an all-male environment would, whatever the deficiencies in other areas of their training, be eminently well-prepared to minister to men. The training principle of withdrawing seminarians from all contact with women is clearly questionable as a strategy for enabling them subsequently to be at ease with women. Similarly the practice until comparatively recently of seminarians spending the vast majority of their time in the company of priests and fellow seminarians is questionable as a strategy for enabling them subsequently to be at ease with men. It was not a particularly well thought-out strategy in either instance, nor, one now imagines, was it much thought about at all by the vast majority of seminary staff who, in theory, were presented as the crème de la crème of the diocesan clergy, but were on the whole and on their own admission as uninspired and uninspiring as some of their charges found them.

A recent publication in the United States of America gave voice to a growing concern over the rising phenomenon of homosexuality in the priesthood. The author links the departure in the United States of America of twenty thousand priests, most in order to marry, with a dramatically altered 'gay/straight ratio [contributing] to the disproportionate number of priests with a homosexual orientation' (Cozzens, 2000, p. 100). Though it is yet unclear how predominantly heterosexual male Catholic parishioners will relate to patently homosexual priests, it is inadvisable for church authorities just to 'wait and see' in the fond hope that it will not serve to disincline straight males from having too much to do with a church that is overtly gay.

One question has been asked concerning seminary training in connection with a ministry that future priests will meet, namely responsibility for ministry to an increasingly elderly congregation: whether clergy who can expect to minister in this milieu are adequately or at all prepared to provide sensitive and appropriate leadership for the elderly (Gulledge, 1992). The evidence appears to point to the conclusion that clergy are neither adequately prepared nor motivated to meet the needs of elderly church members. Only to attend on an ad hoc untrained basis to the pastoral needs of the elderly, who incidentally are the fastest growing section of society, is difficult to justify. Death impinges proportionally more upon the elderly in the population, so one obvious consequence is the importance of bereavement counselling to the elderly. Because it is now extraordinary ministers of the eucharist who, in many parishes, bring holy communion to the sick and housebound, it becomes increasingly important that during their seminary training, the clergy are enabled to instruct and assist their future lay ministers in awareness both of the talents and needs of older people. The paradoxical comment that 'the Church can deal with dying people; it is the living with whom they have trouble', should not, in a truly caring Christian ministry, ring with quite the note of truth that so often in fact it does.

Regarding the commitment of those currently undergoing seminary training for work with people, it is worth reflecting whether the description of his seminarians by one seminary faculty member in the United States of America would fit those now in British seminaries: 'They tend to be a bit narcissistic, taking care of themselves first, saving time for themselves above all. It shows itself in other ways too. The sign-up sheet for holy hours is always full, but it is hard to find anyone to serve a meal in a shelter' (Schuth, 1999, p. 89).

Listening to the priests

Remarkably, in Catholic seminaries before the mid-1960s the underlying presumption cannot but have been that training to work with people could best be achieved by keeping seminarians apart from them. One priest made this point in the following way.

> My seminary days were lecture orientated – leading to ordination. It was very negative – people didn't come into it – rules, regulations, canon law, validity of marriage. Counselling skills, etc. were never considered . . . Now at my age I am increasingly frustrated by being a manager rather than a priest – I have a club/pub to run – I am a tax collector, etc., everything I wasn't ordained for (priest aged between 60 and 64).

There is a nice irony of priest turned into tax collector; precisely the reverse of the evangelical call to Matthew (Matthew 9:9).

One priest welcomed the opportunity to air his views, but what might give cause for concern is the negative perception felt by the priest who patently feels that his opinion is neither sought nor heard.

> I am happy to be asked my opinion about training for ministry etc., because I feel I have very little power to influence things (priest aged between 55 and 59).

If the initial seminary training for work with people was indeed as insubstantial as some priests expressed, even more recent seminary attempts to make up for these deficiencies are not highly considered.

> I hope that the findings of your survey are used in the vital area of formation of priests at seminary which, apart from the purely academic, appears woefully inadequate. Further it is clear that formation is ongoing, maybe throughout one's ministry (priest aged between 45 and 49).

However positively the implementation of seminary reorganization proceeds, what appears to be essential is the formation of priests who are able to work collaboratively with the laity. The story is told of a comparatively recent book-loving Administrator of Westminster Cathedral that, when an elderly lady introduced herself to him as a former parishioner who remembered him as a young priest in her parish, his reply was, 'Madam, had you been a book I would have remembered you. As you are not, I regret that I have no recollection of you at all.' That such a reply was remembered and retold speaks volumes. People expect a consistent, tangible sense of welcome from a parish priest and are keenly aware of situations in which they are made to feel that they do not matter. Although not single-handedly, priests set the tone of welcome in a parish. If they are not gregarious by nature, the bare mechanics of making others feel welcome can be taught and learned.

Shaping the questions

Against this background, the *Catholic Parochial Clergy Survey* developed three main themes concerned with the preparation or training priests perceived themselves as having received for work with people. The first theme focused on work among young people. How well do priests feel that their seminary training prepared them for ministry with children? How well do priests feel that their seminary training prepared them for ministry with teenagers? Given the Catholic Church's continued investment in church schools, these may be crucial areas of ministry for developing the Church's future.

The second theme concentrated on work with adults, but highlighted the differences involved in the priest's work among men and among women. On the one hand, the celibate priest, trained in an all-male environment, may be expected to find some aspects of ministry among women problematic. On the other hand, the celibate priest, set aside by his training from the culture of men in general, may be expected to find some aspects of ministry among men problematic. How well, then, do priests feel that their seminary training prepared them for relating to women? How well do priests feel that their seminary training prepared them for relating to men?

The third theme concentrated on work among people in later life. Given the ageing of church congregations and the Catholic Church's traditional expectations of ministry among the dying and the bereaved, this area of ministry may be of increasing importance to the parish priest. How well, then, do priests feel that their seminary training prepared them for ministry to the elderly? How well do priests feel that their seminary training prepared them for ministry to the bereaved?

Interpreting the statistics

Table 3.1 demonstrates that priests feel that they were ill-prepared by their seminary training for ministry to young people. Fewer than one in five priests felt well prepared for ministry among children, teenagers and women. No more than two in five priests felt well prepared for any other area of work with people.

For every two priests who felt that their seminary training prepared them well for ministry to children, seven felt that their seminary had not prepared them well in this area (18% compared with 63%). For every two priests who felt that their seminary training prepared them well for ministry to teenagers, ten felt that their seminary had not prepared them well in this area (13% compared with 68%). In other words, only one in every six priests felt well prepared by the seminary for ministry to children. The proportion falls further to just one in every eight priests who felt well prepared by the seminary for ministry to teenagers.

Clearly priests felt much less prepared by their seminary for relating to women than for relating to men. Fewer than one in five of the priests (18%) felt that their seminary training had prepared them well for relating to women, compared with three in five of the priests (60%) who felt that their seminary training had not prepared them well for relating to women.

While twice as many priests felt that their seminary training had prepared them well for relating to men in comparison with relating to women, still only two in five of the priests (40%) felt that this had been the case. Even here the seminary is far from receiving a great vote of confidence.

Priests are twice as likely to have felt that their seminary did a good job in preparing them for ministry to the elderly compared with ministry to children. While only 18% of the priests considered that their seminary training prepared them well for ministry to children, the proportion rose to 39% who considered that their seminary training prepared them well for ministry to the elderly.

Although ministry to the bereaved is a central part of the priests' work with people, only one in four of them (25%) felt that their seminary training prepared them well for ministry to the bereaved. Twice this number (53%) were clear that their seminary had not prepared them well for this area of ministry.

Regular and secular

Table 3.2 demonstrates that in some key areas regular priests have felt better prepared than secular priests by their seminary for work with people. Three points are clear from the statistics.

First, regular priests felt slightly better prepared than secular priests for ministry to young people.

While 17% of the secular priests felt their seminary training had prepared them well for ministry to children, the proportion rose significantly among the regular priests to 22%. While 12% of the secular priests felt their seminary training had prepared them well for ministry to teenagers, the proportion rose significantly among the regular priests to 17%.

Second, regular priests felt slightly better prepared than secular priests for relating both to women and to men. While 17% of the secular priests felt their seminary training had prepared them well for relating to women, the proportion rose significantly among the regular priests to 26%. While 39% of the secular priests felt their seminary training had prepared them well for relating to men, the proportion rose significantly among the regular priests to 46%.

Third, there are no significant differences in the proportions of secular and regular priests who felt that their seminary training had prepared them well for ministry to the elderly or for ministry to the bereaved. Thus, 36% of the regular priests and 40% of the secular priests considered that their seminary training had prepared them well for ministry to the elderly. A quarter of the regular priests (25%) and of the secular priests considered that their seminary training had prepared them well for ministry to the bereaved.

Generational differences

Table 3.3 demonstrates that it is the oldest cohort of priests who felt best trained by their seminary for work with people. Overall the middle cohort felt less well prepared than the oldest cohort. Then the youngest cohort felt better prepared than the middle cohort, but less well prepared than the oldest cohort. These generalizations, however, need to be more carefully nuanced in respect of different groups of people.

First, the statistics show that there are no significant differences between the three cohorts in respect of ministry to children and young people. Just 19% of those aged 60 and over felt that their seminary prepared them well for ministry to children, and so did 19% of those under the age of 45. Just 15% of those aged 60 and over felt that their seminary prepared them well for ministry to teenagers, and so did 14% of those aged under 45. Although in both cases the proportions drop slightly among the 45–59-year-olds, the drop is not large enough to be statistically significant.

Second, the statistics show that those aged between 45 and 59 felt less well prepared by their seminary for relating to women and to men than was the case among the older and the younger cohorts. Thus, only 15% of the 45–59-year-olds felt well prepared by their seminary for relating to women, compared with 21%

of those aged 60 and over, and with 21% of those under the age of 45. Similarly, only 36% of the 45–59-year-olds felt well prepared by their seminary for relating to men, compared with 45% of those aged 60 and over, and with 41% of those under the age of 45.

Third, the statistics show that satisfaction with seminary training for ministry to the elderly and for ministry to the bereaved was lower among both those under the age of 45 and among the 45–59-year-olds than among those aged 60 and over. While 43% of those aged 60 and over felt their seminary training had prepared them well for ministry to the elderly, the proportion fell to 36% among the 45–59-year-olds, and rose only marginally to 38% among those aged under 45. While 29% of those aged 60 and over felt their seminary training had prepared them well for ministry to the bereaved, the proportion fell to 21% among the 45–59-year-olds, and rose only marginally to 24% among those under 45. It may be that seminaries are losing confidence in preparing priests for ministry in these areas.

CHAPTER FOUR

Training for the Priestly Life

The Roman Catholic church has tended to adhere to a very distinctive branch of Christianity with its ontological conception of priesthood, the bestowing of sacred gifts upon ordination, and its ontological conception of the Church, so that those located at pinnacle points in the religious hierarchy are necessarily more divine in authority (Ranson, Bryman and Hinings, 1977).

This chapter is concerned with the seminary training received by Catholic priests to equip them for the *priestly life*. The priestly life, broadly conceived and as lived out in England and Wales today, is considered to embrace such features as living on limited means, often living alone, looking after oneself, living as a single man, coming to terms with a life of celibacy, accepting one's sexuality, making a creative use of leisure time away from parish commitments, and developing a spiritual life.

Context

Training for the priestly life appears necessarily to involve a clear notion of what has been called the seminarians' professional self-concept. This may best be explained by instancing a classic study of medical students by Huntington (1957) which found them more likely to think of themselves as doctors the more advanced they were on their training and especially so in their last years of training. Medical students thought of themselves as doctors while interacting with patients rather than with nurses, classmates or faculty staff. It was during their internship, by their interaction with hospital patients, that medical students were provided with their opportunity to identify with being a doctor. Patients provided what is known as 'role support', defined as a set of reactions and performances by others, the expressive indications of which tend to confirm one's detailed and imagined view of oneself as occupant of a position (McCall and Simmons, 1966). In other words, professional identity is a social construction confirmed by various audiences to varying degrees.

It would appear to be similarly advantageous that seminarians should think of themselves as priests, their reference group according to Merton's (1957) notion of 'anticipatory socialization', though still aware that they are technically still students (their membership group) (Ventimiglia, 1978). Perhaps the extent of opportunity to engage in various defined areas of pastoral ministry, at present

44

afforded to seminarians, will facilitate this process of anticipatory socialization. The modern engagement in lay ministries by men who subsequently train for priestly ministry, will also assist the identity transition from layman to priest.

It will be understood that the foregoing analysis has nothing to do with pretending to be something one is not, still less a manifestation of any of those many delusions that seminarians of an earlier age were solemnly warned against. Rather it corresponds more clearly with what one American priest suggested when he said, 'I think one ought to change the preparation structure in favour of adopting the medical model, seminarians as intern then as resident' (Barr, 1993).

The near inevitability of a level of inadequacy in seminary training has long been noted. 'Young people choose the ministry with one set of ideals and occupational images, they are introduced to a radically different set in the seminaries, and when they emerge as neophyte ministers into local parishes they discover additional roles and obligations for which they were never trained' (Jud, Mills and Burch, 1970, p. 93).

'The seminary', said one American priest, 'was an unjust place. We were expected to prepare ourselves to talk with people by not talking to each other' (Dubi, 1993, p. 64). Another berated the monastic discipline, while yet another said, 'The seminaries didn't do a very good job in helping us to build our self image. Part of the very spirituality we were given was to beat up on people, not to find lightness of being. It carries over to our pastoral work. To this day, when my class gather, much of our conversations are about how people were beaten down' (Kenneally, 1993, p. 159). This experience would seem to be more universal than those formally or currently connected with running many seminaries would readily acknowledge. A priest historian pointed out that the clerical culture with which most priests were imbued was one of behaving as if it believed that it knew all the questions and had all the answers. 'There was a lot of intellectual arrogance and cocksureness among the clergy, and it lasted for years' (Ellis, 1993, p. 84).

Many older priests will acknowledge that during their time at the seminary, rather than providing specific or even general information regarding looking after oneself or living on limited means, there was almost what could be construed as a conspiracy against speaking about such matters. Newly ordained priests knew that they would be expected to live in a presbytery and would not be handsomely paid, but in contrast to their seminary existence, living in almost any parish presbytery was an improvement on that experience. Few gave it very much anticipatory thought.

Realistic engagement with instruction in and assessment of the lifelong task of what was involved in living as a single man preparing for the life of celibacy, and accepting one's sexuality, was not attempted by the seminary staff. All that was provided was an occasional spiritualized, exhortatory talk, advocating the embodiment in one's own life of the generosity, spirit of service and self-sacrifice which were characteristic of Jesus. Of course forty and more years ago there was nowhere near the same freedom felt in talking about sexuality, let alone homosexuality as there is today. Sexuality was a largely hidden and forbidden topic due, it is now recognized, to an inadequate appreciation of the role of sexuality in human life. Adolescents are quickly aware that those who are telling them not to worry about their sexuality are in fact worried about telling them (Clark, 1986). One wonders whether the problem of pastoral sexual misconduct, which has surfaced as far more common than was once believed, is due in part to an inadequate personal appraisal during seminary education of the topics of intimacy, loneliness and relationships.

A radically altered world has obliged every major institution to review the training given to its members. It has been questioned whether such a fundamental rethink has similarly and adequately influenced seminary training. Though an indirect financial link exists between parishes and seminaries, little feedback seems to come from parishes or those in specialist ministries to exert leverage on seminary policy. This is nicely exemplified in the account related by a priest attending the Authority and Governance Conference, June 2000 in Cambridge, that in the seven years of his appointment as diocesan director of catechetical formation, an appointment presumably made because of his particular expertise, this priest was not once invited to the diocesan seminary to share either his expertise or experience with its staff or students.

Listening to the priests

The newly ordained diocesan priest prior to the 1960s took his place in the parish structure and quickly became absorbed in maintaining the cultic status quo. As a newly commissioned agent of the bishop, he had been trained to support an institutionalized ghetto-church (Arbuckle, 1996). The newly ordained priest had to learn to live outside a seminary existence of six years of predictable, bell-regulated life, consisting of lectures, meals, religious services, study, sport and sleep. Such a pattern had been better suited to a monastic future than to the comparative unpredictability of the average day in a parish. It quickly dawned on many a young priest on leaving the seminary that he had been given woefully insubstantial training in the practicalities of living as a priest in a parish. One priest wrote about this experience as follows.

> In general my own priestly training in a pre-Vatican II foreign seminary did not, I feel, adequately prepare me for the parochial life although it provided a good theological training and discipline for the spiritual life of a quasi-monastic nature, which I still tend to espouse (priest aged between 55 and 59).

Alongside a personal faith centred in the sacramental life of the Catholic Church, it has long been recognized that the 'core' of priestly spirituality is prayer. The necessity of developing an individual prayer-life was emphasized to seminarians, though the precise form adopted depended upon the particular piety of each priest. Referring to the questionnaire, one priest wrote as follows.

> I am disappointed that prayer figures so little in your questions. I derive immense benefit from contemplative prayer. Without it my life would be pretty empty and my ministry would greatly suffer (age unspecified).

A somewhat different piety is shown by the priest who wrote about his own oratory.

> Every priest needs his own oratory where he and Jesus are personally together with the bonding of the blessed sacrament, which bonds the priests to all, too (priest aged between 65 and 69).

Few would dispute that seminary authorities today are capable of understanding rather better than their predecessors what is conducive to fostering authentic, mature, human development. There are, however, features inherent in the life of the priest in the Catholic Church that preclude those experiences of marriage, mortgage, professional salary and measurable success, to say nothing of fatherhood, that propel many an adolescent male into maturity (Cozzens, 2000). The necessary maturity to be achieved by the celibate priest must be reached by a different route. His lifetime's exertions and his celibacy are thrown into doubt for one priest who wrote about his profound sense of isolation.

> After forty years I feel more isolated than thirty years ago. I feel I am fighting a losing battle against indifference and a Church seeming to be discussed now as being of little consequence. [There exists] no longer the loyalty, enthusiasm and zeal for Catholic life. There is now no understanding of obligation in conscience to worship, share faith with family, attend Catholic school . . . Certainly a celibate priest is not seen to be of much importance (priest aged between 65 and 69).

The perception of not being valued can lead to distressing effects for individuals. The point is made by one priest who wrote about his sense of not being valued.

> If clergy were valued, and this includes proper financial support, then my feelings of depression and frustration would be blessed. There is a general feeling in this diocese that 'the Curia' are not interested in our needs but simply 'impose from on high'. This experience does not help us to feel valued (priest aged between 30 and 34).

The priests in England and Wales taking part in the survey made little comment upon personal finances – evidence perhaps of an overall contentment or example of a general lack of acquisitiveness among them. This is in contrast at least to the anecdotal judgement on their fellow priests working in Ireland. Fifty and more years ago it was quipped that any stranger to Dublin who wanted to know where to dine well needed only follow a group of priests at mealtime. Baseless slander or not, researchers of the seminary scene in the United States of America have alluded to a comparable temptation to which some of their better-off students have fallen of participating in the culture of 'élite affluence', striving to enjoy the best in restaurants, clothing etc., 'possessions [being] perceived as a sign of power and prestige' (Schuth, 1999, p. 89). Most priests in England and Wales just do not have the financial resources to indulge any such proclivity, even if they were minded to do so.

Shaping the questions

Against this background, the *Catholic Parochial Clergy Survey* developed three main themes concerned with the preparation or training that priests perceived themselves as having received for living the priestly life. The first theme focused on the practicalities of living as a priest in the presbytery. In today's context many priests are sent out to parishes to live on their own and to live on limited means. How well, then, do priests feel that their seminary training prepared them for looking after themselves? How well do priests feel that their seminary training prepared them for living on limited means?

The second theme concentrated specifically on the issues of sexuality faced by the celibate priest living, often alone, in the presbytery. How well do priests feel that their seminary training prepared them for living as a single man? How well do priests feel that their seminary training prepared them for the life of celibacy? More generally speaking, how well do priests feel that their seminary training prepared them for accepting their sexuality?

The third theme was concerned with the broader concept of spirituality. In one sense, spirituality may be expressed in the traditional concept of a 'spiritual life' shaped within the tradition of faith. The survey was concerned to ascertain how many priests felt that their seminary training had prepared them well for developing what they were happy to call a spiritual life. In a more contemporary sense, spirituality may be experienced through the concept of developing a rounded appreciation of life. For example, how many priests feel that their seminary training prepared them well for the creative use of their free time?

Interpreting the statistics

Table 4.1 demonstrates that seminary training is rated much more highly for preparing priests to develop a spiritual life, than for living in their parish, for living with their sexuality, and for knowing how to make good use of their time off. These issues will now be examined in greater detail.

Overall, the seminaries were not rated badly for preparing their students for living within their restricted means. Nearly twice as many priests felt that their seminary training had prepared them well for living on limited means, compared with those who took the view that their seminary training had not prepared them well for living in this way (55% compared with 30%).

On the other hand, the seminaries were rated considerably less well for preparing their students for looking after themselves. Only one-third of the priests (34%) considered that their seminary training had prepared them well for looking after themselves, compared with nearly half (46%) who took the view that their seminary training had not prepared them well for the responsibility they found, once away from the seminary, for looking after themselves.

Seminaries were rated quite poorly for the way in which they prepared their students for living without a partner. Thus, less than a third of the priests considered that their seminary training had prepared them well for accepting their sexuality (29%), or had prepared them well for living as a single man (32%). The proportion giving a favourable response rose slightly when the focus turned significantly to celibacy. Even then, however, the proportion rose only to 38% who considered that their seminary training had prepared them well for the life of celibacy.

Looked at from the opposite perspective, the proportion of priests who expressed the view that their seminary training had failed to prepare them well for living without a partner is a clear criticism of the system. Nearly half considered that the system had failed to prepare them well for accepting their sexuality (49%), or for living as a single man (47%). Two-fifths considered that the system had failed to prepare them well for the life of celibacy (41%).

Seminaries were also rated quite poorly for the way in which they prepared, or failed to prepare, their students for making creative use of their free time. Only a third of the priests (33%) considered that their seminary training had prepared them well for creative use of free time, compared with 43% who felt that the seminary had clearly failed to take this area of life seriously.

By way of contrast, the majority of priests felt that their seminary had done a good job on the spiritual front. Two-thirds of the priests (68%) considered that their seminary training had prepared them well for developing a spiritual life, compared with just a quarter of this number (17%) who judged that their seminary had not performed well in this area.

Regular and secular

Table 4.2 demonstrates that the regular priests rate their seminary training significantly more highly than the secular priests in respect of all seven issues listed under the theme of training for the priestly life.

First, the regular priests perceived themselves as having been better prepared for the practicalities of living as a priest. Two-thirds of the regular priests (65%) considered that their seminary training had prepared them well for living on limited means, compared with 53% of the secular clergy. Similarly, 43% of the regular priests considered that their seminary training had prepared them well for looking after themselves, compared with 32% of the secular clergy.

Second, the regular priests perceived themselves as having been better prepared for living without a partner. Half of the regular priests (48%) considered that their seminary training had prepared them well for the life of celibacy, compared with 35% of the secular priests. Over two-fifths of the regular priests (43%) considered that their seminary training had prepared them well for living as a single man, compared with 29% of the secular clergy. Nearly two-fifths of the regular priests (38%) considered that their seminary training had prepared them well for accepting their sexuality, compared with 27% of the secular clergy.

Third, the regular priests perceived themselves as having been better prepared spiritually. Three-quarters of the regular priests (76%) considered that their seminary training had prepared them well for developing a spiritual life, compared with 65% of the secular clergy. Two-fifths of the regular priests (39%) considered that their seminary training had prepared them well for creative use of their free time, compared with 31% of the secular clergy.

Generational differences

Table 4.3 demonstrates some very significant generational differences in the perception of the value of seminary training in preparation for the priestly life. The oldest cohort rated their seminary training more highly in this area than the two younger groups. At the same time, there are some areas in which the youngest cohort rated their seminary experience more highly than is the case among the middle cohort, but other areas in which the youngest cohort rated their seminary experience less highly than is the case among the middle cohort.

Two-thirds of the priests aged 60 and over (68%) considered that their seminary training prepared them well for living on limited means. The proportions fell steadily to 52% among the 45–59-year-olds, and to 40% among those aged under 45. Two-fifths of the priests aged 60 and over (40%) considered that their seminary training had prepared them well for looking after themselves. The proportion fell to 29% among those aged 45–59, and then remained at 30% among those aged under 45.

Nearly half of the priests aged 60 and over (46%) considered that their seminary training had prepared them well for living as a single man. The proportion fell sharply to 24% among the 45–59-year-olds, and then fell slightly further to 21% among those aged under 45. Over half of the priests aged 60 and over (53%) considered that their seminary training had prepared them well for the life of celibacy. The proportion fell sharply to 29% among the 45–59-year-olds, and then fell slightly further to 25% among those aged under 45.

A slightly different pattern, however, obtains to the question regarding sexuality. Almost two-fifths of the priests aged 60 and over (38%) considered that their seminary training had prepared them well for accepting their sexuality. The proportion halved to 20% among the 45–59-year-olds, and then rose again to 28% among those aged under 45. These statistics suggest that seminaries may have placed the issue of sexuality somewhat higher on their agenda in recent years.

The use of leisure time, like sexuality, may be gaining a higher profile on the seminary agenda in recent years. While 39% of the priests aged 60 and over considered that their seminary training prepared them well for creative use of free time, the proportion fell to 25% among the 45–59-year-olds, but rose again to 33% among those aged under 45.

Finally, the statistics suggest that the strength of the seminary in convincing the students that they are being prepared for developing a spiritual life is declining across the generations. While three-quarters of the priests aged 60 and over (76%) considered that their seminary had prepared them well for developing a spiritual life, the proportions fell to 63% among those aged between 45 and 59, and to 59% among those aged under 45.

CHAPTER FIVE

Theology and Priesthood

Priesthood is seen now as the exclusive prerogative of a male whose ordination has endowed him within his very being with power to perform certain actions which the lay members of the Church do not have and which women can never have. The most important of these powers are to consecrate bread and wine so that they become truly the Body and Blood of Jesus and to absolve from sin. The belief in the possession of such power by these privileged persons has led to the concentration of all ruling power in the hands of this clerical élite (McLaughlin, 1998, p. 128).

This chapter is concerned with the *theology of priesthood* which underpins the work of the clergy in the Catholic Church. Broadly conceived, theology of priesthood embraces those theologically motivated practices that give shape to the priestly way of life, including the daily mass and the daily office.

Context

Throughout the history of the church the precise interpretation of gospel demands has been tempered to meet changed and changing circumstances. The English word 'priest' is derived from 'presbyter' and not from the Greek or Latin terms for priesthood. This is not as odd as it sounds. By the third century, when there were more communities than the bishop himself could serve, the presbyter began to be the person to whom the bishop delegated responsibility for pastoral oversight in a given area and the duty of presiding at celebrations of the eucharist. By medieval times the parish priest had become the personification of the Church in the local community who said mass and, except for confirmation and ordination, celebrated all other sacraments and Christian rites. For good or for ill, bishops and priests had virtually taken over the Church and all its ministries.

Until the middle of the twentieth century the prevailing understanding of the theology of priesthood among Catholic theologians had been heavily influenced by the Council of Trent (1545–63). Just as refusal to accept literary and historical criticism had led Catholic scholarship into a cul-de-sac, so ignorance of some of the historical context influencing deliberations of the Council of Trent led to an unbalanced theology of priesthood. The object of Trent was to affirm by anathematizing their contradictions, only those facets of belief about the sacrament of orders denied by the Reformers. It is now generally accepted that the image of priesthood thus presented was a partial, cultic view that ignored equally valid, non-cultic aspects of ministry, which some will remember from the old Catholic aphorism, 'We are priests but they are only ministers.' The polemical circumstances surrounding the Council of Trent resulted in an overemphasis on the cultic aspects of ministry, leading to an understanding of ministry as exclusively priestly and narrowly religious, something done by priests and not by laypeople. The Tridentine understanding, if taken alone, has now been recognized as an impoverishment not only of the evangelical concept of ministry but also of ministerial priesthood (Lawler, 1990).

In emphasizing celebration of the eucharist as central to priesthood, the polemical context of the Council of Trent obscured the Reformers' contention that preaching was central to New Testament ministry. In spite of the existence of the Dominican Order and its preaching mission, the words of the Second Vatican Council came as a surprise to many, 'Since no one can be saved who has not first believed, priests, as co-workers with their bishops, have as their primary duty the preaching of the gospel to all' (Abbott, 1966, pp. 538–9). Of course, preaching the word includes the celebration of the eucharist, but it had taken four hundred years officially to right the balance. It was not that the Council of Trent had denied the priestly activity of preaching and teaching, but in its adoption of anti-positions against the Reformers, the consequence was to stress the cultic activity of the priest. Increasing emphasis over the years was placed upon the priestly powers of consecration and absolution, powers that assumed mysterious and mystical qualities enhancing the status of the priest, but that also served to accentuate a more subservient and secondary role for the laity.

Ordination to the priesthood in the Catholic Church has been interpreted as a rite of passage that brings about a change in status from layman to clergyman, be it priest or deacon. It is difficult to ascertain to what extent deacons share in this popularly perceived 'apartness'. Clergy status confers a sacred aura. Unless the status is revoked, the priest or deacon retains for life this altered status. In other words, 'the priest is not only a religious functionary: he is a symbol, a sacramental person, *theotokos*, bearer of the sacred in the midst of life' (Carroll, 1992). The theological legitimation supporting the secularization of the priestly role arose from the transference in the seventeenth century of the basis of the priesthood of Jesus from the level of his humanity to that of his divinity. The Second Vatican Council reasserted a balance that baptism is the matrix and root of all the sacraments, including that of ordination.

The exalted image of the priest in the popular Catholic mind, common forty and more years ago, has not disappeared, engendered as it is by the believed transformation of the man by his priestly ordination. Social distance was enhanced by the distinctive Roman collar, black suit, cassock and biretta. The strongly felt, but imprecisely defined, attribution of sacredness to the very person of the priest was linked to these characteristics. Perhaps the greatest charisma connected with the Catholic priest's apartness was his commitment to celibacy. In a *Daily Telegraph* article, the journalist Paul Johnson wrote in 1978, 'More important today, however, and obviously of more universal application, is the continuing practice of compulsory celibacy, which transforms the priest into a man, out of this world, who has chosen a form of crucifixion more painful and onerous than any material poverty or deprivation.'

If celibacy was the first defining sacral characteristic of the Catholic priest, the second was that the priest alone communicated from the chalice, denied to the laity. The distinction between the clergy and the laity was further reinforced in the practice of the laity receiving holy communion, not in the hand as in the tradition of other Christian denominations, but directly on the tongue. The laity were fed the eucharist like small children are fed by their parents. A link was established between the sacredness of the eucharistic species and the hands of the priest, which alone were allowed to touch or distribute the sacred elements. Reception of communion in the hand, as it became known, contributed toward a reduction in that attribution of sacredness to the priest, and was further depreciated by the introduction of lay reception of communion from the chalice. The intended purpose was to offer the chalice to the laity: an unforeseen consequence reduced the laity's perception of the uniqueness of the priest.

Though greater accessibility of the sacraments was the ostensible objective of many reforms, the new intimacy and informality of out-of-church worship contrasted sharply with the formal and hushed setting of the Catholic Church, reducing appreciably a sense of the numinous, as well as the sacred nature of the priestly role. Closer association with the erstwhile sacralized person (please not Father: call me John) reduced the mystique of the priesthood itself. The relationship in religion between mystery and majesty had further reinforced an identification of the priest with the sacred rites enacted within the sanctuary, that sacred space delineated by the altar rails, illuminated by candles and sometimes wreathed in incense, where the priest, robed in varying coloured cope, stole or chasuble, sang, spoke or prayed in Latin at the celebration of mass and the sacraments. About his daily work the priest wore distinctive role-symbols of dress. Abandonment of Latin in favour of the vernacular, however beneficial and desirable at one level, reduced the metaphorical distance between priest and laity, as did literally the reversal and forward transposition of the altar, removal of the altar rails and the celebration of mass in private houses.

It seems incontestable that in developed countries Catholicism appears to have forgotten the value of keeping alive in the heart of the religious experience the non-rational element of religion (Otto, 1923). The public or even private recitation of the divine office falls into this category. Few would deny that something of great significance has been lost when less attention is given to the sacramental, metaphorical, symbolic, non-rational dimensions of religion. 'The desire to put everything into familiar no-nonsense language is a clear indication of a movement away from the rich complexity of symbolism toward a supposedly easier but certainly more impoverished form of communication' (Robinson, 1987, p. 59). A twenty-first century perception expressing the loss runs as follows:

When I recall my Catholic youth in the late sixties and seventies, by contrast, I think of the colour beige ... There was a hand wringing and apologetic quality to the Catholicism of my youth. It seemed as though the project was to 'translate' uniquely Catholic doctrine, practice, and style into forms acceptable to the surrounding culture, always downplaying whatever might be seen as peculiar or supernatural (Barron, 2000, p. 5).

The link between money and masses has a long and contentious history. Mass stipends, money given to a priest to celebrate mass for a particular person or intention, has for a long time made up an appreciable proportion of the priest's weekly income. Were not daily masses celebrated by individual priests, the numbers of Sunday masses would have been insufficient to satisfy this demand for particular requests. Though not asserting that daily mass celebration has only continued because of its link with a regular source of income, the underlying theology of the tradition of daily mass seems to have been insufficiently scrutinized. The private devotional aspect of the mass, independent of the public Sunday celebrations, is in need of further analysis.

The New Testament exhortation to pray ceaselessly, allied with the Roman division of the day into four 'hours' (*prima, tertia, sexta, nona*) and the night into four watches (Dugmore, 1986), forms the origin of the canonical hours, those times of daily prayer adopted by the Catholic Church. Since clerics are obliged by Canon Law to recite what are variously known as the divine office, the daily office, or the Liturgy of Hours, this practice resides at the heart of the priestly role. The recitation of the daily office had not always been a tradition gladly undertaken by clergy, instead seen by some parochial clergy as burdensome and intrusive. The pressure of daily work can make it difficult to fulfil the obligation, though a preferred paradigm is that parochial activities should be accommodated around fixed times of prayer, not that prayer be squeezed between the work gaps.

Ambivalent feeling toward the divine office among priests has been well expressed as follows.

So you can imagine that diocesan priests find the office hard. It is so clear that psalms are meant to be sung in common, at clearly defined times of day, and that readings are meant to be read out and listened to. This is liturgy. In however simple a form it merits a certain ceremony. Saying your breviary in a chair, in your living room, by yourself in church, not always at the proper times and with an ear cocked for the telephone, is not satisfactory. We are not monks, and understandably bridle at a basically monastic scheme of prayer. We do on the other hand, need urgently to pray, just as much as monks do (Philpot, 1998, p. 37).

Listening to the priests

Several priests took the opportunity to comment on their theology of priesthood from a variety of perspectives. For example, one priest with a high theology of priesthood wrote about his regular prayer that God:

will help me and my brother priests to be the sort of priest God would wish one to be and to do what He would wish one to do for the glory of God and the salvation of souls. I do hope we can always deserve the beautiful title

'Father' . . . I hope we could find it in our hearts to give God an hour's prayer daily, preferably in the presence of the Blessed Sacrament (priest aged between 65 and 69).

Another priest sharing a high theology of priesthood emphasized what he described as the special calling and the great grace associated with the vocation and ordination to priesthood.

I feel priesthood is a special 'calling' and a great grace . . . that the priesthood is bringing Christ to the people and the people to Christ. I feel that very often it is being regarded from a human point of view and therefore the gospel is not being preached (priest aged between 60 and 64).

Writing out of a very different theology of priesthood, another priest wishes to stress not the ways in which priests were different from other men, but rather the ways in which they shared in the same basic and common humanity. This priest saw the real problem as that of giving priests the courage to look behind their role and to be in touch with their humanity.

Getting priests to admit their needs and to be 'in touch' with their feelings [is] very difficult [as is] trying to get priests to admit to their humanity and not see themselves as consecrated flesh (priest aged between 45 and 49).

Shaping the questions

Against this background, the *Catholic Parochial Clergy Survey* concentrated on three main themes relevant to the priests' articulation of a theology of priesthood. The first theme tackled the direct and obvious question: What proportion of priests today claim to have a clear theology of priesthood?

The second theme focused on the celebration of mass as one of the clearest indicators of what sets the priest apart from the laity within the Catholic community. Today, what proportion of priests continue to value highly saying the daily mass?

The third theme turned attention to the expectation of priesthood in following a spiritual discipline through the daily office. For many the discipline of the daily office may be a constant reminder of living life in close relationship with the traditions of the Catholic Church and with the Lord of the Church. Today, what proportion of priests continue to value highly saying the daily office? Looked at from another perspective, what proportion of priests today would say that most days they do not find time to pray all the daily office?

Interpreting the statistics

Table 5.1 demonstrates that the majority of priests have a clear theology of priesthood and that the majority remain faithful to the traditional discipline of the daily office and of the daily mass.

Only a very small proportion of priests (6%) felt that they do not have a clear theology of priesthood, while another 20% were none too confident about this issue. This still means that three in every four priests (73%) were convinced that they had a clear theology of priesthood.

The daily mass remained a high priority for four out of every five priests: 83% said that they value highly saying a daily mass. Although not quite as highly endorsed as the daily mass, the daily office remained a high priority with three out of every four priests (73%) who said that they value highly saying the daily office. Looked at from the opposite perspective, one in ten priests (10%) did not value highly saying a daily mass, and one in six priests (17%) did not value highly saying the daily office.

It is clear from the data also that a number of priests were conscious of a discrepancy between what they value and what they find they are actually able to put into practice. While 73% of the priests said that they value highly saying the daily office, the proportion declined to 56% who felt that most days they found time to pray all the daily office. Looked at from another perspective, 41% of the priests said that most days they did not find time to pray all the daily office.

Regular and secular

Table 5.2 demonstrates that the differences are not large between regular priests and secular priests in respect of their understanding and practice of priesthood.

For example, there is no significant difference in the proportions of regular priests and secular priests who felt that they have a clear theology of priesthood (76% and 73%). Similarly, there is no significant difference in the proportions of regular priests and secular priests who reported that they value highly saying a daily mass (85% and 82%).

Although regular priests and secular priests hold very close views on the value of saying a daily mass, opinions between these two groups of priests begin to diverge a little over the issue of the daily office. While 79% of the regular priests said that they valued highly saying the daily office, the proportion fell slightly among the secular priests to 72%. While only 33% of the regular priests said that most days they did not find time to pray all the daily office, the proportion rose somewhat to 43% among the secular priests.

Generational differences

Table 5.3 demonstrates that younger Catholic priests are less likely to maintain the discipline of the daily mass and the discipline of the daily office espoused by their older colleagues.

While 91% of the priests aged 60 and over valued highly saying a daily mass, the proportion fell to 79% among those aged between 45 and 59, and then fell further to 75% among those aged under 45. Similarly, while 86% of the priests aged 60 and over valued highly saying the daily office, the proportion fell to 68% among those aged between 45 and 59, and then fell further to 60% among those aged under 45.

The tendency for younger priests to value the daily office less highly is accompanied by a growing reluctance or inability to find time to pray the daily office. While only 28% of the priests aged 60 or over said that most days they failed to find time to pray all the daily office, the proportion rose to 46% among the 45–59-year-olds, and then rose further to 55% among those aged under 45.

The question about having a clear theology of priesthood indicates that the priests aged between 45 and 59 were significantly less likely to have a clear theology of priesthood than was the case among their older colleagues (69% compared with 77%). Young priests under the age of 45 seem to have regained some of the confidence in the theology of priesthood lost by those in the 45–59 year age group. Thus, quite similar proportions of priests under the age of 45 and priests aged 60 and over considered that they had a clear theology of priesthood (74% and 77%).

CHAPTER SIX

Experiencing Priesthood

Most priests, I believe, appreciate not having to worry about money. But the psychological implications of being 'taken care of' well into one's thirties and beyond are often overlooked. According to Robert Hovda (1985), 'Clergy and other professional servants of the churches are kept in a state of economic serfdom and dependency upon fringe benefits, sycophancy and tax evasion, discouraging the very freedom, independence and maturity we are finally beginning to desire of our ministers' (Cozzens, 2000, p. 73).

This chapter is concerned with the practicalities and realities of *experiencing priesthood* in the Catholic parish. The experience of priesthood, broadly conceived, includes making sense of living in the presbytery on the small clerical stipend, dealing with the expectations and demands of parishioners and of society as a whole, and establishing a balance between the demands of the office and the needs for recreation.

Context

Embracing the life and calling of priesthood assumes that the aspirant has high ideals of altruism and personal dedication. Priests in England and Wales are by the standards of other professions poorly paid, so poorly paid in fact that it may confidently be stated that only the misinformed would enter the parochial priesthood for financial reasons. Liverpool diocese in 1998 guaranteed each parochial priest a minimum salary of £5500 per year, additional to board, lodging and motor mileage allowance, with the intention of lessening the disparity between what priests earned from parish to parish, as well as making them less dependent upon inequitable stole fees.

The remuneration of clergy has often been an indication of their relative significance in society. Catholic clergy income, when compared with the average salaries of those in other professions, only serves to accentuate the perception that societies and individuals are generally prepared to pay for what they consider valuable. There was a time when priests were financially much better off than the major proportion of their working class parishioners, many of whom were poorly paid, but for most of the last century it is doubtful whether this has been true.

Traditionally unmarried priests in the Catholic Church are constrained to live comfortable but relatively abstemious lives. Financially responsible only for themselves, the celibate priest may express satisfaction with or tolerance of a life of near evangelical poverty. This lifestyle cannot be a reasonable option for those who are married, especially those with school age children. The difficulty of finding adequately remunerated employment has been a struggle experienced by the Catholic hierarchy in 1995–6 in locating the hundred or so former Anglican clergymen who had joined the Catholic Church in the wake of the ordination of women priests in the Church of England. Many have been directed into ministries, mainly chaplaincies, where either the state or the employing organization pays them appreciably more than they could ever expect from the engaging Catholic diocese. It is worth noting that such unintentional sidelining of these men into military, prison, school and other chaplaincies, done from the best of financial motives, obliges them to work in comparative isolation and cannot but militate against their incorporation and assimilation as married priests into the main body of celibate Catholic priests in a diocese. It is a reasonable assumption that such an intentionally benign policy, adopted with one specific aim in mind, unless countered by alternative action aimed at their integration, could give rise in married, former Church of England clergy, now ordained as Catholic priests, at best to perceptions of marginalization and at worst to feelings of second-class citizenship in the priesthood.

A priest in the Catholic Church is a man who is professionally religious. He is the full-time leader of the local church who probably still sees himself as symbolizing and articulating the belief systems and values of the Catholic Church he serves. According to Beit-Hallahmi and Argyle (1997, p. 63), adopting this role dictates strong behavioural constraints leading to strong identification with the role and to related beliefs, which hitherto has involved the adoption of special dress, lifestyle and sexual rules. Over the past forty years some of this has been eroded.

The position of the priest in his own perception and in that of his parishioners has to some extent been influenced by the raised levels of education of the Catholic laity in England and Wales. As greater numbers of Catholics acquired higher education, some parishioners attenuated their participation in parish life. Other well-educated, often graduate, parishioners, however, chose to continue the link and have acquired the skills to make their voice heard in seeking greater participation in the life of their church. As a consequence, the more lay people have done what formerly had been the unique professional preserve of the priest, the greater has been the tendency to blur the distinction between priests and laity. In turn, this focused attention on the question of the precise nature of the unique competence of the priest (Goldner, Ference and Ritti, 1973). Priests can be seen as status professionals: those who perform their roles because of their position as much as their competence. As a status profession many elements of ministry appear outdated and superfluous in a world emphasizing achievement and specialist competence (Halsey, 1989).

Although there are many frustrations in the role, together with isolation and an often excessive workload, priests are in the main committed to the role. Such role commitment is defined as 'a process which links a person to a position in a social system to the extent that the position provides an individual with a favourable net balance of rewards over costs' (Schoenherr and Greeley, 1974, p. 407). Various studies take account of two important variables: first, the value of what sociologists call the exchanged resource, and second, the presence or absence of valuable alternatives in the exchange relation. This means in effect that a priest is prepared to engage in a disadvantageous exchange if the role of priest is more advantageous than what is exchanged for it. In traditional theological terms the role of priest may be experienced as answering Christ's call, or taking up a sacred vocation. The question at the beginning of the twenty-first century remains whether there still exists within the Catholic priesthood sufficient advantageous elements in what sociologists call the exchange resource to attract balanced individuals to seek to engage in an exchange that may appear to many outside the Catholic Church as apparently so disadvantageous.

Priests have been socialized in the seminary into adopting the view of offering selfless service in the name of the gospel. Pursuit of improved remuneration from the Catholic Church has been considered by some as indecent money-grubbing, while low salaries are counterbalanced by benefits in kind, such as free board and lodging. Accommodation in a tied house, the presbytery, together with the low salary and lack of choice denies the priest any say in where he lives. Entrance upon the scene of convert married priests with families might bring both the topics of salary and of housing into sharper focus.

Listening to the priests

In a newspaper article headed 'Have you hugged your priest today', Ronald Rolheiser drew on the slogan used in a campaign a generation ago alerting parents to the importance of assuring their children of parental love. He was suggesting the responsibility of parishioners to give moral and emotional support to their beleaguered clergy who are working under significant strain, exacerbated by the publicity given to a handful of atypical priest-paedophiles. Unpopularity, hostility even, can be faced with equanimity, he argued, if priests are assured of the love and support of their own people. 'Last Sunday', he continued, 'a distinguished priest summed up in the pulpit his own reason for withdrawing from the ranks of the diocesan clergy to join a religious community after eighteen years in a parish.' Among his own people, he said, 5% gave uncritical support. Another 5% much more noisily complained and without ceasing. The remaining 90% simply gave an impression of cold indifference (*Catholic Herald*, 24 November, 2000).

Religious community, like marriage, is an opportunity for happiness, as the married will attest, not a guarantee of it. One priest made the point in the following way.

> Regulars have a lot of contact with clergy of their own order. Sometimes this is a positive, upbuilding experience, sometimes their confrères become another burden (priest aged between 45 and 49).

It would be to misrepresent the evidence if it were not stated that quite the most frequent and consistent refrain, among those priests who completed the questionnaire, was the level of expressed contentment and satisfaction in the role. Typical was the priest who wrote as follows.

> I am very happy being a priest. I feel that we are in both challenging and exciting times for the Church. It has never been easy to be a priest; each age demands new things but the Church is ever ancient, ever new. Keeping these two in balance is the heart of the priest's ministry (priest aged between 40 and 44).

Many other priests expressed a similar sentiment. One wrote simply:

> I am very happy in the priesthood and could not imagine any other life (priest aged between 30 and 34).

Another made the point in the following way.

> I would add that I am very happy to be a priest and shall always be grateful to the Lord for his many gifts and blessings bestowed on me. As my parish priest said when I told him that I wished to become a priest, 'You will never regret it.' I never have, and hopefully will always be thankful (age not given).

While enjoying similar contentment, one respondent was led to question whether his feelings were at all typical.

> I personally am completely fulfilled in my ministry and am extremely happy in all that God has given me in the priesthood. I feel, however, that there are very few priests who could be as definite as this. In the company of fellow priests, I often feel the odd man out (priest aged between 65 and 69).

Few priests commented on remuneration, though one priest felt bold enough to act as spokesman.

> Can I suggest that there is concern among my brother priests about our financial state of affairs. Some would like to see a countrywide salary scheme. In fairness for brother priests, this is, I believe, well overdue (priest aged between 45 and 49).

Another gave portmanteau expression to a number of topics.

> I like being a priest but the presbytery system with no defined job description or on/off hours is too stressful. I do not feel lonely; rather I long for a place of my own where I can relax and be myself. Hence my 'dream', to retire from a presbytery as soon as I am financially independent, i.e. by 65 years! (priest aged between 35 and 39).

A rather darker picture of the experience of priesthood was expressed by one of the younger priests, who wrote as follows.

As things are there is no future in the priesthood in England and Wales. Too many priests don't give a toss any more and those in responsible positions are generally not interested in the personal well-being of their colleagues unless one is a personal friend (priest aged between 35 and 39).

Many priests remarked on loneliness, or rather, as in the following instance, on aloneness and the need for support from the bishop or his delegate.

As priests are more and more on their own, it becomes imperative that the bishop or a person with full delegated powers is assigned to visit/call-in far more frequently than now to bring assurance, support and above all, to see how things are, not just parish-wise but personally and at a far more humane and down-to-earth level than is now the practice (priest aged between 55 and 59).

Only a minority of priests admitted the major role that television provides in their relaxation. Like some of their parishioners, priests can be found who dismiss as 'rubbish' certain television soaps, but who at the same time appear to be aware in great detail of the day-to-day content of these programmes. An appreciable number of priests experience and admit to loneliness, as evidenced by the following comment.

I experience great loneliness and isolation. I believe that it is very common among us. I believe we need lots of support networks (not necessarily clerical) (priest aged between 40 and 44).

The perception of being over-faced with work was made quite frequently. One priest wrote as follows.

In general I am quite tired out. This is mainly due to not having the opportunity to get away for a proper holiday due to lack of supply [priests] (age not given).

Another priest made the observation that:

Many priests have several extra-parochial duties in addition to running a parish. This aspect of priestly commitment does not appear to have been addressed (priest aged between 65 and 69).

After reading what priests have written about strong feelings of isolation and overwork, one cannot help concluding that in the context of a profession whose *raison d'être* is often seen as essentially caring for others, the Catholic Church appears strikingly deficient in providing that support for its key members (Hemrick and Hoge, 1991).

Shaping the questions

Against this background, the *Catholic Parochial Clergy Survey* framed three main themes relevant to exploring the priests' perceptions and experiences of living out their vocation. The first theme focused on the key issue of money and explored this issue from two directions. On the positive side, the survey explored the proportion of priests who feel that they receive enough money to live comfortably. On the negative side, the survey explored the proportion of priests who feel that they are underpaid.

The second theme examined the extent to which priests feel supported or unsupported in their ministry. In view of the social context in which they work, how many priests now feel irrelevant to the lives of their parishioners? How many priests today feel lonely and isolated in their ministry?

The third theme focused on workload and relaxation. It is sometimes maintained that the conscientious priest is now trying to do the work of several men as a consequence of falling vocations and of the demands of the job. How many priests, then, feel that their workload is excessive? On the issue of relaxation some priests may feel cut off from the lives and experiences of the laity and geographically distant from the company of other priests. For some the television may provide the main or sole source of relaxation. How many priests, then, feel that watching television has become their major source of relaxation?

Interpreting the statistics

Table 6.1 demonstrates that the majority of priests felt properly rewarded for their role, although a sizeable minority raised warning signs about isolation and overwork.

Only one in seven priests (14%) complained that they did not receive enough money to live comfortably. For every one priest who made this complaint, between five and six (79%) affirmed that, in their view, they received enough money to live comfortably. Taking a slightly different perspective on the same basic issue, only 20% of the priests complained that they felt underpaid, compared with 68% who clearly denied that this was the case.

Nearly two out of every three priests (63%) continued to feel relevant to the lives of their parishioners. At the same time, it is important to note that one priest in every six (16%) is resigned to being largely irrelevant to the lives of parishioners, and a further one in every five (20%) is on the edge of feeling that this may be so.

Loneliness and isolation among the priesthood is clearly a very significant problem to be faced by the Catholic Church. As many as one in every three priests (34%) admitted that they often feel lonely and isolated, while a further 8% were unable to deny that this was true for them. If loneliness and isolation lay at the heart of problems like alcoholism, depression and sexual irresponsibility, it may be worth listening to these statistics seriously.

Overwork among the priesthood is also clearly a very significant problem to be faced by the Catholic Church. As many as two in every five priests (43%)

admitted that they feel their workload is excessive, while a further 15% were unable to deny that this is true for them. If overwork leads to exhaustion and to burnout, it may be worth listening to these statistics seriously as well.

For one in every four priests (23%) the major source of relaxation has become watching television. Perhaps a rather sad picture can be constructed of such priests, shut away in their presbytery and isolated from fellow priests, parishioners and other human beings. One in four remains too large a minority to be ignored.

Regular and secular

Table 6.2 demonstrates that there are some key ways in which the experience of priesthood is significantly less positive for the secular priests than for the regular priests.

First, the secular priests were more likely to feel that they are underpaid for their ministry, compared with regular priests (21% compared with 15%). On the other hand, similar proportions of secular priests and regular priests (79% and 80%) felt that they received enough money to live comfortably.

Second, the secular priests were much more likely to suffer from feelings of isolation. Thus, 37% of the secular priests said that they often felt lonely and isolated, compared with 23% of the regular priests.

Third, the secular priests were much more likely to feel overworked. While 30% of the regular priests felt that their workload was excessive, the proportion rose by over half to 46% among the secular priests.

Fourth, the secular priests were more likely to be dependent on the television. While 16% of the regular priests admitted that their major source of relaxation was watching television, the proportion again rose by over half to 25% among the secular priests.

On the other hand, there was no significant difference between the proportions of secular priests (17%) and regular priests (13%) who felt that they were largely irrelevant to the lives of their parishioners.

Generational differences

Table 6.3 demonstrates that younger priests are reporting a less positive view of the priesthood than is the case among their older colleagues. They are less content with their stipend, more isolated and more oppressed by the job.

While 86% of the priests aged 60 and over felt that they received enough money to live comfortably, the proportion fell to 77% among the 45–59-year-olds, and then fell further to 70% among those under the age of 45. Looking at the same issue from another perspective, while only 15% of the priests aged 60 and over felt that they were underpaid, the proportion rose to 20% among the 45–59-year-olds, and then rose further to 28% among those under the age of 45.

The feeling of being largely irrelevant to the lives of their parishioners troubled one in every ten of the priests aged 60 and over (11%). The proportion almost doubled to 19% among the two younger groups, those aged between 45 and 59 and those under the age of 45.

The issue of loneliness and isolation also separates the oldest cohort from the other two cohorts. While one in every four of the priests aged 60 and over (25%) admitted to often feeling lonely and isolated, the proportions rose to 40% among those aged between 45 and 59, and to 41% among those under the age of 45.

The two younger cohorts of priests are much more likely to perceive themselves as being overworked in comparison with the oldest cohort. While one in every three of the priests aged 60 and over (33%) complained that their workload was excessive, the proportions rose to 48% among those aged between 45 and 59, and rose further to 52% among those under the age of 45.

The importance of television in the lives of priests also may be increasing slightly among the youngest cohort, although not to the point of becoming statistically significant. Thus, while one in five priests aged 60 and over (20%) reported that television was their major source of relaxation, the proportions rose to 23% among those aged between 45 and 59, and to 27% among those under the age of 45.

CHAPTER SEVEN

Dress and Deference

The clergy not wanting to look the part has something to do with the dismantling of the Book of Common Prayer. Anxious not to sound like parsons they can hardly be blamed for not wanting to look like them either. The 'underneath this cassock I am but a man like any other' act . . . must be a familiar routine at many a church door . . . Priests have always hankered after the world, or at any rate the worldly, and consorting as he did with publicans and sinners it was Jesus who started the rot (Bennett, 1991, pp. 11–12).

The fact remains . . . that when people meet a priest they feel that they meet the church and all that it stands for in a very special way. This is a precious and valuable asset, because it enables priests to have greater influence and effectiveness than they would on their own merits (Hussey, 1999, p. 26).

This chapter is concerned with examining the significance of those outward signs of priesthood which help to set the priest apart from other men. The consideration of *dress and deference*, broadly conceived, embraces the notion of distinctive clerical dress, use of the clerical collar, and attachment to deferential forms of address, like the title 'Father'.

Context

The distinctive sombre pattern of dress adopted by most Roman Catholic priests until comparatively recently served a tangible function in providing a constant reminder to members of the clergy that they were outside the ways of the world. Dressed all in black as they were for most of the time, with the Roman collar uniquely distinctive of the clerical profession, neither the priests themselves nor those who saw them were likely to mistake them for anything other than the rather peculiar people that they were. It is possible to see in this distinctive garb an institutional defence mechanism, which from the early 1800s to the 1960s can now be recognized to have been an important determinant of clerical attitudes and behaviour. That is not to say that sober clerical dress was a necessary determinant of such attitudes and behaviour, but it appears to have been instrumental in creating and protecting a desired social identity. Its ultimate purpose as a clerical livery is rather better known than the mechanisms that contributed to its effectiveness in designating its wearer as a man apart.

Socialization is the word used to describe the preparation of people for their role or status in life through some form of apprenticeship, training or education. As, for example, the career of the Tudor Cardinal, Thomas Wolsey, has shown, entry into a profession enables individuals to eclipse their origins, in Wolsey's case being the son of a butcher. This has been particularly true for Catholic clergy. Though the aim of those entering the profession of priesthood has the manifest purpose of raising minds and hearts to God, at the same time in many countries it achieved for many priests the latent purpose of notable social mobility and, for some, a level of economic security. This was exemplified most ostentatiously in the late nineteenth century at the Archdiocesan seminary in Chicago where each seminarian had his own bathroom (Unsworth, 1993). Such luxury would have been especially appreciated by Irish-born seminarians, moving as they had from very humble houses and farmsteads where bathrooms were virtually unknown to a mode of living in which the opposite would increasingly hold true for what is now termed 'upwardly mobile' Irish country boys. The fact that as priests they moved into presbyteries that still employed servants long after all except the wealthiest households could no longer afford them, showed precisely how far and beyond most of their peers these men had progressed socially.

There is no question that priesthood has become an avenue of social mobility for Catholic boys from very deprived backgrounds in East European and African countries where seminary recruitment still appears to be holding up. Although there is nothing unusual, still less wrong, in acknowledging mixed motives in the choice of vocation, a clear contrast has been recognized between, on the one hand the continued attractiveness of the priesthood as a vocation in less developed countries, and, on the other hand, the decline in vocations in countries more developed.

It has long been acknowledged that it is not the cowl that makes the monk, but for some years it has also been recognized that a particular identity is not inherited as is one's genetic makeup, but has to be bestowed by others via acts of social recognition (Berger, 1988). It is not at all a question of pretending to be what one is not, such as someone impersonating a police officer, but an essential and gradual transformation into the role. The seminarian progressively adopts the priestly persona to which he aspires. It is precisely through the acknowledgement by others of his embryonic priestly identity that the seminarian may come to think of himself as a priest. In short, the self-image of the priest as priest can be maintained for any period of time only in the social context in which others are willing to recognize him in this identity. The more he is treated as a priest, the more like a priest he becomes. The converse here is also likely to be true. The less like a priest he is treated, the less like a priest he becomes.

Through ordination, the Catholic Church conferred priestly title and status upon the erstwhile seminarian whatever his social origin. The house 'Rules and Regulations' read out annually at one Northern seminary in the United Kingdom included the Victorian adage, 'It is no disgrace to be low-born; it is to be ill-bred.' By the 1960s this dictum was greeted with derisory catcalls by some of the listening seminarians who were increasingly suspicious of such outmoded categories. The same 'Rules' outlawed, even in seminarians, anyone 'singularly and ostentatiously dressed'. A strongly emphasized mechanism of control was operational in the matter of dress. Conformity in the aspect of dress assisted in inculcating conformity in more contentious matters. For example, though it would not have been against Canon Law for a priest to have spoken his mind on a particular issue that the bishop would rather have buried in silence, the likelihood of spending the better part of one's future ministry in parishes on the wrong side of the tracks remained a powerful disincentive to speaking out of turn. Without it ever being formally acknowledged, priests picked up the unspoken message that 'Where human beings live or work in compact groups in which they are personally known and to which they are tied by feelings of personal loyalty, very potent and simultaneously very subtle mechanisms of control are constantly brought to bear upon the actual or potential deviant' (Berger, 1988, p. 87).

An article in *The Tablet* (November 2001, p. 1555) instancing the management style of the recently retired Archbishop Ward of Cardiff who, it was reported, had let it be known for twenty years that it was none of the business of diocesan priests how his diocese was run, is a potent reminder that such an episcopal attitude is not, as some would like to believe, a throwback to the executive style of a less enlightened age, but an example of a prevalent episcopal style used from Rome to Rio in the twenty-first century to keep uppity priests in their place. The growth of management schools worldwide, to say nothing of the British officer training establishments like Dartmouth, Sandhurst and Cranwell, is evidence enough that leadership can be taught. There is no evidence that any competence, least of all competence in religious leadership, comes automatically from the laying on of hands.

Dress was just one of the adjuncts to the behavioural constraints imposed upon generations of Catholic priests. The obligation of living in a specific tied property known as the presbytery, as described in chapter 6, identified the priest more closely with the role. Since before the First World War, if it was ever the case, priests in England and Wales had never been sufficiently well paid to enable them to buy even a modest property of their own. As much, therefore, by necessity as by a sense of commitment to their calling, priests in the Catholic Church remained at their post long after their lay peers had called it a day. In addition, priests did nothing, and still do nothing, to knock on the head the 'working a twenty-four hour day' myth which has been reinforced by their compulsorily 'living above the shop'. Rejecting any separation of life and work (Coate, 1989), priests can still delude themselves that, like the military, they are never off duty, the unspoken but misleading implication being that they are always hard at work. The truth is that the majority of priests work sufficiently diligently to have no need to peddle any such fiction.

One more likely example of the separation of public persona from private identity is illustrated by the vivid, if somewhat dated, example of the wish to separate the role of priest from the role of ordinary person who wished to go swimming. 'Thus some French Canadian priests do not want to lead so strict a life that they cannot go swimming at the beach with friends, but they tend to feel that it is best to swim with persons who are not their parishioners, since the familiarity required at the beach is incompatible with the distance and respect required in the parish' (Goffman, 1990, p. 137).

Priesthood is a status profession in contrast to one manifesting achievement or specialist competence. By representing the sacred in the midst of life, the priest's social identity has a basis in status rather than competence or occupation (Jarvis, 1975). There was often an overemphasis on the priestly persona, the priestly identity that took precedence in all relationships with parishioners. Today people are generally less readily impressed by the priestly persona. The very fact that the persona has been used, infrequently but with sufficiently notorious examples, as a mask for such evildoing as paedophilia has now put people defensively on guard, where once the priest, at least in the United Kingdom, was assumed to be of almost unquestionable probity.

The uniquely distinguishing characteristic of priests in the Catholic Church, when compared with their fellow ministers of other denominations, is celibacy. In an age that accentuates sexuality, sex is used in advertising to sell just about everything. The impression, if not the reality, is of the paramount importance of sex. Freud alerted us to the centrality of sex in the human psyche. The Catholic Church by contrast maintains that abstinence from all sexual contact is a gift from God, and asserts that celibacy is a voluntary self-imposition on all priests. It had for long been esteemed as a higher state of life than marriage, but such a view was unwittingly undermined by the opinion of the Second Vatican Council, which elevated the value of sacramental marriage as equal to, though different from, vowed celibacy as an alternative path to Christian holiness. Increasing publicity given to sexual misdemeanours of Catholic priests, and on occasion of bishops too, has diminished dramatically the respect formerly automatically accorded to priests as celibate 'men apart'.

The training of priests was, and still is, largely controlled by the clergy by whom seminarians are socialized into a number of shared assumptions and attitudes. However uncertain they find themselves today about their changing role and identity, priests still enjoy membership of a large and privileged élite. Priests are one of the few remaining professions enjoying total job security. Their elevated status within the Catholic family is reinforced by that special form of address 'Father' which gives them both symbolic and actual prominence in the life of their parishes (Dyson, 1985). There has, however, always been a price to pay. The obligation to behave by rigid rules and established norms ensures that the Catholic Church controls the priest, but in the main it meant little hardship to men trained and ordained to minister in a milieu of religious certainties. They had endured the quasi-military structure and discipline of seminary training, so priesthood was comparatively easily adopted.

Whether or not that was how they saw themselves, there was no question that clergy were thought of as being *above* the laity. It was a pervasive attitude that is increasingly clearly seen to be theologically wrong-headed. 'To the extent that any priest, deacon, or pastorally trained person clings to worldly privilege, titles, and honours, or maintains an air of false superiority, everything that can be said about the "dignity" of the ordained priesthood and the priesthood of the people becomes insipid, misleading, and totally false' (Häring, 1996, p. 46).

It was such a false concept of dignity that had so shocked Häring in the late 1950s when Cardinal Giuseppe Pizzardo, the head of the Holy Office, had suppressed worker-priests with the argument that the position of a dependent worker contradicted the 'dignity' of priesthood. It would be difficult to quantify precisely how many priests and bishops there are who are still loath to renounce the glamour and privilege of clericalism in all its forms at every level. Delusions of grandeur may afflict the parish priest as much as Pope or president. For example, the story is told concerning a parish priest, at loggerheads with his parishioners, who refused to consider moving to another parish, saying that he had been appointed by Jesus and would only leave at Jesus' command. The bishop, hearing of the impasse, discreetly asked the priest to transfer to a nicer parish. The priest announced on the Sunday that during the week Jesus had asked him to move and that now he was going. Relieved but unimpressed, the congregation immediately rose to their feet and began to sing 'What a friend we have in Jesus'.

Listening to the priests

The fact that so few priests chose to comment on the matter of dress or status could be an indication of its lack of importance in priests' view of life. Just one drew attention to both when he wrote as follows.

I do hope we can always deserve the beautiful title 'Father', that we can be proud of our priestly garb and see the vital necessity of pastoral visiting (priest aged between 65 and 69).

Shaping the questions

Against this background, the *Catholic Parochial Clergy Survey* framed three main themes relevant to exploring the priests' perceptions and experiences of dress and deference in their ministry. The first theme focused on two aspects of clerical dress, distinguishing between the overall concept of clerical dress and the particular significance of the clerical collar. What proportion of priests today consider that it is important that priests should wear distinctive dress? How do priests feel today about wearing a clerical collar when on duty?

The second theme examined the priests' attitude toward the use of a distinctive mode of address. What proportion of priests today actually prefer parishioners to address them as Father?

The third theme examined the priests' perceptions of the way in which they are treated by their parishioners. To what extent do priests feel that their parishioners treat them with *too* much deference?

Interpreting the statistics

Table 7.1 demonstrates that the balance of opinion remains in favour of clerical dress and the continuing use of the title Father, although a considerable minority of priests express dissatisfaction with both. Only a minority of priests feel that parishioners treat them with too much deference.

Half of the priests (48%) considered that it was important that priests should wear distinctive dress, compared with one-third (34%) who took the view that it was not a matter of importance that priests should wear distinctive dress. The fact that one in five priests (18%) claimed to have no fixed view on this issue shows the extent to which the maintenance of clerical dress in the Catholic Church may be in flux. Looking at the same statistics from a different perspective indicates that while 48% of the priests currently considered distinctive dress to be important, 52% were not willing to sign up to this view.

Confidence among the Catholic clergy remained higher in the clerical collar as a badge of office when on duty than in the wider apparatus of clerical dress. While 48% of the priests supported the wider apparatus of clerical dress, the proportion rose to 58% who maintained the importance of wearing a clerical collar when on duty. Indeed, twice as many priests supported the value of the clerical collar when on duty, compared with those who dismiss its value (58% compared with 27%). Three out of every twenty priests (15%) were unclear where they stood on the use of the clerical collar. For the immediate future, therefore, the clerical collar is likely to remain the recognizable badge of office for priests in the Catholic Church.

The use of the title 'Father' assumed a similar profile among the Catholic clergy to the importance of wearing distinctive dress. Overall nearly half of the priests maintained the importance of both attributes of ministry: 48% maintained the importance of distinctive dress and 47% preferred parishioners to call them Father. While half of the priests (48%) were positively in favour of being addressed as Father, a lower proportion (33%) were clearly against this practice. Once again, the fact that one in five priests (20%) claimed to have no fixed view on this issue shows the extent to which the maintenance of clerical titles in the Catholic Church may be in flux. With 53% of the priests either no longer in favour of or positively against the style 'Father', this familiar title may begin to become discouraged in Catholic parishes.

Around one in six of the priests (16%) felt that their parishioners treated them with too much deference. The majority of the priests (61%) did not feel that this was the case and a further 23% had no clear view on the matter. Whatever the current relationship between priests and people in Catholic parishes, only a small proportion of priests may feel concerned to dismantle existing structures of deference.

Regular and secular

Table 7.2 demonstrates that there are no significant differences in the perceptions of dress and deference between secular priests and regular priests. Thus 45% of the regular priests and 49% of the secular priests considered that it is important for priests to wear distinctive dress. Three-fifths of the regular priests (59%) and of the secular priests (58%) considered that priests should wear a 'clerical collar' when on duty. Just under half of the regular priests (47%) and of the secular priests (47%) preferred parishioners to call them Father. Just 18% of the regular priests and 16% of the secular priests felt that parishioners treated them with too much deference.

These statistics suggest that parishes served by secular priests and by regular priests may share similar experiences regarding their clergy's attitudes toward such issues as wearing clerical dress and being addressed as Father.

Generational differences

Table 7.3 reveals some interesting age trends in the attitudes of Catholic priests toward issues of clerical dress and deference. It is, overall, the priests in the 45–59 age category who are the most liberal in their attitudes on these issues.

Parishes in the care of priests aged 60 and over are the most likely to experience the maintenance of traditional values in clerical dress and in clerical style. Thus, 60% of the priests aged 60 and over supported the view that priests should wear distinctive dress. In this age category the proportion who believe that priests should wear a clerical collar when on duty rose to 70%. Two out of every three priests in this age category (64%) preferred parishioners to call them Father.

By way of contrast, parishes in the care of priests between the age of 45 and 59 are the least likely to experience the maintenance of traditional values in clerical dress and in clerical style. Thus, only 37% of the priests aged between 45 and 59 felt that it was important that priests should wear distinctive dress, although the proportion rose to 48% who felt that priests should wear a clerical collar when on duty. One out of every three priests in this age category (36%) preferred parishioners to call them Father.

Priests under the age of 45 appear to be reacting against some of the liberalizing tendencies demonstrated by priests in the 45–59 age band, although they are not demonstrating the same levels of certainty displayed by priests aged 60 and over. For example, while the proportion of priests who maintained the importance of clerical dress fell to 37% among the 45–59-year-olds, it rose again to 48% among those under the age of 45. While the proportion of priests who felt that they should wear a clerical collar when on duty fell to 48% among the 45–59-year-olds, it rose again to 56% among those under the age of 45.

Although the youngest cohort of priests tends to re-emphasize the importance of clerical dress, they do not wish to revitalize the style 'Father'. While the proportion of priests who prefer parishioners to call them Father fell from 64% among those aged 60 and over to 36% among the 45–59-year-olds, the proportion stayed at the level of 36% among those under the age of 45.

Finally, no significant differences were found among the three age cohorts in respect of the perception that parishioners treat them with too much deference. This view was taken by 16% of those under the age of 45, by 17% of the 45–59-year-olds, and by 15% of those aged 60 or over.

CHAPTER EIGHT

Relating to the Laity

Celie, tell the truth, have you ever found God in church? I never did. I just found a bunch of folks hoping for him to show. Any God I ever felt in church I brought in with me. And I think the other folks did too. They come to church to *share* God, not find God (Walker, 1983, p. 165).

If lay ministry is ever to become the genuinely secular ministry it can and must be for the salvation of the world, all the people, lay and clerical alike, will need to be on guard against this creeping *clericalisation* of Christian ministry (Lawler, 1990, p. 48).

This chapter is concerned with the proper place of the *laity* within the Catholic Church and with the current relationship between laity and clergy. This discussion involves an analysis of the change in perspective brought about by the Second Vatican Council and the ways in which laity and clergy have responded to these changes.

Context

It is from the Greek word for people, '*laos*', that English gets the word 'laity'. Christians referred to themselves as the people of God (1 Peter 2:10), distinguishing themselves from those who were not God's people. Irrespective of the particular functions of apostles, overseers, presbyters, prophets or teachers, there was but one people. There is a growing realization that in distinguishing laity as a less important part of the Church than clergy, the Catholic Church had strayed away from its understanding of itself as the people of God (Lawler, 1990).

Prior to the Second Vatican Council the prevailing ecclesiology saw the church as a divinely constituted, hierarchical organization in which the Pope at the apex of a pyramidal structure oversaw and directed the cascade of truth via bishops, priests and religious to the passive laity at the base. This description of the commonly accepted culture, written by Arbuckle (1993, pp. 82–4), would be recognizable to any Catholic above middle age who had experience of the Catholic Church in their youth. There could be something very reassuring, at least on the surface, of belonging to an organization possessing such authority and such self-assurance, but the truth was that the theology underlying this view of the relationship between the organization's members was alarmingly skewed in its presentation of a clergy-centred Church. Some have argued that, in spite of the fact that the theology underlying such an ecclesiology has been called into question, much of the model still persists in practice and, until its final abandonment, the tendency of the laity will be to continue to let priests and bishops get on with running the Church.

Retired priests and priests who are within a few years of retirement grew up and were trained in that Church in which, for all practical purposes, the priest did all the ministering. Even religious sisters too, in the main, did as they were told. Not only were the laity not expected to do anything more than they were told by the clergy, but they were also made so conscious of their own lack of Christian status that they expected no more of themselves than to 'turn up, pay up and shut up'. That crude old generalization summed up for far too long what was the expectation of the vast majority of churchgoing Catholics.

In a devastating reply to a pastoral letter written in 1908 by Cardinal Mercier, Archbishop of Malines, Belgium, naming an English priest, Father George Tyrrell SJ, as an arch-Modernist, Tyrrell wrote the following.

> Tell the layman, as the Encyclical [of Pius X *Pascendi Dominici Gregis* (1907)] does, that his religious thought in no way contributes to the penetration and better understanding of the Christian faith; that he has no business to meddle with or investigate a subject which is the exclusive concern of the episcopate; or rather, of the Pope; tell him moreover, that there can be no real progress in religious knowledge; that the fullness of Catholic truth was stereotyped once and for all two thousand years ago, and is stored up in the secret archives of the Vatican; that uncertainties are to be solved not by mental struggle, but by a simple reference to those archives; tell him all this, and why, in Heaven's name should he trouble his head about religion any more than about the further development of the multiplication table? (Tyrrell, 1994, pp. 41–2).

The contrast with the elevated status of laity as described in the Second Vatican Council's decree on the Apostolate of the Laity (Abbott, 1966, pp. 500–1) could not be more marked. The idea that the latter position adopted by the teaching authority of the Catholic Church is a natural progression or development flowing from the former position cannot be sustained. It need only be observed to see that the teaching of the Second Vatican Council completely contradicts the declared status of the laity expressed in *Pascendi Dominici Gregis*.

Greater access to education, coupled with a rediscovery of alternative theologies, was to alter much of this ecclesial worldview. No longer content with seeing themselves as passive recipients of teaching from above, individual access to higher education and increasingly to theological education had been given to large numbers of laity, both male and female, the means whereby evaluation could be made of what being a Christian meant, independently of whatever picture had previously been presented by local parish clergy. There was a growing perception that the authoritarian, clerical, judicial, triumphalist model of the Catholic Church was insecurely grounded both scripturally and theologically.

It was the late theologian Charles Davis in his book *A Question of Conscience*

(1967) who wrote that many Catholics had escaped the pressures of a rigidly dogmatic church by remaining uncommitted in regard to any definite doctrinal statement. Considered by many at the time to be an opinion that grossly exaggerated the reality, it has since become increasingly difficult to contradict Davis' evaluation, in spite of any lack of tentativeness underlying the content of the *Catechism of the Catholic Church* (1994). Not for a long time in developed countries have priests preached to largely peasant congregations, but increasingly to college-educated and professionally trained men and women whose access to news and information, as well as whose ability to think critically about issues of importance, including theological ones, in many instances is at least as good as their own.

Referring to the place in the Catholic Church of what has been styled 'the baby boomers' generation', Klimoski (1999, p. 42) made the following point:

> Research on the baby boomers provides pervasive evidence that the freedom to make up one's own mind on virtually every issue is now taken for granted no matter where one falls along the liberal–conservative continuum. Thus membership in the parish is no longer assumed to be the principal means of gaining access to a spiritual relationship with God. Moreover what I as an individual determine is sufficient for parish membership takes precedence over external criteria imposed by an institutional authority.

This phenomenon could be seen as a good example in practice of the *sensus fidelium*. In such a comparatively short space of time, in marked contrast to the previous restrictions upon what those not in holy orders have been permitted to do in the church, the engagement of the laity in the Catholic Church is now welcomed and encouraged. Some may justifiably wonder whether it is expediency driven by the fall in priestly vocations rather than theological conviction of the proper role of the laity that drives the process. This seems almost inevitable in the light of a statement such as the following from the encyclical letter, *Christifideles Laici*.

> When necessity and expediency in the church require it, the pastors according to established norms from universal law can entrust to the lay faithful certain offices and roles that are connected to their pastoral ministry but do not require the character of orders (John Paul II, 1989, p. 23).

Tridentine theology whose focus was the sacramental power belonging to the priest alone had emphasized the priesthood as the principal ministry of the church. The document *Lumen Gentium* of the Second Vatican Council righted the balance somewhat by stating that the Church is the entire community of believers and that the term 'people of God' refers to the total community of the Church that includes priests and bishops (Abbott, 1966, p. 25). Although it might appear to be a statement of the obvious, it is useful to be alert to one consequence of the concept of the Church being the entire community of believers. It is that the public work of the Church – the liturgy – becomes once more the task of all the people who belong to the Church, not just of a clerical élite. The entire community celebrates the liturgy at which the bishop, and by extension the priest, presides. The mission of the Church is, therefore, the responsibility of all of the baptized, not simply of the clergy. No longer is it the people's role merely to support the priest in his ministry and behave as little more than onlookers when he celebrates the liturgy. Instead the priest as a baptized Christian is ordained to minister to his fellow baptized Christians and support them in *their* ministry. The transition from the teaching of the Council of Trent on the priesthood as primarily the power of consecrating the eucharistic elements and of forgiving and retaining sins is quite marked. According to the document *Presbyterorum Ordinis* of the Second Vatican Council, the diocesan priest is less an *alter Christus* than an *alter Episcopus* with the consequence that his traditional role and significance has been unintentionally undermined and his clear, if flawed, self-image rendered more complicated if not obscured. His link with the bishop is emphasized and his rather questionable autonomy somewhat diminished.

Some strands of recent research, however, suggest that the dualism between clergy and laity in the church remains prominent. For example, one relevant paragraph of the Lay Formation Study, published in June 2000, reads as follows.

> Many interviewees' comments amounted to the conclusion that there is an unhelpful dualism in the prevailing culture of the church that separates the clergy and the laity. That is not to misunderstand the way in which priests and people *are* different . . . This dualism [is] characterised by a notion of clericalism infused with superiority, extra-giftedness and power, and a notion of laity infused with obedience (to clergy), unworthiness and lack of ability in matters of faith. It was generally agreed that this is not a healthy state of affairs either for lay people or for priests (Mannix, 2000, p. 22).

If what is conveyed in the Lay Formation Study is representative of the overall parochial experience in England and Wales, the clergy's espousal of lay involvement might in fact be more notional than real.

Two quotations from priests in the report of the Lay Formation Study blame the role of the seminary. The first quotation states that 'The culture of the seminary is no place to develop an understanding of collaborative ministry.' It might reasonably be supposed, therefore, that considering the inadequate pastoral training given to priests who were trained thirty and more years ago, the obstructive priests referred to by the Lay Formation Study report could only have been these older men. However, the second quotation critical of seminary training states, 'Seminaries have got worse over the last ten years. The model of relationship in the seminary is not a good preparation for ministry.' This additional evidence, then, does not support the older priest supposition. There appear to be young fogies as well as old. It is significantly stated that the seminaries' failure was not the last word and that deficiencies there could be supplemented later in another context. 'Priests in this study felt that they had been formed by other opportunities, especially living in parish life. This was felt to be the significant element in their formation but it was recognised that the poor preparation in the seminary meant that some parish clergy are not equipped to learn even through the practice of their ministry' (Mannix, 2000, p. 13).

The Lay Foundation Study also drew attention to a consensus regarding an uneasy relationship between some clergy and active laity. Mannix (2000) remarked that such a consensus 'was not the symptom of a church that has rediscovered . . . the egalitarian model of church as described in the gospel'.

Listening to the priests

Their relationship with the laity was not one of those issues on which many of the priests chose to comment at length. The comments received were mixed.

For some priests it was clearly the opportunities for shared ministry and for support from the laity that gave sense, purpose, and hope to their ministry. For example, one priest noted the support that he received from the greater involvement and engagement of the laity and writes as follows.

I do not feel threatened by the challenges that face us thanks to the support I receive from the laity (priest aged between 40 and 44).

One of the images used to express the active collaboration of clergy and laity is that of shared pilgrimage. Using this image, one of the priests said:

We are a pilgrim people. That means we walk together and value those who have walked with us and have allowed me to journey at my own pace (priest aged between 30 and 34).

Far from seeing lay involvement and engagement as a form of provisional ministry brought about by expediency consequent to the possibly temporary decline in the number of priestly vocations, many priests spoke about the positive steps being taken to ensure the transition from a clergy-led church to a lay-led church. In this connection one priest spotted the relevance of the *Catholic Parochial Clergy Survey* for providing an empirical basis on which to structure change. This priest wrote as follows.

I was happy to take part because it hopefully will provide an excellent insight into where we are today in the ordained ministry and enable us to face the change in people's attitudes toward ministry in general especially in fostering more and more non-ordained ministries (priest aged between 30 and 34).

A very different perspective was taken by the priest who saw no potential for change toward greater lay involvement and who rejected the possibility that the *Catholic Parochial Clergy Survey* could make any contribution toward shaping the future. This priest wrote as follows.

I doubt very much the efficacy of such an enquiry. The Roman Catholic Church is totally autocratic and obviously intends to remain so. In a sense this survey is a big joke which I have for some vague reasons decided to go along with (priest aged between 60 and 64).

Shaping the questions

Against this background, the *Catholic Parochial Clergy Survey* developed three main themes relevant to exploring the priests' perceptions and experiences of relating to the laity. The first theme focused on the key issue of the priests' attitude toward greater involvement of the laity in parish life. This issue was approached from two directions. To what extent do the clergy actually welcome the greater involvement of the laity in parish life? To what extent does the increasing influence of laity in the Catholic Church generate anxiety among the clergy?

The second theme turned attention closer to home and looked at the priests' perceptions of what was happening in their own parishes. How many priests actually feel that laypeople have too much power and influence in their parish?

The third theme focused on the priests' perceptions of their personal abilities to relate to their parishioners. This broad issue was sharpened by distinguishing between three groups of parishioners: men, women, and children. How well do priests feel that they relate to men in their parish? How well do priests feel that they relate to women in their parish? How well do priests feel that they relate to children in their parish?

Interpreting the statistics

Table 8.1 demonstrates that the majority of priests feel confident about their ability to relate to the lay people in their parish, to men, women, and children. The majority of priests feel really positive about the greater involvement of the laity in parish life.

There was almost total unanimity among the priests to welcome the greater involvement of the laity in parish life. None of the priests (0%) said that he did *not* welcome the greater involvement of the laity in parish life. Just 2% felt sufficient reservation not to endorse the statement positively, leaving 98% who signed up to welcoming greater involvement of the laity in parish life.

Although there was almost total unanimity among the priests in welcoming greater involvement of the laity, a significant minority of the priests nonetheless saw this development as a source of anxiety. As many as seven priests in every hundred (7%) were clear that the increasing influence of laity in the Catholic Church made them anxious, while a further six priests in every hundred (6%) wondered whether this could be the case for them as well.

Just three priests in every hundred (3%) felt that laypeople have too much power and influence in their parish, compared with 90% who did not feel this way about the laity in their parish.

The majority of priests felt that they related well to all sectors of their parishioners. They were most confident about their ability to relate to men and a little less confident about their ability to relate to women and to children. Thus, 90% of the priests considered that they relate well to men, 88% considered that they relate well to women, and 84% considered that they relate well to children. Looked at from the opposite perspective, just one in a hundred priests (1%) felt that they did not relate well to men, just two in a hundred (2%) felt that they did not relate well to women, and three in a hundred (3%) felt that they did not relate well to children.

Regular and secular

Table 8.2 demonstrates that the secular priests and the regular priests hold very similar views on the ways in which they relate to the laity, although there are two very small, but statistically significant differences. First, although overall only a small minority of priests felt that laypeople have too much power and influence in their parish, the proportion was significantly higher among the regular priests than among the secular priests (5% compared with 3%). Second, although there was no significant difference in the proportions of secular priests and regular priests who reported that they relate well to children (84% each) or that they relate well to women (88% and 91%), a significantly higher proportion of the regular priests reported that they relate well to men (93% compared with 89%). These differences are, however, too small to be of much practical significance.

Generational differences

Table 8.3 demonstrates that there is no significant relationship between age and attitude toward the involvement of the laity in parish life, although there is a significant association between age and the priests' perception of their ability to relate to some sectors of the laity.

Between 98% and 99% of all three age cohorts welcomed the greater involvement of laity in parish life. Between 5% and 8% of all three cohorts felt that the increasing influence of laity in the Catholic Church makes them anxious. Between 2% and 4% of all three cohorts felt that laypeople have too much power in their parish. None of these differences reached a level of statistical significance.

Overall it is the youngest cohort of priests who felt that they relate best to both women and men. Thus, 93% of the priests under the age of 45 felt that they relate well to women, compared with 86% among the 45–59-year-olds, and 88% among those aged 60 and over. Similarly, 93% of the priests under the age of 45 felt that they relate well to men, compared with 88% among the 45–59-year-olds and 91% among those aged 60 and over. On the other hand, there is no significant difference in the way in which the three age cohorts perceive their ability to relate to children. Thus, 87% of those aged under 45, 83% of those aged 45–59, and 84% of those aged 60 and over considered that they related well to children.

CHAPTER NINE

Celibacy and Priesthood

Pope John Paul won't let priests leave the priesthood to marry unless they say they were mentally unstable at ordination (Cornwell, 1995).

Schillebeeckx (1981) calls attention to a kind of double hermeneutical standard applied to the actions of Jesus. Why, he asks, must the fact that Jesus chose only men as apostles have absolute and immutable theological significance, while the fact that he chose for the most part only married men is granted no significance whatever? He could have appended a long list of similar questions about cases where the action of the Roman Catholic Church is at variance with the actions of Jesus (Lawler, 1990, p. 111).

This chapter is concerned with the pivotal teaching of the Catholic Church which links priesthood with celibacy. Although Pope John Paul II has forbidden official debate of the topic of priestly celibacy, the debate clearly continues. The situation in England and Wales was given a new twist by the reordination into the Catholic Church of married former Anglican clergymen.

Context

Whether the newspaper article by Cornwell was inaccurate or the reported action of the Pope a misrepresentation, the very substance of the article was itself evidence that the topic of priestly celibacy is one of the most visible and volatile issues affecting the Catholic Church. This should be unsurprising as the issue of celibacy affects so many levels of church life. Celibacy affects the churchgoing laymen and laywomen for whom there are now notably fewer priests than there were half a century ago. Celibacy, of course, has affected the lives of former Catholic priests who have left and married. Celibacy affects not only those already ordained priest, but others who might feel called to priestly ministry but not to obligatory celibacy. Celibacy affects potential recruits to the priesthood who are aware of the salvific value of sacramental marriage as an alternative path to true Christian holiness, which in the words of the Second Vatican Council is equal to, though different from, vowed celibacy (Abbott, 1966). Celibacy affects potential recruits to the priesthood who are aware of the clerical status of married deacons and of the growing extent of lay participation in ministry that has considerably narrowed what had hitherto been considered exclusively priestly ministry.

Pope John Paul II has forbidden official debate of the topic of priestly celibacy. Such an embargo among Catholics might encourage an impression that at an official level there is unanimity of opinion on the matter. The reality is that a body of informed, theological opinion dissenting from the current orthodoxy has not been suppressed. As Sipe (1992, p. 1118) writes:

> By not facing the difficult and as yet partially unanswerable questions about celibacy, the Church, or that part of the Church which has responsibility for the training of celibates, avoids the pain of uncertainty, but at the same time inhibits the development of spirituality and even ensures severe irresponsibility and, in some cases, hypocrisy.

Beginning with the support of Paul the Apostle, through much of the history of the Catholic Church a body of literature has been amassed supporting the view that the concentration of all one's efforts to spiritual matters without the burden of family obligations is adequate justification for the conjunction of celibacy and priesthood. The experience of clergy and of laity within the Catholic Church has not, however, remained static.

> Within the last 40 years a growing number of men and women who clearly do not have the charism of celibacy have become convinced that they have a call to ministry. Their argument is not with the sublimity of the celibate ideal or the validity of the celibate charism. Rather they question the wisdom of a church law that identifies priestly ministry with celibacy (Sipe, 1992, p. 1118).

Bishop Rheinhold Stecher, when retiring as bishop of Innsbruck in 1997, broke ranks with the imposed silence of his fellow bishops. In a letter critical both of papal and Vatican policy, he asserted that continued insistence on an exclusively male, celibate priesthood within the Catholic Church by an exclusively male, celibate, clerical élite involves an unavoidable implication that such a priesthood accords better with the mind of Christ and that a compulsorily celibate priesthood is also in the best interest of the people of God. Stecher's interrogation of the Western Catholic practice of compulsory celibacy gave voice to what in future might be seen as prophetic words.

> To regard remaining unmarried as the imitation of Christ *par excellence*, the endeavour literally to mimic the state of Christ especially in his unmarriedness and impose it upon the vast majority of priests by linking the charism of celibacy as a condition of ordination to the Roman Catholic priesthood appears increasingly, theologically questionable (Stecher, 1997, p. 1668).

In the United Kingdom the anomalous nature of Canon Law concerning priestly celibacy was highlighted in the mid-1990s paradoxically by an event occurring in the Church of England. Catholic priests to whom marriage is forbidden by Canon Law have historically been obliged to abandon the exercise of priesthood if they wish to marry. Following the decision to ordain women as priests in the Church of England, a number of married, former Anglican clergymen converted to the Catholic Church and were reordained as Catholic priests. Their welcome by those same bishops who had to uphold, according to Canon Law, the expulsion from active priesthood of cradle-Catholic priests wishing still to minister as married men, only serves to accentuate a curious anomaly. Apparent confusion should not mask important alterations in official attitudes. For instance, Schillebeeckx (1985) reported that in the 1971 Synod of Bishops 'many members of the Synod clearly looked on marriage in pre-Vatican II terms: as procreation and pure sex. They said things about married ministers which were a slap in the face for many married, Reformed pastors.'

The comparative ease and lack of controversy accompanying the acceptance for ordination to the Roman Catholic priesthood of married, former Anglican clergymen contrasted with the distressing experience of so many of those who departed during the unprecedented exodus of priests from active ministry in the 1960s and 1970s. Those departures had been met by alarmed church authorities with a mixture of incomprehension, hostility and vindictiveness toward those leaving, attitudes that in retrospect appear unworthy, uncharitable and profoundly unchristian. Though Pope Paul VI reluctantly released many priests from their promises or vows when they were resolved to marry, his successor Pope John Paul II dramatically slowed the process down. Now little spoken of from the distance of decades, the aftermath of such unsympathetic attitudes shown by bishops and religious superiors toward priests who resigned their ministry bequeathed a legacy of sadness, not to say bitterness, largely unaddressed and unresolved to this day.

In the face of the serious decline in numbers of priests in many parts of the world at the start of the twenty-first century, the imperative to review the theological rationale underpinning a celibate priesthood was summed up by Professor Jack Dominian in a letter to *The Tablet* (1999, p. 665) evoking the following suggestion.

> The marriage of the clergy should not be seen either as an emergency measure to make up for the diminishing numbers nor as a concession to the predilection of our time. Rather it should be seen as a God-appointed time for clergy to enter a rich vein of sexual spirituality through marriage.

From an analysis based on Eriksonian developmental psychology, Kennedy and Heckler (1972) produced evidence linking loneliness to psychological and psychosexual factors in the causal process leading to a decision to resign from the priesthood. On a continuum indicating 'maldeveloped' at one end and 'well developed' at the other, their 1972 study found that the majority of Catholic clergy in the United States of America were in the 'underdeveloped' and 'developing' categories. That the majority of priests resolve this maturing-adult and intimacy crisis in favour of remaining in the priesthood still leaves the problem of loneliness and celibacy that influences a significant number of young priests to change their minds and opt for marriage (Schoenherr and Young, 1993).

Listening to the priests

Priests over the age of fifty do not too readily permit themselves to forget a curious mindset with which they were once familiar that could extol marriage only so long as, at least subconsciously, it was kept separate from the subject of priesthood. Memories of such an attitude, so strongly evocative of the seminary ethos of the day, are perfectly caught in the words, 'Where there is a right under-standing of the potential holiness of sex and marriage, to allow priests to marry is no longer repugnant' (Davis, 1967, p. 31). It is the word 'repugnant' in reference to a possible married priesthood, used by the theologian Charles Davis, that embodies the attitude many older priests might wish to forget. Combined with a scarcely suppressed disgust even of married sexual activity was a neo-pagan esti-mation of cultic priestly purity. That it is an attitude still extant is shown in the words of a young priest in the United States of America when he says, 'Celibacy was asked for [by the people of the Church] because it is tied to the sacredness of the eucharist. I can't think of a better way to capture sacredness' (Keehan, 1993, p. 154). This is nothing but a reiteration of Old Testament cultic purity at best; at worst it is a theologically shocking statement in its implicit debasement of married sexuality. That it used to be a common clerical attitude inculcated in the seminary will be acknowledged by numerous priests trained in that era, and still reported by some priests who responded to the survey. For example, one priest wrote as follows.

[At my seminary] As for celibacy – we weren't 'giving up much; marriage wasn't all it was made out to be' (priest aged between 60 and 64).

Some of the clergy clearly decided to speak out in favour of celibacy. For example, one respondent noted some of the practical advantages of the link between celibacy and priesthood.

Celibacy is preferable from an operational point of view – money, houses, moves, etc. (priest aged between 65 and 69).

Some others were as forthright and unequivocal as the priest who gave the following opinion.

I decided to complete the questionnaire because I feel it is important to give the views of one who is completely loyal to a great Pope and to the Church. I am completely happy with Pope John Paul's ruling on celibacy . . . I feel that those whom God calls to the priesthood are also called to the celibate life. What I find distressing are the criticisms of priests who disobey the Pope and the Church and try to tear the church apart (priest aged between 55 and 59).

Another wondered whether celibacy had an updated prophetic role.

It feels as though ordained (celibate) ministry has become more strongly counter-cultural than ever before (priest aged between 30 and 34).

It is questionable whether mandatory celibacy as a counter-cultural statement speaks with quite the clarity that is intended. Though a powerful rationale still exists for a freely chosen celibacy, the question remains whether the same argument holds true at all for enforced celibacy, especially in the face of the growing shortage of men prepared to accept celibacy with priesthood.

A greater number of clergy, however, chose to speak out against the current situation regarding celibacy in one way or another. Some attacked the theological bases for celibacy and the theological issues surrounding it. For example, in retaining celibacy the Catholic Church is de facto not only implying the superiority of celibacy over marriage for priests, but, as one priest noted, also may appear to be elevating celibacy above the eucharist, since restricting priesthood exclusively to celibate males deprives millions of regular eucharistic celebration.

Other priests attacked what they saw to be incoherence and contradiction in the current practice of accepting within the priesthood convert married Anglican clergymen. One priest wrote as follows.

If married Anglican clergy are converting solely on the issue of women priests, then I feel they should not be accepted. This is how it appears to be happening (priest aged between 50 and 54).

Priests expressed clearly the paradox posed by the welcome of still-married former Anglican clergymen and the departure of reluctant celibate priests.

What are we to make of the situation whereby a priest is leaving to marry and is being replaced by a former Anglican who is married?!! (priest aged between 40 and 44).

One priest, prepared to raise the practical problem of paying married former Anglican clergymen a much more substantial salary than Catholic priests enjoy, repeated a rather scurrilous libel.

Married former Anglican priests ordained Catholic priests cause a financial burden for the Catholic community, not thoroughly thought through by bishops. 'Prams in presbytery means hands in till' (priest aged between 45 and 49).

Another priest gave evidence of what he saw as certain injustices inherent in the exercise of Canon Law with regard to celibacy. One cannot help being reminded of the ancient adage that though the church preaches justice, as an organization it often behaves unjustly.

Celibacy is a powerful charism of the gospel to be affirmed and honoured and preserved especially for the priest. The canonical obligation [of celibacy] with its system of dispensations does more harm than good and in some cases is unjust and inhuman. If there is to be a law imposing the obligation, the obligation must automatically cease when the priest is willing to return to the lay estate. The dispensation process is cruel. I speak from talking to my ex-brethren (priest aged between 65 and 69).

Many priests who participated in the survey and many who refused to do so took the trouble to express an anxiety that the results of the survey might be used for media mischief-making at the Church's expense. Much of this anxiety focused on the media's interest in celibacy and in the sexual misdemeanours of clergy. Largely for this reason the questionnaire had included no direct questions on the priests' actual sexual behaviour and experience. Some of the respondents, nonetheless, decided to provide data on this issue. One priest commented as follows.

You didn't ask if we had indulged in sexual relationships since ordination, which I think is a question many would be interested in (NB No, I haven't!) (priest aged between 40 and 44).

Another priest noted the omission, but provided no personal information.

I am surprised at no questions on celibacy, marriage, promiscuity or gay issues among the clergy (priest aged between 55 and 59).

Shaping the questions

Against this background, the *Catholic Parochial Clergy Survey* developed two main themes on the topic of celibacy and priesthood. The first theme focused on the principles of chastity and celibacy. What proportion of priests today believe that celibacy should remain the norm for entry into priesthood? How many priests continue to maintain that chastity is essential for a priest in the Catholic Church? What is the current perception regarding the extent to which priests remain faithful to their commitment to celibacy?

The second theme approached the issue from the opposite perspective of framing questions about clerical marriage. What proportion of priests today believe that married men could validly be ordained priests? As a specific test issue, how many priests feel that the Catholic Church has too readily ordained married convert Anglican clergymen? Given the readiness of the Catholic Church to ordain married convert Anglican clergymen, how many priests consider that priests who left the Catholic Church and married should be read-mitted to ministry?

The final question in this section faced the direct issue of enquiring how many priests would wish to get married and to stay in priestly ministry if it were per-mitted. One view might be that the exodus of clergy from the priesthood has now left a solid core totally committed to the pattern of celibacy and chastity. Another view might be that many of those who remain in the priesthood operate within a system that is inimical to their personal convictions. This final question may help to adjudicate between these conflicting perspectives.

In shaping these questions, it was decided not to ask a direct question regarding sexual practice. One of the authors considered it more than priests would tolerate to have been asked directly whether they had been true to their vow or promise of perpetual chastity. Based upon this consideration, the less contentious alternative was to include a statement asking for a level of agreement or disagreement with the proposition, 'Most priests are faithful to their commitment to celibacy.' The supposition underlying the proposition was that each priest would himself know of his own fidelity to celibacy as well as having some idea by general knowledge of the incidence over the years of the failure of fellow priests in this regard or of priest friends and acquaintances admitting to sexual involvement.

Interpreting the statistics

Table 9.1 demonstrates that among priests currently engaged in parish ministry in the Catholic Church, there is a high regard for the principles of chastity and celibacy and a balance of opinion in favour of retaining celibacy as the norm for entry into the priesthood. Comparatively few serving parochial priests would wish to get married. On the other hand, there is general acceptance of the view that married men could be ordained priest.

Nearly three-quarters of the priests (73%) signed up to the view that chastity is essential for a Catholic priest. As many as one in six (17%), however, were prepared to deny this view, while a further 10% were still pondering the issue. Looked at from another perspective, one in every four priests (27%) currently engaged in parish ministry in the Catholic Church were no longer convinced about the need for chastity.

Nearly three-quarters of the priests (72%) were of the view that most priests remain faithful to their commitment to celibacy. Only a handful (6%) felt that the tide has turned the other way and could say with confidence that most priests are unfaithful to their commitment to celibacy. It is interesting, however, that as many as one in every four of the priests (23%) felt uncertain about this question. In other words, they were not willing to take it for granted that the majority of priests remain committed to their vows of celibacy.

While nearly three-quarters of the priests (72%) felt that those who had entered the priesthood aware of the rules of celibacy remain committed to those rules, the proportion dropped to less than half (46%) who felt that celibacy should remain the norm for entry to the priesthood. On this issue, as many as a third (34%) of the priests who themselves entered the priesthood under the rule of celibacy and have remained in the priesthood felt that celibacy should no longer remain the norm for entry to the priesthood. A further one in five of the priests (20%) were continuing to debate this issue.

The vast majority of the priests (91%) believed that marriage should not pose a complete barrier to priesthood and that a married man could validly be ordained priest. Only one in twenty of the priests (5%) took the position of denying the validity of the ordination of a married man, while a further 5% remained uncertain about the validity of such orders.

Although the balance of opinion was divided on whether or not Catholic priests who left and married should be readmitted to ministry, the weight of opinion was in favour. For every three priests who supported this view (45%), there were two priests who stood against it (29%), and nearly two more who had not made up their minds (26%).

Once again the balance of opinion was divided on the appropriateness of the way in which the Catholic Church had received into priesthood married Anglican clergymen who had left the Church of England over the issue of the ordination of women. The weight of opinion, however, was in favour. For every two priests who thought that the Catholic Church had too readily ordained married convert Anglican clergymen (32%), there were three priests who rejected this criticism (46%), and a further 22% who were still forming an opinion on the issue. Among the priests currently serving in the parish ministry, one in five (18%) said that, if it were permitted, they would get married and stay in priestly ministry. Another one in four of the priests (24%) were not so sure of their personal intentions, but would want to keep the options open. The majority (58%), however, are clear that they would not entertain thoughts of marriage while remaining in priestly ministry.

Regular and secular

Table 9.2 demonstrates that on most of the issues raised in this section there are no significant differences between the views espoused by secular priests and the views espoused by regular priests. For example, 74% of the regular priests and 73% of the secular priests maintained that chastity is essential for a Catholic priest, and 71% of the regular priests and 72% of the secular priests believed that most priests are faithful to their commitment to celibacy. The clear majority of the regular priests (89%) and the secular priests (91%) believed that a married man could validly be ordained priest, and 45% of the regular priests and 45% of the secular priests argued that Catholic priests who left and married should be readmitted to ministry. The view that the Catholic Church has too readily ordained married convert Anglican clergymen was taken by 29% of the regular priests and by 33% of the secular priests.

The gap seems to begin to widen, however, between regular priests and secular priests on whether celibacy should remain the norm for entry to the priesthood. This view was taken by 51% of the regular priests and by 45% of the secular priests, although this difference did not reach statistical significance. The one statistically significant difference concerned the question about the desire to get married. While one in five of the secular priests (20%) said that, if it were permitted, they would get married and stay in priestly ministry, the proportion fell to 12% among the regular priests.

Generational differences

Table 9.3 demonstrates that, overall, priests in the 45–59 age category take a more liberal view on the issues surrounding celibacy in comparison with the position adopted by priests aged 60 and over. Priests in the youngest age cohort, under the age of 45, however, are less liberal on most of the questions than those aged between 45 and 59.

While eight out of every ten priests aged 60 and over (79%) agree that chastity is essential for a Catholic priest, the population fell to seven out of every ten priests between the ages of 45 and 59 (69%) and then fell slightly further to 66% among the priests under the age of 45.

While eight out of every ten priests aged 60 and over (79%) agreed that most priests are faithful to their commitment to celibacy, the proportion fell to 66% among the 45–59-year-olds and then rose slightly to 68% among the priests under the age of 45.

Three-fifths of the priests aged 60 and over (59%) wished to maintain celibacy as the norm for entry to the priesthood. The proportion almost halved among the 45–59 age group to 35% and then rose again to 41% among the priests under the age of 45.

Among all three age cohorts, the proportions of priests who believed that a married man could validly be ordained priest were very high. The proportion was highest, however, among the 45–59-year-olds at 95%, compared with 88% among those aged 60 and over, and with 90% among those under the age of 45.

One in three of the priests aged 60 and over (35%) agreed that Catholic priests who left and married should be readmitted to ministry. The proportion increased significantly among the 45–59 age group to 57% and then dropped back to 45% among the priests under the age of 45.

The age category of priests most likely to want to consider marriage comprises the 45–59-year-olds. One in every four of the priests in this age group (24%) said that, if it were permitted, they would get married and stay in the ministry. The proportion halved among those aged 60 and over to 12%. Young priests under the age of 45 were less likely than the priests in the 45–59 age group to express an interest in getting married and staying in the priesthood (18% compared with 24%).

The one issue in this section that does not follow the same clear pattern with age concerns the reception of married convert Anglican clergymen into the priesthood in the Catholic Church. On this issue, the most liberal position was adopted by the oldest cohort of priests. One in every four of the priests aged 60 and over (24%) felt that the Catholic Church has too readily ordained married convert Anglican clergymen. The proportions then rose steadily to 35% among the 45–59 age group, and to 43% among those under the age of 45.

CHAPTER TEN

Fallen Priests

BISHOP'S NIGHTS OF SIN AT THE HOLIDAY INN (Tabloid headline on the former Scottish Bishop of Argyll and the Isles, Roderick Wright's elopement with a divorcee).

If two gay priests go to a conference and share a hotel room, the bishop praises them for saving money. But if a heterosexual priest shared a room with a woman! Ha! (McBrien, 1993).

If a married couple use contraception, they're complicit in evil. If a priest molests a child, he gets a new parish. Indeed, sex itself seems in the cardinals' minds, entirely an abstraction. It's a sin or an act rather than a relationship (Andrew Sullivan, *The Sunday Times News Review*, 28 April 2002, p. 4).

This chapter is concerned with *fallen priests*. There are a number of ways in which priests can fall from the standards that the Catholic Church expects of them, that society at large expects of them and that they expect of themselves. This chapter focuses on four specific issues: alcohol abuse, homosexuality, heterosexual relationships and paedophilia. Some would argue that each of these issues should lead to expulsion from ministry. Others would wish to grade the gravity of the issues more subtly.

Context

Regarding the first of these issues, alcoholism, alcohol addiction and alcohol dependency describe those whose psychological or physical state is affected by alcohol. The condition has long been known and described, although it was as late as 1939 that alcoholism was first categorized as a disease. Clergy are not immune from this condition. Given the view that recovery from alcoholism is itself sometimes seen as a spiritual process (Alcoholics Anonymous, 1986), clergy might be thought to be good candidates for rehabilitation.

Several studies conducted in the United States of America have given particular attention to the incidence and correlates of alcoholism among the clergy. For example, Sorensen's (1976) sociological study, comparing alcoholic and non-alcoholic priests, found that alcoholics tended to come from alcoholic families and that a high proportion held higher degrees. The surprising discovery was that alcoholic priests apparently had no more conflict with colleagues and parishioners than did their sober counterparts. A study by Jean and Peterson (1988), investigating the differences between religious and secular clergy alcoholics, found in general that there were no significant differences between these two groups.

Fichter (1982) in an empirical study involving 138 dioceses in the United States of America estimated alcoholism among secular clergy as lower than the incidence among the population as a whole. On the contrary, Royce (1987) estimated that a higher percentage of priests than among the general population have their ministry impaired by alcohol.

Ryan (1993) identified two difficulties in the way of accurate assessment of the problem of alcoholism among the clergy. The first difficulty is the prevailing notion of stigma among clergy when speaking of alcoholism, in spite of generalized acceptance of alcoholism as a disease. It is unsurprising, therefore, that clergy should see alcoholism as a moral problem. The second barrier to accurate assessment of the disease is the all-pervasive practice of denial both by those afflicted with alcoholism and by those people associated with them. The Catholic Church appears to have been as likely as other professions to underestimate the incidence of the problem. Some would argue, however, that the Catholic Church should have a particular responsibility to take this problem seriously.

> The Church regards itself as a healing community and so it needs to be actively involved in combating so destructive and pervasive an illness as alcoholism among its clergy. It does have a special role, particularly as many authorities see recovery as involving a psychic change which is spiritual in nature (Ryan, 1993, p. 44).

Regarding the second issue, in 1102 Saint Anselm, Archbishop of Canterbury, demanded that the punishment for homosexuality should be moderate because 'this sin has been so public that hardly anyone has blushed for it, and many, therefore, have plunged into it without realising its gravity' (Zeldin, 1994, p. 123). It was probably only in the twelfth and thirteenth centuries that a mass condemnation of homosexuality began in Europe. The total obloquy heaped for so long by the Church on homosexuals and homosexuality moderated considerably in the final decade of the twentieth century with the distinction now being made by Catholic Church authorities between homosexual orientation and homosexual genital activity, forbidding the latter while tolerating the existence of the former.

A report from the United States of America by Sipe (1990) alerted a wide English-speaking audience to the reality of homosexuality in connection with the Catholic priesthood. Barry and Bordin (1967) had written: 'As a confirmed bachelor in the "world" a man might be subject to the real or fancied taunts of his fellows: as a priest he can live a bachelor's life and be praised for it.' Verdieck, Shields and Hoge (1988) summarized that the weakened impact of desire to marry on the decision to continue at the seminary might be in part a function of altered social norms regarding the legitimacy of various lifestyle alternatives, suggesting even that of homosexuality. One of the statements in a paper for the

Catholic Bishops' Conference of England and Wales stressed a potential drawback to a preponderance of homosexual seminarians: 'With a higher proportion of homosexually inclined entrants, very often the heterosexual can feel he is in the wrong place. The image of the seminary is compromised' (Smith, 1993, p. 14). The conclusion of Wolf (1989) and Sipe (1990) was that the percentage of priests in the Catholic Church who admitted to being gay or were in homosexual relationships was well above the national average for the United States of America. The research by Rovers (1995) on Canadian seminarians indicated considerable sexual orientation confusion, again more than had been commonly expected from what was known of the proportion of homosexual males among the general Canadian population.

Some years ago in an article in *Commonweal*, the priest chairman of the theology department at the University of Notre Dame, Indiana, disturbed and alarmed the hierarchy of the Catholic Church in the United States of America when he asked, 'Do homosexual bishops give preference, consciously or not to gay candidates for choice pastorates?' (McBrien, 1987, p. 380). On the one hand, it has been tacitly acknowledged for years that homosexually inclined bishops had submerged such tendencies under power play and watered silk but consistently gave the game away by surrounding themselves with good-looking priests. Many priests, on the other hand, it is said, submerged their ambivalent and unresolved homosexual feelings with drink.

On the matter of homosexuality, as on the fidelity of priests to their promise or vow of celibacy, bishops, superiors and seminary rectors tend to be defensive. Unsworth (1993), writing about the experience in the United States of America, reports that one seminary professor at a large diocesan seminary stated that an entire floor in his theologate was occupied by gay seminarians. It is common diocesan clergy knowledge that as long as twenty and thirty years ago, and possibly ever since, one corridor of the senior northern seminary in the United Kingdom began to be referred to by the students as Queens' Walk for obvious reasons.

It is not just in the so-called 'lavender rectories' of parishes in the United States of America that homosexual priests have claimed a distinction between priestly life and sexual life. Such a point of view involves a novel casuistry that was never claimed for illicit heterosexual activity by clergy. The heterosexual priest remains as celibate as his efforts will allow, but some homosexual priests are proud of their homosexual activity and assert that 'celibacy applies only to heterosexual priests'. How widespread is such a view is unclear, but a characteristic of one part of the homosexual scene, at least before the advent of AIDS, was promiscuity.

Regarding the third of these issues, according to Sipe (1990), speaking of the experience in the United States of America, seminaries do little to train the clergy in celibacy during the years spent there. In many seminaries the topic was never formally mentioned. Newly ordained priests move from the comparative social isolation of the seminary into a world in which sex is the engine that drives much of the entertainment industry, is central to most advertising and shapes our consciousness and unconsciousness. The life of a vowed celibate in such an environment becomes exceedingly difficult even if voluntarily chosen, but mandatory celibacy is increasingly challenged from within the Catholic Church as dysfunctional and questioned by a culture that relishes sex (Fox, 1995). One American priest-theologian claims that celibacy

> sends a negative message to the rest of the world, a message that says that sexual intimacy and marriage somehow detract from one's relationship with God. It says that the ideal form of life is one that is lived without intimacy ... obligatory celibacy has no theological status (McBrien, 1993, p. 199).

A melancholy reflection in the same book by one Monsignor in the United States of America adds, 'I find it hard to believe that God takes pleasure in our loneliness.'

The view has been expressed that before the Second Vatican Council, at least in the United States of America, celibacy was relatively easy because the priests rarely left the rectory, never took off their black suit and collar, had to be home by 10.30, and largely saw the down side of marriage. Although largely unacknowledged fifty and more years ago, in this more forthright age it is common knowledge that there are now many reluctant celibates in the Catholic Church. Studies point to a general consensus that about 20% of priests are at any one time involved either in a more or less stable sexual relationship with a woman, or with more than one woman, and that between 8% and 10% are at a stage of heterosexual exploration involving sexual contacts (Dominian, 1991).

Regarding the fourth of these issues, until comparatively recently the sexual proclivity and behaviour of those priests now recognized as paedophiles or ephebophiles seems to have been condoned in practice, if not defended theologically, by a clerical culture of denial and secrecy. It ought not be forgotten that 'The custom of sweeping such things under the carpet was actually condoned by the police in those days' (Longley, 2000, p. 272). Wholesale denial by bishops, reassignment of perpetrators and attempts to discredit accusers encapsulated a topsy-turvy world in which clergy perpetrator was defended as victim and victim portrayed as perpetrator.

Referring to the sexual scandals that broke around the Catholic clergy in the United States of America early in 2002, *The Tablet* wrote as follows.

> The Church was inclined to put fear of scandal and compassion for its priests before the safety of children. Wary of transparency bishops tried to keep the civil authority out and so regarded the sexual abuse of minors as a sin, whereas it is also a crime. The price is now being paid, not just in punitive legal settlements but in the shattering of the Church's moral authority (*The Tablet*, 20 April 2002, p. 3).

The policy has been one that ultimately magnified the harm done, but literally and metaphorically has proved disastrously expensive to the Catholic Church.

In all of this is the alarming impression that harm done toward the individual has been seen as less important than harm to the institution. Such an inversion is mirrored in the Pope's address to the cardinals in the United States of America when he says 'The Church will help society to understand and deal with the crisis in its midst' (*The Tablet*, 27 April 2002, p. 29). It is society that has forced the hand of the Catholic Church to acknowledge and face up to the evil within its own priestly ranks, not the other way round. The Pope's words would attempt to turn that reality on its head. Such mishandling by Church authorities has been seriously damaging both in moral terms and in terms of morale (Rossetti, 1997).

Few clergy would now publicly condone the longstanding clerical culture of secrecy, which allowed paedophile priests to feign repentance and amendment only to continue their activities when relocated by their trusting if gullible bishop or religious superior. That bishops may still override structures supposedly in place to promote good practice in child safety was manifested in the behaviour of the Archbishop of Cardiff in 2000, who was able to bypass advice and fail to take account of warnings by some of his own senior diocesan priests that two priests in his diocese could be paedophiles. Both of these priests have subsequently been given lengthy prison sentences. Even after the event, the Archbishop of Cardiff, with dismaying self-righteousness, persisted in justifying his handling of the affair, when even the most sympathetic observer could see it had been lamentably handled. This avoidable episode appeared to have precipitated his unsurprising but reluctant resignation.

In England and Wales, at least, diocesan priests are in law neither employed nor self-employed; they are what are known as office holders. This relationship between priests and the Catholic Church means that legal cases for compensation against the Catholic Church are difficult to pursue, as the Catholic Church is said in law not to be responsible for its priests. The recent breast-beating by the Catholic hierarchy of England and Wales regarding their past failure adequately to deal with sexual abuse cases by priests lies uneasily with the adopted legal position which denies the victims financial compensation in England and Wales by the Catholic Church's denial of responsibility for the criminal activity of the priest. Such ambivalence gives pause for reflection. Where responsibility is denied for the behaviour of wayward priests, it is difficult to comprehend in a theological context what possible meaning lies in an apology made by the Catholic hierarchy of England and Wales. Feelings of demoralization reported by priests caused by accounts of child sex abuse by the clergy are understandable and predictable.

The Times, Saturday, 15 June 2002 reported a landmark ruling of the previous day that the High Court in London had for the first time given permission to a 36-year-old former altar boy to proceed with a £100,000 action for negligence against the Catholic Church for the sexual abuse he suffered as a child over an eight-year period at the hands of a priest of the Birmingham Diocese. The significance was less that the archbishop and the trustees of the diocese had predictably denied liability but that for the first time they were potentially to be held responsible for the wrongdoing of one of their priests.

Listening to the priests

The heading 'Fallen Priests' is shorthand for a particular group of priests specified by the wording associated with that era when an unmarried mother was referred to as a fallen woman. In a Church where celibacy is the norm and secrecy still remains the order of the day it was thought unlikely by one of the authors that many priests would be forthright when speaking about sexual activity of any kind, whether heterosexual or homosexual. Unsurprisingly this proved to be the case, with the consequence that few priests chose to offer comments in this area.

Denial and secrecy still seem, therefore, to be the most prevalent reaction to most sexual problems among priests, not least because sexual issues themselves can become terribly complicated. Such secrecy about clergy sexuality is paralleled among clergy in the United States of America of whom it has been written that 'priests over fifty-five appear to be extremely reluctant to discuss such issues, even with classmates they have known for decades – and most priests are over fifty-five' (Unsworth, 1993, p. 249).

One priest who decided to break the rule of silence made it clear that he had no inclination toward homosexual orientation himself, but respected priest colleagues who were practising homosexuals.

> I know several priests who are gay and in longstanding relationships with another man. Their priesthood does not seem to be impaired by this – their ministry in fact seems to be enhanced (priest aged between 55 and 59).

There was less reticence, however, on the subject of alcoholism. Some of the replies were unusually honest, as in the case of the priest who wrote as follows about his responses to the questions in the survey concerning signs of physical and mental poor health.

> In my alcoholism I could have ticked them all, but fifteen years of sobriety have changed my whole life (priest aged between 65 and 69).

Perhaps such honesty should be less surprising since the first step in any worthwhile alcohol rehabilitation programme demands acknowledgement of the problem and the need of help.

One respondent took exception in the survey to the wording 'becomes alcoholic', asserting:

> Bad question. A person doesn't become an alcoholic. The sickness is there and manifests itself with drink (usually the first) (priest aged between 55 and 59).

Shaping the questions

Against this background, the *Catholic Parochial Clergy Survey* framed four main themes relevant to this chapter on fallen priests. This section of the survey remained committed to attitudinal approaches rather than behavioural approaches. The aim was not to uncover the extent to which the priests had themselves experienced these dimensions of life. Rather the aim was to assess how tolerant the priests felt the Catholic Church should be toward priests who behaved in these ways.

The first theme examined the priests' attitude toward alcoholism among the clergy. To what extent do priests believe that a priest who becomes alcoholic should be barred from ministry?

The second theme examined the priests' attitude toward homosexuality among the clergy. To what extent do priests believe that a priest who practises homosexuality should be barred from ministry?

The third theme examined the priests' attitude toward heterosexual relationships among the clergy. This theme distinguished between relationships with married women and with unmarried women. To what extent do priests believe that a priest who has sex with an unmarried woman should be barred from ministry? And to what extent do priests believe that a priest who has sex with a married woman should be barred from ministry?

The fourth theme turned attention to paedophilia. To what extent do priests believe that a priest who practises paedophilia should be barred from ministry? In view of the high profile attention currently given to the issue of paedophilia, a second question on this theme assessed the priests' personal reaction to this scandal within the Catholic Church. What proportion of priests feel demoralized by reports of child sex abuse by clergy?

Interpreting the statistics

Table 10.1 demonstrates how sharply the priests distinguish between the differing levels of importance that should be ascribed to these different ways of falling from the high standards that may be expected from the priesthood. Paedophilia is to be taken very seriously, and homosexuality is to be taken quite seriously too. Sex with a married woman and sex with an unmarried woman are to be treated much more lightly. Alcoholism is regarded as a matter of little significance. Many priests feel demoralized by reports of child sex abuse by clergy.

Nine out of every ten priests (90%) took the view that a priest who practises paedophilia should be barred from ministry. This means that one in every ten priests did not feel that the Catholic Church's child protection policy should automatically rule out such priests from active ministry. According to the data 4% actively argued against paedophiles being barred from ministry and another 6% kept the possibility of leniency open to paedophiles.

Practising homosexuals were regarded as unacceptable in the priesthood by two out of every three priests (65%). By way of comparison only 21% actively argued against barring practising homosexual priests from ministry and another 14% kept the possibility of leniency open to practising homosexuals.

Overall the priests took a much more lenient attitude toward adultery than toward practising homosexuality. While two-thirds of the priests (65%) considered that a priest who practises homosexuality should be barred from ministry, the proportion fell to one-fifth (20%) who considered that a priest who has sex with a married woman should be barred from ministry. By way of contrast, 61% actively argued against barring adulterers from ministry and a further 20% wavered between the two sides of this debate. Clearly the fear of homosexuality is more powerful among priests in the Catholic Church than the fear of breaking the sixth commandment.

The priests distinguish between the severity of a priest having sex with a married woman and with an unmarried woman. While 19% of the priests took the view that a priest should be barred from ministry for having sex with a married woman, the proportion dropped further to 14% who took the view that a priest should be barred from ministry for having sex with an unmarried woman. Looked at from the opposite perspective, while 61% of the priests actively argued that having sex with a married woman should not debar a priest from ministry, the proportion rose further to 67% who actively argued that having sex with an unmarried woman should not debar a priest from ministry.

Only a small minority of priests saw alcoholism as a barrier to ministry. Just 7% of the priests took the view that a priest who becomes an alcoholic should be barred from ministry. On the contrary, four out of every five priests (79%) took the opposite view that a priest who becomes an alcoholic should not be barred from ministry. The remaining 14% have not formed a clear opinion on the matter.

The contribution of scandals involving paedophilia toward the demoralization of priests in the Catholic Church is made clear by the following statistic. Two-thirds of the priests (68%) reported that they felt demoralized by reports of child sex abuse by clergy, compared with just a third of this number (22%) who did not feel demoralized by such reports. The failure to deal adequately with paedophilia within the Catholic Church is damaging not only for the child victims and for the reputation of the Church in society, but for morale within the Church as well.

Regular and secular

Table 10.2 demonstrates that the secular priests and the regular priests adopted very similar attitudes toward the Church's treatment of fallen priests in respect of paedophilia, heterosexual relationships and alcoholism. Thus 91% of the regular priests and 90% of the secular priests wished to bar paedophiles from ministry. Similar proportions of the regular priests (18%) and of the secular priests (19%) wished to bar priests who have sex with a married woman from ministry and the same proportions of the regular priests (14%) and of the secular priests (14%) wished to bar priests who have sex with an unmarried woman from ministry. The view that alcoholics should be barred from ministry was taken by 9% of the regular priests and by 7% of the secular priests.

The demoralization caused by priest paedophiles affected equal proportions of regular priests and secular priests. Thus, 69% of the regular priests and 68% of the secular priests said that they felt demoralized by reports of child sex abuse by clergy.

There is, however, a significant difference in respect of attitude toward practising homosexuals. On this issue secular priests took a more accepting line than regular priests. While 63% of the secular priests felt that a priest who practises homosexuality should be barred from ministry, the proportion rose to 72% among the regular priests.

Generational differences

Table 10.3 demonstrates that there are some key differences in the attitudes espoused by the three age cohorts. The most interesting, and possibly the most disturbing of these differences concerns the profile of the youngest cohort, the priests under the age of 45. While these young priests adopted a more severe attitude in comparison with the 45–59 age cohort in respect of heterosexual relationships, they are more accepting of paedophilia. The young priests, under the age of 45, are also more accepting than their older colleagues of homosexuality and alcoholism.

While nine out of every ten priests aged 60 or over (92%) or between the ages of 45 and 59 (90%) maintained that a priest who practises paedophilia should be barred from ministry, the proportion fell to 85% among the priests under the age of 45. The greater willingness of the younger priests to condone paedophilia is a matter of concern in light of the long-term hurt caused to the victims of abuse, the criminal nature of such activity, and the Catholic Church's need to embed robust child protection policies.

The statistics show a general trend toward the greater acceptance of homosexuality among the clergy. While four out of every five priests aged 60 or over (79%) took the view that a priest who practises homosexuality should be barred from ministry, the proportions fell to three out of every five among the 45–59 age group (61%) and to 47% among those under the age of 45. The greater acceptance of homosexuality among the youngest cohort of priests may simply indicate a greater willingness to accept alternative sexualities, or it may indicate a higher predisposition toward homosexuality among the younger priests themselves.

The statistics show a movement toward a greater acceptance of heterosexual activity among priests from those aged 60 and over to those aged between 45 and 59. Thus, while only 24% of the priests aged 60 or over considered that a priest should be barred from ministry for having sex with a married woman, the proportion halved to 13% among the 45–59-year-olds. Similarly, while only 19% of the priests aged 60 or over considered that a priest should be barred from ministry for having sex with an unmarried woman, the proportion more than halved to 8% among the 45–59-year-olds. At the same time, the proportions rose again among the youngest age cohort. Thus, while 13% of the priests in the 45–59 age groups considered that a priest should be barred from ministry for having sex with a married woman, the proportion rose to 20% among those under 45. Similarly, while 8% of the priests in the 45–59 age group considered that a priest should be barred from ministry for having sex with an unmarried woman, the proportion rose to 15% among those under 45. The puzzle is to explain why an age group that is more accepting of practising paedophile priests and of practising homosexual priests should be less accepting of practising heterosexual priests.

The statistics also demonstrate a progressive liberalization of attitude toward alcoholic priests. Although only 10% of the priests aged 60 and over considered that a priest who becomes an alcoholic should be barred from ministry, the proportions fell further to 6% among the 45–59-year-olds, and to 4% among those under 45. In other words, only four in every hundred priests under the age of 45 felt that alcoholism should be a bar to ministry. The willingness to accept alcoholism among their fellow clergy may indicate a low resistance to alcohol abuse in themselves.

Finally, the statistics demonstrate that the demoralization engendered by the scandal of paedophilia in the Catholic Church affects all three cohorts of priests equally. Thus, 67% of the priests under the age of 45, 68% of the priests between the ages of 45 and 59, and 69% of the priests aged 60 and over reported that they felt demoralized by reports of child sex abuse by clergy.

CHAPTER ELEVEN

Jesus and Mary

Years ago in theological college, students were told to preach certainties not problems. This was bad advice then and could be even worse if given today. Problems must be confronted. Certainties can only be defended if problems are attacked (Hull, 1985).

It needs to be recognised ... that biblical language is often poetic, mythical or metaphorical. The language of exhortation and love differs from the language of doctrine. Although the bible does contain propositional statements, excessive concentration on this aspect of scripture can lead to an impoverishment or distortion of true meaning (Dulles, 2000, p. 72).

This chapter is concerned with the question of doctrinal orthodoxy and the extent to which priests remain committed to the doctrinal teachings of the Catholic Church. These wider principles are tested against specific beliefs concerning *Jesus* and *Mary*. Inevitably consideration of such issues involves a broader consideration of the way in which Christian beliefs have been shaped and formulated.

Context

An important enquiry at the heart of the Christian teaching asks what is enduring and central to the faith and what is not. God, we are told, has spoken to us through creation, through human experience and conscience, through the scriptures, and from within societies throughout human history. But God did not speak in the sense that Winston Churchill spoke to the British nation in wartime broadcasts. God's word is speech in a metaphorical sense. It is a mediated message picked up by prophets, priests and kings who attempted to express and transmit their understanding of what they had learned at a deeper level. The author of the Gospel of John described Jesus as the word of God that had existed from the beginning. It was Pope John XXIII who reminded the Catholic Church that, although the propositional formulae of the faith are important, they do not necessarily encapsulate the whole of the truth, nor do they express it in the only way it can be expressed. The repeated disregard of this realization throughout the history of the Catholic Church made so memorable the Pope's reiteration of the caveat.

The account of any given experience is shaped by interpretation, expectation, expression and insight within the language, symbol systems and usage of any culture.

> In this context the kinds of claims to final and unchangeable certitude about the truth of verbal formulations (which are not uncommonly still made for Catholic doctrinal statements) need to become more cognisant of the nature of our access to the mystery of the transcendent God (Hellwig, 1992, p. 32).

It is an exegetical commonplace now to say that neither Paul, the Gospel writers, nor those who had a hand in producing the books now making up the New Testament were interested simply in reporting the events of which they had close experience. The modern notion of recording an objective account of witnessed events was foreign to those early Christian writers. They saw their role as interpreting the meaning of the events that had been witnessed in a way that would convince and encourage those who heard what they had to tell. They preached and wrote from the standpoint of belief, with the aim of encouraging similar belief in the hearer and reader. The writings relating the Christian message, the Gospels especially, gave us a new form of literature, *euangellion*, good news, whose purpose was 'so that you may believe that Jesus is the Christ, the Son of God and that believing you may have life in his name' (John 20:30). The earliest expectation of this predominantly Jewish group that life as they knew it was soon to end with Jesus' second coming was in practice abandoned quite quickly, with a consequence that involved a radical reinterpretation of the person and message of Jesus.

The scriptural evidence that Jesus himself believed that the kingdom would come in the near future provides a useful example of the development of understanding by the Church of the person and role of Jesus. When the kingdom did not arrive in any sense that could readily be understood by his followers, the residual expectation (it was a very Jewish notion), as has been said, did not last for more than a few generations. The focus then shifted and an image of Jesus took shape as the one whose death and resurrection brought salvation to a world that would last a considerably longer time than had first been thought.

It was C. S. Lewis (1955) who made popular the apologetic argument that anyone claiming to be God must be either mad, bad, or God; and since Jesus could be shown to be neither mad nor bad, he must have been God. It is generally agreed among New Testament scholars of all persuasions that it is no longer possible to argue to the divinity of Jesus by reference to the claims of Jesus simply as related in the New Testament. What becomes remarkable is that the Christology defined at Nicaea (325) and Chalcedon (451) was based upon such a literal understanding of the words of scripture and also the belief that Jesus was cognizant of his divine nature and of his identity as the Second Person of the Trinity. That is to say that for fifteen or so centuries of the Church's existence, it was Christian doctrine that Jesus was the self-proclaimed God the Son living a truly human life. However, the Church's understanding of the scriptural basis for this assertion is now subject to proper academic scrutiny and debate.

The doctrine of the virginal conception of Jesus, leaving aside the problem of Jesus' genetic makeup, poses a very serious problem in reconciling the infancy narratives with the modern understanding of how Jesus could formulate his own identity. The problem is nicely focused by the New Testament scholar Raymond Brown.

> If Joseph and Mary knew that their son had no human father but was begotten of God's holy spirit; if it had been revealed to them from the start that the child was to be the Messiah, and if they had not kept this secret from Jesus, how can he not have affirmed that he was the Messiah or that he was the unique Son of God? Obviously this conflict between the infancy narratives and the (reconstructed) Jesus of the ministry is based on many 'ifs' all of which can be questioned (Brown, 1973, p. 46).

At the same time, Jesus' assertion of knowledge of what God wanted of humankind and his claim to possess powers (exorcism and forgiveness) belonging strictly to God raise the question regarding whether Jesus had any specific knowledge that he was uniquely God's son. If Jesus had specific knowledge of his origins, it is puzzling that he was unable 'to formulate his role in christological titles (the titles given to him in the annunciation of his birth) or in clearer descriptions' (Brown, 1973, p. 47). What do the average parish priests make of an incarnate God who can appear to be ignorant of his own divinity, and what words do priests use Sunday by Sunday to enlighten their parishioners?

In his letter published in the opening pages of the *Catechism of the Catholic Church* (1994, p. 5) Pope John Paul II states that in every age the Catechism expresses with assurance and authority 'a statement of the Church's faith and of Catholic doctrine attested to or illuminated by sacred scripture, the Apostolic tradition and the Church's magisterium'. The major criticism made of the *Catechism of the Catholic Church* is that all problems are made to appear to have been satisfactorily solved and all questions to have been authoritatively answered.

Marian devotions arose in the East and it was there that Mary was first invoked in prayer, and though called 'Mother of Jesus' in scripture, was in the fifth century defined as 'Mother of God'. There seems little doubt that, at least in popular devotion, Mary's createdness and humanity played only a minor role. The idea of Mary's ascension or assumption into heaven derives in part from the classical tradition of the apotheosis of a hero who attained to glory beyond death's long reach. Ancient texts are cited in support of the belief that such had happened to Mary, leading to the promulgation by Pope Pius XII in 1950 of the dogma that 'Mary, after completing the course of her life on earth was assumed to the glory of heaven both in body and soul.' This was the climax of centuries of Marian tradition, in spite of the absence of any scriptural sources. In a bewildering complex world, Catholics like others seek beliefs to make ultimate sense of their lives, and it has been said that beliefs, however implausible, accepted without criticism within a supporting community can have immense power. There is, however, a very real problem of turning a story into a matter of historical or factual truth rather than spiritual truth.

It might be asked, however, whether the inspirational nature of Mary necessitates a belief in her assumption into heaven, whatever that really means in a world where bodies grow old, die and corrupt. Of course, biological reality does not exhaust the explanation of things, but as a statement of fact bodily assumption is scarcely intelligible to present-day thought. Can the assumption of Mary's body be an intelligible answer to the question, what actually happened? Might there not be a confusion here of mythopoeic language with historical literalist language? As has been stated, there is no remaining mention about Mary's assumption either in scripture or even in the traditions of the first five centuries. That is uncontested. There is some difficulty in coming to terms with the obligation upon every Catholic to believe in an assertion about which Jesus said nothing and of which the majority of Christians of the first five centuries would not have heard. The Second Vatican Council put an end to excessive Marianism in the closing chapter on 'The Church' exhorting theologians and preachers, 'in treating of the unique dignity of the Mother of God, they carefully and equally avoided the falsity of exaggeration . . . and the excess of narrow-mindedness' (Abbott, 1966, p. 95). The theological secret might be found in the realization that 'Mary appears consistently as a symbolic character, and that therefore symbolism, not history, is the key to Mariology' (Rausch, 1982).

Listening to the priests

Within Roman Catholicism, at least before the Second Vatican Council, existed a general presumption that it was well known what every Catholic believed and that within Catholicism could be found a uniformity of belief the likes of which existed in no other Church. Just how wrong was that presumption is supported by the subsequent evidence of the existence of many forms of belief within Catholicism. If truth were told, there never had been quite that uniformity of belief among Catholics worldwide that was once so strongly assumed and often asserted.

There is still, nonetheless, a strong expectation among many Catholics, often the older people, that the priest is responsible for delivering the correct thinking about God. The priest becomes the professional God-defining expert. Some priests have clearly become so accustomed to assuming the role of defending the received faith that they found the questions on belief in the survey to be quite offensive. For example, concern was expressed by one priest over the very possibility of having a different belief from that handed down to him by the Catholic Church. He wrote as follows:

> It would be very worrying if priests do not believe in bodily resurrection, or indeed any of the creed (priest aged between 40 and 44).

Another priest made the same point in a somewhat different way.

> I am surprised at questions on dogma which if not believed would put [a] layperson out of the Church or they would live a false life (priest aged between 60 and 64).

Similar concern appeared to have led one priest to make the equivalent mistake to assuming that to ask whether it was believed that the earth was spherical implied that there was a strong belief that the contrary were true. To him asking questions about the context of faith

> seems to assume that there is a great deal of uncertainty on the teaching of the Church among Catholic clergy. I do not find this to be so (priest aged between 70 and 74).

Some of the other respondents wanted to engage in intelligent dialogue with the range of beliefs posed in the survey. One priest, for example, reflected on belief in the bodily resurrection of Jesus in the following way, allowing himself to show some interrogation of the tradition:

> What do *you* mean by bodily resurrection? I believe it but it is not the same as physical resurrection, or is it? (age not given).

Very few priests, however, wrote about their rejection of traditional beliefs.

Shaping the questions

Against this background, the *Catholic Parochial Clergy Survey* framed three main themes relevant to exploring the priests' perceptions of doctrines concerned with Jesus and concerned with Mary. The first theme focused on the classic heart of Christology concerning the two natures. Is the Jesus of the Catholic priest both fully God and fully man? Do all priests believe that Jesus is fully human? Do all priests believe that Jesus is fully God?

The second theme focused on the two key doctrines of the virgin birth and of the resurrection of Jesus. Do all priests believe that Jesus was conceived in the womb of a virgin without a human father? Do all priests believe in the bodily resurrection of Jesus?

The third theme turned attention to Mary and focused on the doctrine of the assumption promulgated by Pope Pius XII in 1950. Do all priests believe that Our Lady was taken up body and soul into heavenly glory as Catholics are meant to believe?

Interpreting the statistics

Table 11.1 demonstrates the very high levels of orthodox belief professed by Catholic parochial clergy. Only a very small minority dissent from the doctrinal teaching of the Catholic Church.

The two natures of Jesus were affirmed by forty-nine priests out of every fifty. Thus, 98% believed that Jesus is both fully human and fully God. The bodily resurrection of Jesus was affirmed by 97% of the priests and the virginal conception was affirmed by 94% of the priests. Acceptance of the assumption of Mary was slightly lower than acceptance of the key doctrines concerning Jesus, and yet 91%

of the priests affirmed that Our Lady was taken up body and soul into heavenly glory.

By way of contrast, only a handful of priests directly denied any of these doctrines concerning Jesus and Mary. Just 1% of the priests did not believe that Jesus is fully human, did not believe that Jesus is fully God, or did not believe in the bodily resurrection of Jesus. Just 2% of the priests did not believe that Jesus was conceived in the womb of a virgin without a human father, or did not believe that Our Lady was taken up body and soul into heavenly glory.

The other very interesting feature of this set of statistics concerns the low level of endorsement for the uncertain response. While a much higher proportion of the priests could allow themselves to express uncertainty over a number of issues raised in the survey, very few allowed themselves to remain uncertain over core matters of doctrine concerning the person of Jesus or over what some might see as more peripheral doctrines like the assumption of Mary. Clearly those who remain committed to the priesthood also remain committed to the whole array of beliefs that the priesthood is expected to propagate within the Catholic Church.

Regular and secular

Table 11.2 demonstrates that there is very little discrepancy between the patterns of belief espoused by regular priests and by secular priests. Thus, 99% of the regular priests and 98% of the secular priests believed that Jesus is fully human and the same proportions believed that Jesus is fully God. The same proportions (97%) of the regular priests and of the secular priests believed in the bodily resurrection of Jesus. The same proportions (91%) of the regular priests and of the secular priests believed that Our Lady was taken up body and soul into heavenly glory.

The only significant difference between regular priests and secular priests concerns the level of belief in the virginal conception of Jesus. While 97% of the regular priests subscribed to the belief that Jesus was conceived in the womb of a virgin without a human father, the proportion dropped slightly to 93% among the secular clergy. While the difference is statistically significant, it is far from demonstrating a serious erosion of orthodoxy among the secular clergy.

Generational differences

Table 11.3 demonstrates a slight tendency among the younger cohorts of clergy to depart from the very high levels of orthodoxy maintained by the oldest cohort of clergy on the two doctrines of the virginal conception of Jesus and the assumption of Mary.

Levels of belief in the two natures of Jesus and in the bodily resurrection of Jesus remained consistent across all three age cohorts. Between 98% and 99% of priests across the age range believed that Jesus is fully human. Between 98% and 99% of priests across the age range believed that Jesus is fully God. Between 96% and 98% of priests across the age range believed in the bodily resurrection of Jesus.

By way of contrast, however, belief in the virginal conception declined a little across the age range. While 97% of the priests aged 60 and over believed that Jesus was conceived in the womb of a virgin without a human father, the proportions fell to 91% among the 45–59-year-olds, and to 93% among those under the age of 45.

Belief in the assumption of Mary dropped even more noticeably across the age range. While 95% of the priests aged 60 or over believed that Our Lady was taken up body and soul into heavenly glory, the proportions fell to 88% among the 45–59-year-olds, and to 87% among those under the age of 45. Given the tendency toward greater conservatism among the youngest cohort of priests in other areas, it is interesting that the doctrine of the assumption of Mary may be losing its hold over this group of priests. The questioning of faith in one area can so easily lead to the questioning of faith in other areas as well.

CHAPTER TWELVE

Marriage, Sex and Death

While the ambiguity of religion and its ongoing need for redemption is a commonplace for biblical scholars, this need has been minimised or even forgotten by Christian teachers and theologians. The claim that in Jesus Christ the ancient promises have been fulfilled and the final age of the world has arrived has led the Church to look upon itself too uncritically as God's holy people and become insensitive to the ambiguity of its piety, its teaching, its life and practice, in short its religion (Baum, 1975, p. 63).

When God told Adam and Eve to increase and multiply, the population density was two persons per square world (Wynn, 1988, p. 107).

This chapter is concerned with the moral teaching of the Catholic Church and the extent to which priests remain committed to moral orthodoxy on issues concerned with *marriage*, *sex* and *death*.

These wider principles are tested against teaching concerned specifically with abortion, euthanasia, artificial contraception, remarriage after divorce, and annulment.

Context

The Catholic Church is a unique institution in which celibate males occupy all major positions of authority. Far from being seen in the twenty-first century as a historical social anomaly, the claim is that within historical Christianity this state of affairs is in accordance with the will of Christ himself. It is a peculiar claim considering the greater proportion of women than men who make up faithful adherents to the Catholic Church. It is more peculiar still that when it comes to authoritative voices concerning so many matters intimately affecting women, such as female identity, fertility, pregnancy, giving birth, raising children, and the role of women in general, it is the voice of celibate men that has been heard within the Catholic Church. That it still has not struck church authorities as curious is bolstered by the unspoken residual predicate that such a state of affairs is by extension the will of God.

As education worldwide, both secular and theological, is made accessible to women as well as to men, to state the case at its more extreme, it should become increasingly unremarkable that more and more educated women might no longer be listening to the religious worldview of a seemingly blinkered, apparently unhearing, exclusively male leadership (Fox, 1995).

Discoveries in reproductive biology, if not calling into question the Catholic Church's insistence that abortion is wrong in any instance, at least according to some Catholic theologians, raise the problem whether the Church's statements on abortion are really saying what they appear to say. For example, if the foetus must be viewed as sacred from the first moment of conception, then it follows that:

> Human life must be respected and protected absolutely from the moment of conception. From the first moment of his (her) existence, a human being must be recognised as having the rights of a person, among which is the inviolable right of every innocent being to life (*Catechism of the Catholic Church*, 1994, p. 489).

If, then, the foetus must be viewed as sacred from the first moment of conception and protected as such, the question is asked, what is this saying about the estimated 55% of embryos lost before and during the process of implantation? The eminent moral theologian Karl Rahner, who died in 1984, asked what it means to say that over half of all 'human beings', real human beings with immortal souls and an eternal destiny, will never get beyond this first stage of human existence (Tauer, 1988, p. 55).

Significantly, the absolute ban on all abortion is looked upon by the Catholic Church as the touchstone of ethical and moral orthodoxy. Admirable though its grounding may be, based as it is upon the sacredness of all human life, it has increasingly been observed that, whereas in consideration of other moral matters basic Christian principles are nuanced having regard for circumstances, the methodology underlying the official attitude of the Catholic Church on sexual morality appears much more law bound, rigid and uncompromising. In an ecclesial atmosphere where a sign of apparent orthodoxy and fundamental loyalty is believed to be demonstrable in a simple litmus test, it would be understandable if most priests, without thinking too deeply on the matter, gave their support to the official teaching of the Catholic Church on the unmitigated evil of abortion.

Whatever its motives and means, direct euthanasia consists in putting an end to the lives of the handicapped, sick or dying persons. It is morally unacceptable (*Catechism of the Catholic Church*, 1994, pp. 490–1). The consistency of such an attitude is matched by the belief that burdensome or dangerous medical interventions that are disproportionate to any expected advantage to the sufferer may be discontinued on the principle that the intention is not to cause death, but rather to acknowledge an inability officiously to try and prevent it. Advances in medical technology capable of staving off death in those who, without such intervention, would surely die have obliged ethicians to scrutinize positions previously adopted and to ask how much treatment should be given to a dying person.

A curious anomaly in the teaching of the Catholic Church refuses holy communion to those Catholics who have divorced and remarried, but on the supposition of their having repented of their misdeed will give communion to the abortionist, the rapist and the mass murderer. This is in contrast to the Catholic Church's attitude to the divorced who have not remarried. The moral state of each of the parties in a divorce is not considered by the Catholic Church to be automatically sinful although the official view asserts that 'Divorce is a grave offence against the natural law . . . is immoral also because it introduces disorder into the family and into society.' From this viewpoint the new marriage is considered as adding 'to the gravity of the divorce putting the remarried spouse in the situation of public and permanent adultery' (*Catechism of the Catholic Church* 1994, pp. 510–11).

Giving expression in extreme terms to what has occurred, by which even the innocent party of the earlier marriage is castigated, cannot help but remind older priests that the age of intemperate language in the service of theology is not past. They might recall that expression in the Good Friday liturgy of the prayer 'for the perfidious Jews', solemnly intoned within living memory. Sensitive priests at the time, while acknowledging that the wording sounded milder and even melodious when chanted in Latin, claimed that the ultimate objective of the prayer was kindly meant. The literalists declared the wording to be no more than a correct and true description of those named. Of the Jews then, and of the divorced and remarried now, proponents of the retention of the status quo argue somewhat alarmingly and apparently with more emphasis on logical categories than with pastoral concern, that both groups had brought their lamentable condition upon their own heads.

Few issues in the past one hundred years have stood out and symbolized the serious rift between official Catholic Church teaching and Catholic attitudes and practice more than that regarding human sexuality, especially in the matter of contraception. The condemnation of contraception by Pope Pius XI in the encyclical *Castii Connubii* (1930) had been based both on an appeal to natural law and to the Bible. Following the discovery of a more accurate estimation of the infertile days in the female ovulation cycle, it was consequently considered permissible to limit births if intercourse only took place on these naturally infertile days. The so-called rhythm method was declared a natural, not an artificial form of birth control.

What was unique about this judgement of the legitimacy of this form of contraception was the contraceptive intent, as the objection previously had specifically been against contraceptive intent. So long as the couple did not interfere with the integrity of the act, their intention to avoid conception was declared licit. The rhythm method enabled couples to avoid conception by restricting their intercourse to days when it was deemed the woman was infertile. What was new was the recognition that the sexual union of a couple had a legitimate end in itself, even when it is not directed toward procreation.

When in the 1960s Pope John XXIII established and Pope Paul VI subsequently adopted a commission to look again at the vexed subject of birth control, initially it had been generally expected that it would reaffirm the Catholic Church's traditional ban on artificial forms of birth control as most recently set out in the encyclical letter *Castii Connubii*. The issue of contraception was removed from the agenda of the Second Vatican Council and assigned to a now enlarged special commission. A crucial turning point was reached on 23 April 1966 when the four theologians on the commission who upheld the traditional opinion admitted that they could not show the intrinsic evil of contraception on the basis of the natural law alone (Hebblethwaite, 1975, p. 212). In spite of the sixty four to four recommendation of the committee to reformulate the Catholic Church's teaching that all use of contraceptives is immoral, Pope Paul VI published *Humanae Vitae* on 25 July 1968.

Largely because a change was expected, the reaffirmation by the encyclical of the previous teaching provoked an unprecedented response worldwide. While there were those who saw in the encyclical a reassertion of the unitive and pro-creative meaning of sexuality in marriage, there were others who publicly dissented. They pointed out the apparent inconsistency that the central teaching that every act of sexual intercourse must remain open to the transmission of life was contradicted by the simultaneous teaching that the rhythm method of contraception may be used when it was known that the woman was infertile. In subsequent years, it is no exaggeration to say that the conflict between the decision of Pope Paul VI and the findings of conscience has resulted in the fact that Catholics worldwide have made up their own minds, and have done so at the expense of a serious depreciation in the strength of papal authority.

The term 'annulment' first reached the universal Catholic psyche in the last fifty years by its association with that annulment granted to Caroline Lee Radzi-will to release her from her marriage to Michael Canfield and enable her to marry Prince Stanislaus Radziwill, a Polish nobleman. Caroline Lee Radziwill will be remembered as the sister of Jackie Kennedy, née Bouvier, wife of John Fitzgerald Kennedy, the thirty-fifth president of the United States of America (1961–3). Rightly or wrongly her annulment looked to many suspiciously like Catholic divorce for those who could afford it. While divorce and remarriage is forbidden in the Catholic Church, annulments have for long been granted by ecclesiastical courts if it can be established for some reason that the marriage was not valid from the start. Though incontestable grounds for granting annulments can be found (for example, non-consummation), the process can be a something of a legal lottery. Because marriage has been based upon a contractual view of a sacrament that is indissoluble, this contractual 'sacrament' presently binds the couple even though the union, the relationship, is irretrievable. That 'this interpretation of sacrament should be dispensed with once and for all' (Häring, 1996, p. 106) is an opinion increasingly voiced by notable theologians.

What one layman in the United States of America writes about local church preaching on these matters is revealing:

> News reports about Catholicism seem to return again and again to matters like birth control, abortion, clerical celibacy or whether women can be priests, yet in twenty years of regular attendance at mass in one church followed by twenty years in another I have never heard a sermon that touched on any one of those things ... One answer could be that the gospels do not have anything to say about birth control or abortion, married priests or women priests and that the great truths of the faith, the Trinity, the Incarnation, are more central to our beliefs than are these controversial items of the day ... But to tell the truth, I do not hear much about these mystical doctrines of the faith in our course of Sunday sermons (Wills, 2000, pp. 2–3).

Listening to the priests

Considering the furore the subject provoked at the time and for the subsequent decade, remarkably little comment was made by priests taking part in the survey on the matter of contraception. In two brief sentences one priest encapsulates some of the confusion.

I don't agree that the Catholic Church totally bans artificial contraception. I agree with the Church that to use it in principle is wrong (priest aged between 40 and 44).

Regarding the question of divorce and remarriage what one priest wrote is worth quoting in full.

The Church says a marriage between two baptised people is indissoluble. Scripture says those who marry in the Lord may not divorce. The Church equates the two, but they are not the same. A whole number of baptised agnostics and even baptised atheists marry. This is because they were font Catholics and font Anglicans. So I very much hold to the gospel teaching but not to the way the Church assumes that because a person has been baptised that person is therefore a Christian (priest aged between 75 and 79).

In deciding on what comment to make regarding their views of the Catholic Church, overall the priests who participated in the survey remained strangely silent on the controversial issue of abortion.

Shaping the questions

Against this background, the *Catholic Parochial Clergy Survey* framed five main themes relevant to exploring the priests' views on the Catholic Church's teaching on key moral issues concerned with life and death, sex and marriage. The first theme focused on the controversial issue of contraception. What proportion of priests support the Catholic Church's total ban on artificial contraception?

The second theme examined the priests' attitude toward abortion. What proportion of priests support the Catholic Church's total ban on abortion?

The third theme moved from abortion to euthanasia, and changed the thrust of the question from one of support for the position adopted by the Catholic Church to one of moral theology. What proportion of priests would maintain that direct euthanasia is morally unjustifiable?

The fourth theme turned attention to the Catholic Church's teaching on divorce and remarriage. This issue was approached from two directions in order to generate insight into the priests' attitudes toward both the teaching of the Catholic Church and pastoral practice. What proportion of priests would want to see the Catholic Church's teaching on divorce and remarriage liberalized? What proportion of priests consider that the divorced and remarried should be admitted to communion?

The fifth theme examined the issue of annulment. What proportion of priests consider that annulment is too easy in the Catholic Church?

Interpreting the statistics

Table 12.1 demonstrates that priests exercise a considerable degree of discretion regarding the support that they give to different aspects of the moral teachings of the Catholic Church. While there is almost unanimous support for the Catholic Church's teaching on abortion and euthanasia, there is much less support for the Catholic Church's teaching on artificial contraception. There is also significant support for a major overhaul of the Catholic Church's teaching on divorce and remarriage.

The statistics show that only a very small number of priests (3%) came out against the Catholic Church's total ban on abortion, with just a further 5% feeling somewhat uneasy and uncertain about this position. The overall support for the Catholic Church's total ban on abortion was, therefore, overwhelming, with 92% of the priests signing up to the official line.

Overall the priests also held very tightly to the traditional line on euthanasia. As in the case of abortion, the proportion of priests who wavered on the issue was very small, with just 5% refusing to come down on one side of the fence or the other. What makes the response to the question on euthanasia different from the response to the question on abortion is the somewhat larger proportion of priests who step out of line with official teaching. While only 3% stood up against supporting the Catholic Church's total ban on abortion, 10% stood up against accepting the view that direct euthanasia is morally unjustifiable. Although 85% of priests support the view that direct euthanasia is morally unjustifiable, chinks have begun to appear in the united front of Catholic moral teaching.

It is the question of contraception, however, that really begins to expose the lack of priestly solidarity behind the moral teaching of the Catholic Church. The statistics on this issue reveal two important insights into the strain that this teaching places on the Catholic clergy. The first insight comes from the proportion of priests who checked the 'uncertain' response to the question. While only 5% of the priests were uncertain about their responses to the Catholic Church's teaching on abortion or euthanasia, 19% were uncertain about their response to the Catholic Church's teaching on contraception. If these priests are being confronted with real pastoral situations by their sexually active parishioners, they may continually confront the anxiety generated by uncertainty. How are they to advise and what are they to say? The second insight comes from the nicely balanced proportions of priests who support and who contradict the teaching of their Church. While 39% of the priests supported the Catholic Church's total ban on artificial contraception, another 43% did not support that position. The advice that laypeople receive may well depend on the parish to which they belong.

Like contraception, the question of divorce and remarriage divides the Catholic clergy. Once again there is a fairly even support balance between those who support the status quo and those who are anxious for change. While 43%

of the priests maintained that the Catholic Church's teaching on divorce and remarriage should be liberalized, another 40% did not seek change in this direction. Once again nearly one in every five priests (17%) had not settled this issue in their own minds.

It is the pastoral practice of refusing communion to the divorced and remarried that confronts the Catholic parochial clergy more directly than the more abstract teaching of the Catholic Church on divorce and remarriage. While 40% of the priests maintained that they saw no reason for liberalizing the Catholic Church's teaching on divorce and remarriage, the proportion dropped to 23% who wished to hold to the traditional line that the divorced and remarried should not be admitted to communion. On this issue the proportion of the priests who still sit on the fence rose to 28%. So how do these priests respond when parishioners whom they know to be divorced and remarried present themselves for communion? How do they deal with the conflict between a pastoral heart that cares for the individuals and a loyal mind that wishes to remain faithful to the teachings of the Catholic Church?

Very few priests voiced the view that annulment has become too easy in the Catholic Church. While 7% of the priests considered that this was the case, eleven times that number (79%) took the opposite view and twice that number (15%) remained sitting on the fence.

Regular and secular

Table 12.2 demonstrates that there are no significant differences over this range of issues between the positions adopted by regular priests and by secular priests. In this sense parishioners served by regular priests and by secular priests can expect to be met by similar views from their clergy on issues like abortion, contraception, euthanasia, remarriage after divorce and annulments.

Support for the Catholic Church's total ban on abortion was given by 91% of the regular priests and by 92% of the secular priests. The view that direct euthanasia is morally unjustifiable was taken by 84% of the regular priests and by 85% of the secular priests. Support for the Catholic Church's total ban on artificial contraception was given by 42% of the regular priests and by 38% of the secular priests. Similar proportions of the regular priests (41%) and of the secular priests (43%) argued that the Catholic Church's teaching on divorce and remarriage should be liberalized. Similar proportions of the regular priests (47%) and of the secular priests (49%) argued that the divorced and remarried should be admitted to communion. Just 5% of the regular priests and 7% of the secular priests took the view that annulment is too easy in the Catholic Church.

Generational differences

Table 12.3 demonstrates that parishioners served by priests under the age of 60 can expect a more liberal attitude among their clergy to issues like contraception, euthanasia and remarriage after divorce, compared with parishioners served by priests aged 60 or over. On the issue of abortion, however, the priests under the age of 60 held almost as tightly to the traditional teaching of their Church as the priests aged 60 and over.

On the issue of abortion, 94% of the priests aged 60 and over supported the Catholic Church's total ban. The proportion dropped significantly, but only marginally, to 90% among the 45–59-year-olds, and to 91% among those under the age of 45. The Catholic Church's teaching on this issue is continuing to hold widespread support among the clergy.

Shifts in attitude toward euthanasia are more pronounced than shifts in attitude toward abortion. While 89% of the priests aged 60 and over held the view that direct euthanasia is morally unjustifiable, the proportions dropped to 81% among the 45–59-year-olds, and to 83% among those under the age of 45. The Catholic Church's teaching on this issue is being maintained less firmly by younger priests.

Attitudes toward artificial contraception have undergone a considerable change. While 52% of the priests aged 60 and over gave their support to the Catholic Church's total ban on artificial contraception, the proportion dropped almost by half to 28% among those aged between 45 and 59, and then rose again only slightly to 33% among those under the age of 45. Here is very clear evidence that the views of Catholic clergy on matters of morality can be shaped by their generation as well as by the unchanging teaching of the Catholic Church.

Pressure for change in the Catholic Church's teaching on remarriage after divorce is considerably higher among the clergy under the age of 60 than among the clergy aged 60 and over. At the same time, there is a tendency for the youngest cohort of priests, those under the age of 45, to be less insistent on change than those aged between 45 and 59. Thus, while 31% of the priests aged 60 and over supported the view that the Catholic Church's teaching on divorce and re-marriage should be liberalized, the proportions rose to 52% among the 45–59-year-olds, and then dropped slightly to 48% among those under the age of 45. While 39% of the priests aged 60 and over supported the view that the divorced and remarried should be admitted to communion, the proportions rose to 59% among the 45–59-year-olds, and then dropped to the mid-way position of 50% among those under the age of 45. The comparison between the 45–59-year-olds and those under the age of 45 may reveal a younger generation of priests who once again wish to assert the authority of the Catholic Church above the pastoral needs of their parishioners.

Priests aged 60 and over were more likely than their younger colleagues to take the view that annulment is too easy. While one in every ten of the priests aged 60 and over (10%) argued that annulment is too easy in the Catholic Church, the proportions dropped to 4% among those aged between 45 and 59, and remained at the level of 4% among those under the age of 45.

CHAPTER THIRTEEN

Church and Sacrament

The following brief address was given within the last twenty years to a primary school classroom of Scottish Catholic children by one of their last 'prince bishops'. 'Now children, unlike you, I am very fortunate that the house in which I live is sufficiently large to have room for a chapel on the first floor. As in your chapel alongside the school here, so in the chapel in my house, resides our blessed Lord, a prisoner in the tabernacle. I have no need to tell you, children, why we should visit Jesus in the tabernacle, have I? Yes, that's right. Well, every night, children, on my way up the stairs to bed, I call into my chapel and whisper "Good night" to Jesus in the tabernacle and in my mind's ear, I imagine I can hear the gentle voice of Jesus replying, "Good night my Lord"' (Scottish Army Chaplain, 1996).

This chapter is concerned with theological beliefs about the divine nature of the *Catholic Church* and the special character of the *blessed sacrament* within the Catholic Church. Special consideration is also given to the hierarchical structure within the Catholic Church.

Context

Immediately following the Second Vatican Council the question was posed whether changes within the Catholic Church, such as those proposed, were even possible considering the seemingly immutable nature of so much connected with the Catholic Church. Though at one level a distinction might have been made between the permanent and the transient in the Church, so little had in fact changed substantially in the lifetime of any Catholic believer that the necessary distinction had scarcely ever adequately been insisted upon. Consequently, there has been a tendency to believe that many more of the structures, practices and beliefs of Catholicism than could possibly have been the case, were of divine ordinance. It was such a deep-lying attitude that some, even now, find difficulty in acknowledging it, even when attention is drawn to the evidence. Structures, it has been observed, 'are seen as given by God, intrinsic to what Jesus handed over to his earliest followers. Even if some aspects of Church organization, sacramental rites and formulations of teaching are shown to have appeared much later in history, it is assumed that this is only an inevitable unfolding of the original design and intent. It is a design understood to have been made in eternity, therefore having a timeless quality that distinguishes it from all other human events, societies and ceremonies' (Hellwig, 1992, pp. 2–3).

One such presumption of 'original design and intent' is precisely the hierarchical structure of the Catholic Church. As Jesus seems not to have ordained anybody either a priest or a bishop, the notion of apostolic succession providing a connecting link to persons chosen by the apostles and therefore implicitly by Jesus is increasingly suspect as a vehicle by which empowerment or authenticity is conferred. It does not seem to have been entirely beneficial that hierarchical structures have been presented as divinely constructed mechanisms through which the laity are shepherded by the successors to the apostles.

It is Ignatius of Antioch who is repeatedly quoted as having said that the Christian community should do nothing without its bishop. It is important to realize that Ignatius could not possibly have anticipated how a modern bishop would assume authority *over* the church. After all, the Christian community had chosen the bishop and, as Paul had insisted, Christians as a group are the body of Christ – the authentic presence of Jesus on earth after his resurrection. The idea of an individual believing himself to be superior to the body of believers in the fashion subsequently adopted by bishops, is clearly a notion foreign to any intelligible idea of being 'servant'. What Ignatius realized was that the bishop symbolized the unity of the believers. The plea of Ignatius in his letters was that only when Christians are united, as opposed to factionalized, are they with their bishop the body of Christ.

The history of the Catholic Church bears witness to the reality that hierarchical structures, however spiritualized, have shown themselves to be closer in origin to the exercise of ordinary temporal power than to divinely inspired activity. It was not sufficient that the bishop of Rome should claim the title servant of the servants of God, while his imperial style made him unique among servants of any sort. When a delegation of German bishops who had not shown sufficient acquiescence to the proposed definition of papal infallibility were received in advance by Pope Pius IX, he did not offer his hand to be kissed but moved forward the papal foot, which his fellow bishops felt obliged to kiss, one by one (Wills, 2000). We can see the amusing side from the distance of over a hundred years but, when compared with the teacher from Nazareth who washed his disciples' feet, some may feel that there is something preposterous in such taken-for-grantedness of the majesty of papacy.

The legitimation of the Catholic Church in the fourth century resulted in the adoption by bishops of the insignia and privileges of imperial authority with a style closer to 'lording it over' than 'servant'. It was only the fact that there had been a number of patriarchs in the Eastern empire that on its break-up enabled the Church in the East to avoid the monarchial structure of the Western 'Latin' Church. By whatever route the Catholic Church claims to have arrived at its leadership style, for most of its history the manner adopted by the Pope still reflects more of Caesar than of Jesus. The language is Christian; the style is inappropriately regal.

The sense of embarrassment experienced by older Catholics on recollection of youthful espousal of the teaching that 'outside the church there is no salvation' may be lessened by the knowledge than an identical claim had been shared in equal measure by many non-Catholics, similarly convinced of the consignment to damnation of all papists. What is worse was our common conviction of the rightness and justice of it all. How we formulate our beliefs has a direct impact on the way we see our position in the world. How we denigrate others confirms us in our superiority and justifies their maltreatment. The statement that the Catholic Church is uniquely the one true Church founded by Jesus no longer carries the unspoken corollary that the religious practices of non-Catholics are entirely without virtue, which was the accepted Catholic view until well into the twentieth century. There is now among a growing number of theologians the appreciation of a need to be more circumspect in claiming final and unchangeable certitude in theological formulations, though it continues to be recognized that the creeds and some liturgical and catechetical texts maintain a pre-eminent position within the tradition. There is at large a growing and greater humility about the nature of Catholic access to what is true and a preparedness to conclude that other approaches or interpretations might also have some validity.

It has proved too easy for those committed to the need for certainty to forget the remarkable words of the Second Vatican Council document on ecumenism:

> Christ summons the Church, as she goes on her pilgrim way, to that continual reformation of which she always has need, insofar as she is an institution of men there on earth. Therefore, if the influence of events or of the times has led to deficiencies in conduct, in Church discipline, or even in the formulation of doctrine (which must be carefully distinguished from the deposit itself of faith) these should be appropriately rectified at the proper moment (Abbott, 1966, p. 350).

One could do worse than draw a distinction between the 'visible' and the 'invisible' church, as advocated by one writer who points out that the 'visible' church is a mixture of asceticism and affluence, courage and compromise, faith and frailty, prayer and perfidy, sanctity and sin and that so often the 'visible' church has forgotten this tangled mixture when it has spoken of itself. 'Invisible' church language has been used to inflate and legitimate some far-from-divine attributes adhering to the visible church. 'There is thrown up around the "visible" church the smokescreen of irreproachability. There is the attempt to convince us that we are dealing with a divine reality and should consequently watch what we say' (Dyson, 1985, p. 14).

The Second Vatican Council made one remarkable change to the teaching of the Council of Trent. That Council had stated that 'If anyone says that there is not, by divine ordination in the Catholic church a hierarchy which is composed of bishops, priests and ministers, let him be anathema' (Denzinger and Schoenmetzer, 1965, p. 1776). The Dogmatic Constitution on the church reads, 'Thus the divinely established ecclesiastical ministry is exercised on different levels by those who from antiquity have been called, bishops, priests and deacons' (Abbott, 1966, p. 53). What is remarkable is the substitution for the word 'hierarchy' of the words 'ecclesiastical ministry'. It is a critical change intended to emphasize the incontrovertible historical evidence that the *ministry* of the church and not *the hierarchical form* of that ministry is what is believed to be divinely established. In other words, it is acknowledgement that from the beginning in the church there were many ministries and that ministry ought not be connected exclusively to hierarchy, as it has for most of the church's history. The idea of ministry as an ecclesial function exercised by all those who serve on behalf of the church is thereby restored to its rightful place (Lawler, 1990).

Listening to the priests

A number of priests took the opportunity provided by the survey to comment on aspects of the hierarchical structure of the Catholic Church, on bishops in partic- ular, on aspects of sacramental theology and on the Catholic Church's claim to hold the only path to salvation. It was, however, this last issue that drew the most comment. One priest, for example, tried to explore the different levels of meaning which could be attached to the established doctrinal statement that outside the Catholic Church there is no salvation. He commented that the doctrine is either:

> a statement about the saving work of Christ or a piece of bigotry, depending on the meaning of the words theological or popular. I am for or against the statement depending on its meaning (priest aged between 60 and 64).

Another priest tried to re-interpret the traditional doctrinal statement in the following way.

> 'salvation outside the church' should mean ultimately through the salvific death of Christ, not simply nullifying non-Christian religions (priest aged between 70 and 74).

This doctrine restricting salvation within the confines of the Catholic Church has, of course, considerable implications for the path of ecumenism. The problem of ecumenism was neatly solved, at least to his own satisfaction, by one priest who wrote as follows.

> Also, I see unions as all Christians acknowledging the leadership of the Pope (and hence 'Catholic') but not as exercised by the present one (priest aged between 75 and 79).

Bishops came in for quite a lot of comment by the priests, and not all of the comment was complimentary. One of the most memorable comments was as follows.

> It is an abiding wonder to priests what real or imagined gifts are possessed by many of those men who are appointed bishops (priest aged between 55 and 59).

A few priests commented on their sacramental understanding of the real presence of Christ in the eucharist. One priest set out his own understanding by distinguishing between the theology of the real presence and the theology of transubstantiation. He wrote:

> I believe in the real presence but not in transubstantiation (priest aged between 75 and 79).

Another priest considered the very asking of a theological question about the understanding of the eucharist to be unforgivably subversive.

> Most problematic of all is asking priests whether or not they accept a dogma of faith, such as 'I believe in the real presence of Christ under the species of bread and wine.' A priest makes a solemn act of faith that he accepts all the solemn teaching of the magisterium of the Church at his ordination and at his induction as parish priest. No doubt you will insist that you are attempting to bring out the priests' 'real feelings' in this survey. Another interpretation could be that you are inciting a priest to express in writing his doubts as to faith which should rather be the subject of conversation in the total confidentiality of the confessional (priest aged between 55 and 59).

Shaping the questions

Against this background, the *Catholic Parochial Clergy Survey* framed four main themes relevant to understanding how the priests interpreted the claims to uniqueness made by the Catholic Church and the claims made by the Catholic Church concerning the sacrament of bread and wine. The first theme examined the claim that the Catholic Church derives its unique authority from being founded by Jesus. What proportion of priests would agree that the Catholic Church is uniquely the one true Church founded by Jesus?

The second theme examined the claim that no other churches can lead their adherents to eternal salvation. What proportion of priests would agree that outside the Catholic Church there is no salvation?

The third theme examined the claim that the hierarchical structure of the Catholic Church is God-given. What proportion of priests would agree that the hierarchical structure of the Catholic Church is divinely ordained?

The fourth theme turned attention to eucharistic theology. What proportion of priests would sign up to belief in the real presence of Christ under the species of bread and wine?

Interpreting the statistics

Table 13.1 demonstrates that Catholic priests have a well nuanced understanding concerning their commitment to the doctrines about the nature of the Church. Generally they accept the view that the Catholic Church is uniquely the one true Church founded by Jesus. They are less concerned about the hierarchical structure of the Catholic Church being divinely ordained. They are generally unconvinced by the doctrine that outside the Catholic Church there is no salvation. Belief in the real presence of Christ in the eucharist is very high.

The statistics show that between eight and nine priests out of every ten (85%) believed that the Catholic Church is uniquely the one true Church founded by Jesus. By way of comparison, just one priest in every ten (9%) were unconvinced by this tenet of faith and a further 6% remain sceptical about it. A clear implication of this belief should be the view that only the true Church founded by Jesus can lead men and women to salvation. Very few priests, however, wished to take this belief to its logical conclusion.

While 85% of priests signed up to the belief that the Catholic Church is uniquely the one true Church founded by Jesus, the proportion dropped dramatically to just 12% of priests who signed up to the belief that outside the Catholic Church there is no salvation. On the contrary, 81% of priests rejected this belief outright, leaving just 6% who had not resolved the issue in their own minds. This more generous attitude holds promise for the ecumenical agenda of many of the Reformed Churches.

Nearly three out of every five priests (57%) held the belief that the hierarchical structure of the Catholic Church is divinely ordained, compared with fewer than half that number (25%) who actively distanced themselves from that view. A further 19% had ceased to be convinced that the hierarchical structure of the Catholic Church is divinely ordained but were not prepared to fight against the doctrine.

Belief in the real presence of Christ under the species of bread and wine is one of those beliefs that continue to unite the Catholic clergy. Thus 99% of the priests affirmed this belief and the remaining 1% expressed uncertainty rather than disbelief. As far as the Catholic clergy are concerned, from an empirical perspective at least, this belief in the real presence of Christ under the species of bread and wine constitutes an immutable bedrock of faith.

Regular and secular

Table 13.2 demonstrates that there are no significant differences in the profile of belief concerning the nature of the Catholic Church held by regular priests and by secular priests. Both groups of priests held strongly to the view that the Catholic Church is uniquely the one true Church founded by Jesus (86% and 84%), held less strongly to the view that the hierarchical structure of the Catholic Church is divinely ordained (58% and 57%) and generally no longer believed that outside the Catholic Church there is no salvation (12% and 12%). At the same time, 99% of both the regular priests and the secular priests believed in the real presence of Christ under the species of bread and wine.

Generational differences

Table 13.3 demonstrates that it is the priests aged 60 and over who are most likely to espouse a traditional theology concerning the nature of the Catholic Church, while it is the priests in the 45–59 age category who are most likely to take a radical approach. The youngest priests under the age of 45 are reverting more in favour of the traditional beliefs.

Among the priests aged 60 and over, 92% affirmed the belief that the Catholic Church is uniquely the one true Church founded by Jesus. The proportion fell to 78% among priests in the 45–59 age group and rose marginally to 80% among priests under the age of 45.

A similar pattern is found, much lower down the percentage scale, concerning the doctrine that outside the Catholic Church there is no salvation. Among the priests aged 60 and over, 16% accepted this doctrine. The proportion halved to 8% among the priests in the 45–59 age group and then rose to the mid-way position of 12% among the priests under the age of 45.

Among the priests aged 60 and over, two-thirds (67%) affirmed the belief that the hierarchical structure of the Catholic Church is divinely ordained. The proportion fell to 46% among the priests in the 45–59 age group and then rose to the mid-way position of 56% among the priests under the age of 45.

Although beliefs concerning the divine origin and nature of the Church have suffered some erosion among younger priests, belief in the real presence of Christ under the species of bread and wine has remained resilient, with 99% of the priests in all three age cohorts staying firm to this immutable bedrock of faith.

CHAPTER FOURTEEN

Rome and the Vatican

Louis Duchesne's three volume history was a casualty of the reign of terror of Pope Pius X, being placed on the Index of Forbidden Books. Shortly after this bitter sentence, Duchesne, holidaying in Egypt met in Cairo an acquaintance from Paris.

'Monseigneur', the man said, 'what brings you to Egypt?'

'My dear fellow', Duchesne replied, 'I am waiting for the death of King Herod.'

This chapter is concerned with *Rome and the Vatican* and discusses in particular the balance of power between the central structures in Rome and the local dioceses and parishes. Attention is also given to the role of the Second Vatican Council.

Context

By the decree *Lamentabili* (3 July 1907) Pope Pius X (1903–14) branded Modernism 'a synthesis of all heresies'. In his encyclical *Pascendi Dominici Gregis* (8 September 1907) he warned the Catholic Church against what he saw as contemporary evils. By imposing an obligatory oath against Modernism on all Catholic university and seminary teachers, Pope Pius X in the decree *Sacrorum antistitum* (1 September 1910) stifled its scholars and condemned the Church to a dark age of decades of intellectual thrall and conservatism. It is no surprise that Pope Pius X should have undertaken to reform the code of Canon Law, indicative of a Church whose legal style and peremptory tone had been the expression of her teaching for sixteen centuries. Canon 329 of the new code of Canon Law published in 1917 exemplified the massive increase in the centralization of authority by declaring that 'all bishops were to be nominated by the Roman pontiff, setting the seal of legal timelessness on a radical extension of papal responsibility which had taken place virtually in living memory' (Duffy, 1997, p. 304). In spite of what many saw as a largely repressive and retrogressive papacy, Pope Pius X was canonized a saint in 1954 by Pope Pius XII, on account of his personal piety evidenced in the promotion of frequent reception of communion and the restoration of Gregorian chant.

Few now remember Louis Duchesne, but a succession of eminent men, including Hans Urs von Balthasar (1905–88), Marie Dominique Chenu (1895–1990), Yves Congar (1904–95), John Courtney Murray (1904–67), Pierre Teilhard de Chardin

(1881–1955), Jean Danielou (1904–74), Bernard Häring (1912–), Hans Küng (1928–), Karl Rahner (1904–84), Henri de Lubac (1896–1991) and Edward Schille-beeckx (1914–), all in their turn had been marginalized, pressurized or silenced by the Vatican, although the ultimate irony was that their philosophical, sociological and theological insights were significantly to influence the content of many of the documents of the Second Vatican Council (1962–5). The tragic anti-modernist witch-hunt arose from a self-understanding by the Catholic Church implying, if not directly claiming, that it was a 'perfect society' possessing total truth, which had nothing to learn from anyone outside itself in a changing world. 'It did not see itself as a culture in its own right with layer upon layer of uncritically accepted Euro-centric customs, aristocratic values and habits' (Arbuckle, 1993, p. 23).

Pope Pius XII (1939–58) showed a welcome willingness to engage in a positive dialogue with the post-war world, encouraging biblical scholars and theologians to pursue their research. To a greater extent then than now, Catholics with an intellectual background inherited from the era of Pope Pius IX (1846–78) and Pope Pius X (1903–14) had an understandable difficulty in acknowledging even the possibility of ignorance or weakness in the Catholic Church, still less in admit-ting the necessity of its constant reform and renewal. With such a heritage, it is unsurprising that as soon as Pope John XXIII (1958–63) in 1961 called a Council, plans were drawn up by some senior members of the Roman Curia, the Vatican's papal bureaucracy, to dictate the agenda to be used at the Council with the inten-tion of ensuring that as little as possible should be changed in an already 'perfect society'. How such a predetermined, closed, Council agenda was circumvented by a few perceptive non-Curial cardinals is now part of history. Roman Curial offi-cials, however, like civil servants the world over, are disposed to take the long view and are capable of subverting and frustrating the intention and purpose of legitimate decision-makers. 'In the long run, the church may be guided by the Holy Spirit, governed by canon law, and defined by dogma; but in the short run personalities, ideologies, and power influence the direction the church takes' (Gillis, 1999, p. 44). In the religious sphere also, it should not be forgotten that it is generally the victors who write both the history and the theology.

From the time that the Catholic Church was adopted by the state in the fourth century, an understandable but questionable alteration took place in the attitude which the Church, from the beginning, had held toward civil power-structures. The transformation from being the object of repressive state activities to eleva-tion as agent of state resulted in a natural tendency for the Church to equate humanly constructed patterns of society with the will of God and to accept them uncritically (Hellwig, 1992). A near inevitable consequence was that because fallible, frail human beings are its constituents the Catholic Church was increas-ingly identified with the powerful, the privileged and the wealthy. It is an identification from which the Catholic Church has, in practice, shown a reluctance to disassociate. The unquestionable humanizing role of religion has shown itself at various times in history to be capable of coexistence, if not co-operation, with what may be seen in retrospect as un-Christian structures such as self-aggran-dizement, to say nothing of acquiescence in torture, slavery, colonialism and of aping the role of civil power.

The absorption of the Papal States into a unified Italy in 1871 led to a prolonged denial by the Vatican of the legitimacy of the Italian State until 1929 when the full and independent sovereignty of the Holy See in the Vatican was recognized by concordat. Pope Pius XI showed both wisdom and courage in relinquishing claim to the former Papal States, thereby disowning appreciable political power. Nonetheless, he and his successor Pope Pius XII insisted on maintaining the self-imposed style 'prisoner of the Vatican' in sympathy with the vow made by Pope Pius IX to stay put until the Papal States were restored. This barren gesture was finally abandoned by Pope John XXIII when he left the Vatican and visited prisoners in a Roman city jail at Christmas 1958.

The accredited diplomatic representatives of the Holy See are generally archbishops who have ambassadorial status with the title 'nuncios'. 'One of the principal tasks of the nuncio is to act on behalf of the Congregation for the Doctrine of the Faith in pursuit of supposedly errant theologians, thus bypassing the local bishop. Nuncios also play a crucial role in the nomination of bishops who are chosen above all for their soundness and orthodoxy' (Hebblethwaite, 1975, p. 180). If not the manifest purpose of the obligatory five-yearly visit of every national hierarchy to Rome, submitting itself to Curial inspection, the principal consequence has been to strengthen Rome's control over the life of the local churches. This can be seen to call into question any theological reality to the notion of local church.

To all intents and purposes Rome has appropriated the function of the local church in the selection of its bishops. When over the centuries civil rulers had usurped the right, for their own ends, to appoint bishops, there had been justification that the Catholic Church in the person of the papacy should have intervened to wrest back the independence of the Church from secular control. Such centralized authoritarian control and obedience to Rome has resulted, as Duffy (1997) points out, in such an institutional structure being erroneously seen as an essential and ancient characteristic of Catholicism. The principle of subsidiarity that maintains that larger social structures should not usurp functions which can be undertaken successfully by smaller, simpler units, is here ignored. Yet subsidiarity had been declared by Pope Pius XII to be 'valid for social life in all its organisations and also for the life of the Church without prejudice to its hierarchical structures' (*Acta Apostolicae Sedis*, 1946, p. 14). Sufficient reason has obviously been found to justify why subsidiarity does not apply in the matter of episcopal appointments.

In effect the selection and appointment of diocesan bishops by nuncios and Roman Curial officials is the operational method by which Roman views, if not imposed, are obtruded into local churches. Local insight, to say nothing of the expertise of the local community of believers, is increasingly liable to be disregarded in a structure that acts as if only one part of 'hierarchic authority has certain access to the truth about how [any] issue is predetermined' (Hellwig, 1992, p. 58). When the experience of the faithful is continually disregarded, that the so-called traditions of the Church will tend to sound less and less intelligible or convincing to the faithful is a fairly predictable outcome.

Roman Catholicism has developed an authoritative, impressive and rigorously defined belief-system. Rome has displayed a historical tendency to promulgate authoritative statements on various topics obliging the assent of adherents, but later quietly to abandon some such positions when they have been shown to be demonstrably untenable. Perfectionism is a characteristic of Catholicism. It means claiming always to know the answers and never admitting to making mistakes, or at least only owning up to the worst of them hundreds of years later.

Papal infallibility was itself observed by theologians over four decades ago to cast an aura 'over papal teaching authority, as though it could be equated with divine authority absolutely and beyond question in every detail of every utterance (in a way no longer accorded to the text of scripture)' (Hellwig, 1992, p. 67). A similar aura surrounds the day-to-day functioning of the Roman Curia. An impression is fostered of access to a special revelation providing the right answers to complex pastoral issues arising in all parts of the world. Once more is revealed a church acknowledging in theory but unprepared in practice to admit to uncertainty. For instance on clerical celibacy: '[Such] treatment of human regulations as though they were absolute' (Stecher, 1997, p. 1688) contributes to and prolongs theologically questionable 'creeping infallibility'. It cannot be good theology to make exaggerated claims of certitude over disputed subjects. As John Henry Newman wrote, it only serves to create 'in educated Catholics a habit of scepticism or secret infidelity as regards all dogmatic truth' (Wills, 2000, p. 9). This is not to dispute that the Catholic Church has the right to speak authoritatively in some matters but to draw attention to a widening gap between the experience of believers and official declarations of the Church.

It should not be forgotten or denied that millions of Catholics lived their lives and faced their death believing the teaching of the magisterium that one could be damned for eating 'not less than two ounces' of meat on Friday. Either they *were* damned or we can laugh about it. If we do, it is undeniable that the magisterium has obliged the faithful to believe falsities.

> It could be thought that Christ's promise of a special assistance to the apostles also included a divine assurance that the magisterium in the church would be free from all error and even imperfection in the teachings of ethical norms in the region of natural law, but neither the bible nor historical events favour such a position (Häring, 1969, p. 95).

It is worth remembering the Latin adage, 'He who proves too much proves nothing.'

The Second Vatican Council decree on the pastoral office of bishops in the Catholic Church states that the synod of bishops, 'acting in the name of the entire Catholic episcopate, will at the same time demonstrate that all the bishops in hierarchical communion share in the responsibility for the universal church' (Abbott, 1966, p. 400). Though the Council unequivocally tempered the principle of papal authority with the principle of episcopal collegiality, the paradoxical result that has evolved is not a development of episcopal conferences and synods, but a restriction of them. The revised Code of Canon Law (1983) helped tip the balance by its accentuation of hierarchical structure to the detriment of collegiality. The synod of bishops referred to in the Council document was envisaged as more than a rubber stamp for contemporary papal policy. Yet moderators of the synod of bishops are doubly papal appointees, indebted to the Pope both for their episcopal election as well as their synodical appointment. Increasingly far from being, as it was meant to be, a powerful voice calling to account all sections of the Catholic Church – and in theory at least the only authoritative body capable of withstanding the Curia – that forum at least has shown itself to be unprepared or unable to dissent from any official Vatican viewpoint though it is known that a plurality of responsible views is held on currently embargoed topics by individual bishops all over the world.

The bishops themselves exercise their office in the context of a one-sided teaching from the First Vatican Council on the position within the Catholic Church of the bishop of Rome together with a development of that teaching in the theological tradition that followed. If the Catholic laity had been infantilized for generations in the face of their clergy, episcopal office holders have been emasculated in the face of the papacy. From a milieu in which beliefs and practices are deemed to have been derived from a single infallible source, the one who would gainsay any of them lays himself open to accusations at best of disloyalty and at worst heresy. Appointed in a conservative age for their conservatism, loyalty and orthodoxy, present-day bishops are an unlikely source even of loyal opposition.

Listening to the priests

The comments of the priests to this part of the survey drew attention to a number of interesting issues alive in the Catholic Church in England and Wales today. The first of these issues concerns the clear existence of a body of priest dissenters who do not see the Second Vatican Council as a suitable paradigm for the church of the future. This trend toward a growing neo-conservatism in the Catholic Church in the United States of America is referred to in Schoenherr and Young (1993), Unsworth (1993), Cozzens (2000) and Schuth (1999). The fact that this movement in England and Wales is not about to die out with the demise of those priests trained before the Second Vatican Council is evidenced by the comments made by one of the younger priests in the sample, who wrote as follows:

> I find great support in the Traditionalist Movement; the mainstay of my life as a priest is the Tridentine mass and ministering to those marginalised by the post Vatican II reforms (priest aged between 35 and 39).

The comments from another young priest illustrate how lack of confidence in the local bishops can encourage great hopes being placed in the more distant central control of the papacy. This young priest both bemoaned what he saw to be the weak lead of the bishops in England and Wales and at the same time applauded a strong papal leadership.

I feel much of low morale among secular clergy is due to lack of leadership
from our bishops. Most clergy are dissatisfied with the bishops but no one is
allowed to say so. If it were not for Rome, and the Pope's clear leadership,
the Catholic Church in England and Wales would be in an even greater state
of decline (priest aged between 30 and 34).

Another slightly older priest also made the point that he considered the future
hope of the Catholic Church to rest in closer solidarity with the Pope.

I feel strongly that unity with the Pope is essential today and that the media
has too much influence on the way most people think about the faith and the
church. We have become too political in the church and tend to categorise
priests as liberals or conservatives (priest aged between 45 and 49).

The second issue concerns the way in which many priests still see in the Second
Vatican Council a great deal of hope and of promise for the future. They bemoan
the extent to which the promise remains unrealized. For example, one priest
points to so much evidence for the lack of change in the Catholic Church, but
nonetheless looks forward with confidence to the day when it will occur.

There is so much spiritual power to be unlocked if we become people of
faith, hope and charity. We have still to become the Vatican II church (priest
aged between 55 and 59).

It is, of course, known that Christianity itself and Roman Catholicism in particular is a conservative organization. The burden of preserving the religious heritage
is borne principally by bishops and priests. In alarmed response to what was perceived as the new conservatism, on 27 January 1989, 163 German-speaking
theologians issued the Cologne Declaration. It expressed a growing concern over
the appointment by Rome of bishops with no regard to the recommendation of
the local church, over the suppression of theological debate by the silencing of
theologians, over the centralizing tendency of the papacy limiting the freedom
and effectiveness of the local church, and over the questionable connection
between teachings on birth control with fundamental truths of the faith. This bold
step by the theologians had been occasioned by the appointment of Joachim
Meisner as Archbishop of Cologne in opposition to the recommendation of the
Cathedral chapter. Bernard Häring was quoted as saying that the theologians had
spoken because the bishops seemed not to dare to play their role of collegiality
and subsidiarity (McCarthy, 1998).

A number of priests reflected a similar anxiety.

I do think I have a positive value as a priest and contrary to what may
appear, think I have and can continue to help people in future despite
attempts of the Vatican to put the clock back, which I find very demoralising
(priest aged between 45 and 49).

Another in much the same vein wrote as follows:

> I am increasingly frustrated by 'Rome's' negative approach and the lurching
> back to the past rather than preaching the good news of God's kingdom
> (priest aged between 60 and 64).

The priest who wrote the following catches the majority position in favour of the
Second Vatican Council:

> Vatican II was a Godsend. There is too much power vested at the top and I
> see its authority as a great obstacle to growth. Too much secrecy; closed doors
> (priest aged between 60 and 64).

Shaping the questions

Against this background, the *Catholic Parochial Clergy Survey* framed three basic
themes relevant to exploring the priests' attitude toward Rome and the Vatican.
The first theme focused on the Second Vatican Council itself and tried to assess
how large the movement is among clergy to revert to an earlier model of the
Catholic Church. How many priests would prefer, if it were possible, a return to
the pre-Vatican II Church? How many priests would go as far as to say that the
Second Vatican Council was a disaster for the Catholic Church?

The second theme examined the reactions of the priests to the recentralization
that has taken place under Pope John Paul II. What proportion of priests have
actually welcomed the way in which Pope John Paul II has recentralized in Rome
the authority of the Catholic Church?

The third theme focused on the involvement of Rome in the appointment of
diocesan bishops. What proportion of priests feel that Rome should have decisive
say in appointing diocesan bishops and what proportion of priests feel that Rome
should *not* have decisive say in this matter?

Interpreting the statistics

Table 14.1 demonstrates that the vast majority of priests remain thoroughly
behind the Second Vatican Council and only a very small minority would want to
turn the clock back to the days of the pre-Vatican II Church. Many more priests
are against the way Pope John Paul II has recentralized the authority of the
Catholic Church in Rome than are in support of it, although there is an equal
balance of opinion over the role of Rome in appointing bishops.

One priest in every twenty-five (4%) said that he would prefer, if it were
possible, a return to the pre-Vatican II Church. An equal number (4%) seem as if
they may not take a lot of persuasion to go the same way. However, this leaves
92% of priests who see no future whatsoever in turning the clock back.

Given the opportunity by the survey to vote the Second Vatican Council to be
a disaster for the Catholic Church, only one in fifty (2%) cast their vote in that
direction, and a further 3% were still wavering. Great unanimity behind the

Second Vatican Council, however, is shown by 95% of priests dismissing this vote of no-confidence out of hand.

The way in which Pope John Paul II has been seen to recentralize in Rome the authority of the Catholic Church has clearly been welcomed by some priests and deplored by others. The balance of opinion is by more than two-to-one against this process of recentralization. While one in four priests (24%) welcomed the way Pope John Paul II has recentralized in Rome the authority of the Catholic Church, over half (55%) did not welcome this trend. The remaining 22% reported that they were still uncertain about their own reactions to the process.

Opinion was quite evenly divided on the role of Rome in appointing diocesan bishops. Just under two in every five priests (38%) supported the view that Rome should have decisive say in appointing diocesan bishops. At the same time, just over two in every five (42%) argued that Rome should *not* have decisive say in appointing diocesan bishops. The remaining 20% reported that they were still uncertain about their own reaction to the process.

Regular and secular

Table 14.2 demonstrates that there are no significant differences between the views of the regular priests and secular priests concerning the issues examined in this section. Just 4% of the regular priests and 3% of the secular priests preferred a return to the pre-Vatican II Church. Just 2% of the regular priests and 2% of the secular priests regarded the Second Vatican Council as a disaster for the Catholic Church. Similar proportions of the regular priests (27%) and the secular priests (23%) welcomed the way Pope John Paul II has recentralized in Rome the authority of the Catholic Church. Similar proportions of the regular priests (41%) and the secular priests (42%) maintained that Rome should not have decisive say in appointing diocesan bishops.

Generational differences

Table 14.3 demonstrates that there are no significant differences in the levels of support given to the Second Vatican Council across the three age cohorts. On the other hand, the three age cohorts do behave differently in respect of the central power of Rome. Both the priests under the age of 45 and the priests aged 60 and over show more support for centralizing power in Rome than is the case among the priests in the 45–59 year age group.

The proportion of priests who would prefer, if it were possible, a return to the pre-Vatican II Church has remained fairly stable, at 5% among those aged 60 and over, 3% among the 45–59-year-olds and 3% among those under the age of 45. The proportion of priests who regard the Second Vatican Council as a disaster for the Catholic Church has also remained fairly stable, at 2% among those aged 60 or over, 1% among the 45–59-year-olds and 2% among those under the age of 45.

Welcome for the way in which Pope John Paul II has recentralized in Rome the authority of the Catholic Church was clearly strongest among the priests aged 60 and over (32%). The level of welcome halved from 32% to 15% among the priests in the 45–59 age cohort and then rose again to the mid-way position among those aged under 45 (23%).

The age group to stand most in favour of Rome having decisive say in appointing diocesan bishops was the under-45-year-old cohort. Among this youngest group of priests, 34% endorsed the view that Rome should *not* have decisive say in appointing diocesan bishops, compared with 49% of the priests in the 45–59 age cohort and 39% of the priests in the 60 and over age cohort. The younger and more recent recruits to the priesthood are clearly those most in favour of maintaining and extending the power of Rome in the Catholic Church.

CHAPTER FIFTEEN

Catholic Institutions

Earth's crammed with heaven
And every common bush
Aflame with God.
But only those who see
Take off their shoes.
The rest stand around
And pick blackberries (E. B. Browning).

I must believe in Apostolic Succession, there being no other way of accounting for the succession of our bishop from Judas Iscariot (Anonymous).

This chapter is concerned with *Catholic institutions* and gives particular attention to bishops, Opus Dei, Catholic schools and the Catholic press.

Context

From a very early stage in Church history, the essential role played by the people in the choice of bishop was recognized by the Church. In practice their participation moved from being an essential one to one that was required. It was then acknowledged as desirable, but due to practical difficulties their participation was finally agreed to be impossible. Laymen and women may be forgiven some bemusement to hear anew of the essential nature of their ministry in the Church.

Without any formal rules concerning the participation of believers in the choice of bishop, the precise mode of appointment varied from place to place (Schillebeeckx, 1985). It is known that in the first three centuries in the life of the Church one man later called bishop had to all intents and purposes risen above his fellow presbyters to a position of eminence as the ruler of a local church community. Cyprian, who became bishop of Carthage in 249, bequeathed to the Church a theology of episcopate that concluded in making the bishop the ruler of a diocese. With Cyprian originated the view that without a bishop, there was no Church, implying that the priesthood of the people of God was a derivation of the powers of the bishop, not the other way round.

There is now a greater concern than formerly to look at the history of the structures that the Church ultimately possesses today. For instance, the presumption that the position and role of bishops was set by Christ and could not possibly be changed is now seen increasingly by some theologians to be a rather mistaken one. The Catholic Church embodies a history of repeated theological legitimation of power brought about by mere historical opportunism (Duffy, 1997).

Election of bishops by local clergy was the norm well into the middle ages. It is not generally appreciated that the election of the Pope by the college of cardinals, ironically, is the last remaining example of the practice of episcopal election by the clergy of the local church since the predecessors of present-day cardinals were simply the clergy of the churches of the diocese of Rome. From this may be seen the remaining tradition of appointing international cardinals as titular deacons and priests of churches in the city of Rome (Dunn, 1996).

The long democratic tradition of electing both male and female leaders of religious orders helps contradict the often-repeated generalization that the Church is not a democracy.

> And it is surely rather ironic that in today's world, the more sophisticated secular societies – above all, let us say proudly, the 'Anglo-Saxon' English speaking societies – have developed a variety of constitutional mechanisms by which governors are both chosen by the governed and obliged to consult them and ask them what they think their interests are; while several Christian Churches and above all the Holy, Catholic, Apostolic and Roman Church, the standard bearer of Christ's kingdom, remain locked in the forms of imperial Roman, Byzantine autocracy, tied to the centurion's model of authority (Hill, 1997, pp. 312–13).

In one of the heady years following the Second Vatican Council, a large proportion of priests of the Liverpool diocese met with their archbishop George Andrew Beck and the apostolic delegate to discuss the appointment of an auxiliary bishop for Liverpool. The appeal was for the appointment, if not of a Liverpool priest, then at least the election of a pastorally aware priest from the North of England. The papal delegate smiled a lot, made sympathetic noises and showed every sign of listening. Following Archbishop Cardinale's departure, Archbishop Beck assured his priests that they had been listened to and that he himself supported them in their reasonable and modest petition. Furthermore, he added, Rome would not oppose the wishes of a metropolitan. In a space of time impossible for the deliberations of that meeting to have been registered in Rome, the name of an auxiliary bishop was announced. Joseph Gray was the Vicar General of the Birmingham diocese, a native of the Irish Republic and a Canon lawyer with little pastoral experience. The Liverpool meeting, it was universally agreed, had been a crafted charade and, as one theological magazine article subsequently stated, a paradigm in 'How not to appoint a bishop'. The cynicism the whole exercise engendered among those diocesan priests left a bitter legacy that took years to dissipate.

The national figure shows that 9.7% of secondary schools in England and Wales are Roman Catholic. An attempt in the early 1980s to analyse what was distinctive about the practical goals of Catholic education, led Winter (1985, p. 101) to the conclusion that he had seen no definition of what is 'sufficiently specific to justify the retention of our school system'. The precise nature of the theological or ethical influence of Roman Catholic schooling might need to be examined if just one conclusion ten years later of a major survey of secondary schools is considered: 'Roman Catholic clergy need to be aware that Roman Catholic teaching on abortion is far more widely accepted among the young than its teaching on birth control' (Francis and Kay, 1995, p. 219).

From studies in England and Wales there is evidence that Catholic primary schools exerted a positive effect on their pupils' attitude toward Christianity. The studies did appear to show that Church schools could have a positive influence in young people adopting a positive attitude toward Christianity. What was very significant was the debate over the assumption that Catholic schools function as an extension of the faith community. They are effective for children of practising parents but there is a question mark over their influence on the children of non-practising parents (Kay and Francis, 1996).

There is an almost complete lack of empirical evidence regarding the effectiveness of Catholic secondary schools in England and Wales. Instead there has been an understandable presumption of the effectiveness and beneficial characteristics not only of Catholic schools but also of 'faith' schools at all levels. The Labour government re-elected in the United Kingdom in 2001 perceived advantages in schools they coyly term 'faith-based' and declared itself keen to establish more of them without being too precise about what these advantages are. In an article in *The Times*, 24 November 2001, a journalist Hannah Betts claimed that the advantage of many such schools might lie as much in the catchment area from which the pupils are drawn as the attitudes such schools in general engender in their pupils. Betts claimed that 'In the main the ethos under discussion is less religious than middle-class.' Whether advantage does follow from education in a Catholic school or any faith-based school, the reality of such advantage, if such there is, should be capable of verification by some kind of empirical evidence.

The stated purpose of Opus Dei is to spread the life of sanctity among people of all walks of life especially those of intellectual pursuits. A lay organization founded in Madrid in 1928 by Monsignor Josemaría Escrivá de Balaguer (1902–75), who in spite of considerable criticism at its indecent haste was beatified in 1982 and canonized in 2002, Opus Dei has been described as a conservative and reactionary religious organization striving to restore Tridentine theology and medieval structures. In the same year as the beatification of its founder, Opus Dei was named a personal prelature by Pope John Paul II, which allows it to operate independently of the local bishop, to establish seminaries and to ordain candidates for the priesthood. The movement has made a point of cultivating members of national hierarchies, priests and influential laypeople, particularly in South America. Paradoxically at one and the same time Rome is seen to do the 'right thing' according to the values of the Second Vatican Council in supporting racial justice especially with regard to South America, but along with Opus Dei sees Base Communities as undermining the authority of the Catholic Church and message of Christ (Arbuckle, 1993, p. 52). The scarcely concealed aim of gaining political and ecclesiastical influence engenders equally strong feeling in Opus Dei supporters and detractors.

The Church does speak out and makes calls to conversion and eventually recognises its historical error ... unfortunately conversion is interpreted in such a way that allows the power structure to remain as it is. If conversion does not reach the institution of the Church, if it does not call into question the way in which power is exercised ... then we cannot speak of gospel conversion. We end up with extremely good-willed individuals with pure intentions but who are faithful, loyal, and uncritical toward the institution who through this institution cause serious damage to people and to the Church. Blaise Pascal noted that evil is not so perfectly achieved as when it is done with 'good will and purity of heart' (Boff, 1985, pp. 55–6).

A Catholic press would appear to be important, not least because the Catholic Church loves secrecy but should not be indulged in this. History should alert us to the truth that precisely because the Catholic Church is what she is, she needs an observant and benevolent critic to alert her to the constant proclivity to see the speck in the eye of others while ignoring the beam in her own.

Listening to the priests

A number of priests who participated in the survey made quite severe criticism of the processes by which bishops are appointed. For example, a growing appreciation that recent precedent is not necessarily the most desirable practice, still less the most evangelical, led one priest to write as follows.

I want to see changes in the ministry – especially in election of bishops and liberal policies in the Catholic Church (priest aged between 45 and 49).

Another priest who might have been expected from his declared position within a diocese to defend the status quo wrote as follows about his own recent experience and feelings.

As a priest I feel 'left out' of the process of the Church and decision-making. As a [diocese named] priest, this has been very evident in the appointment process of our new bishop. I say this as a priest who has had far more say and influence than others (priest aged between 40 and 44).

Had there been genuine participation in episcopal appointments, such involvement in the process might have made the following comment of one priest somewhat less heartfelt.

I am most concerned by the lack of leadership given by our bishops – an uninspiring muddle-minded bunch (priest aged between 35 and 39).

Apparently much more focused, but inspiring strong feelings of support or antipathy, are attitudes concerning the personal prelature of Opus Dei. Hostile to many of the changes of the Second Vatican Council, their vision is of a return to the authoritarian, coercive patriarchal culture of the pre-Vatican II Church (Tapia, 1998). Some priests adopt a particularly aggressive attitude when Opus Dei is mentioned. For reasons not altogether clear the subject is evidently an emotive one. Considering the positive expression in wording the survey statement about Opus Dei, the following strong reaction by one priest illustrates that point:

> I take positive exception to the suggestion that Opus Dei has been singled out as being possibly harmful to the life of the Church (priest aged between 45 and 49).

Comparable with Opus Dei in its oblique antagonism to the Second Vatican Council and similarly fundamental in its theology, the Neo-Catechumenate, also founded in Spain, has been for some priests a source of inspiration.

> I have been influenced and helped greatly by the Neo-Catechumenical Way. It has renewed my priesthood (priest aged between 45 and 49).

More comments were made by priests in criticism of Catholic schools than in support of them.

For example, one priest criticized Catholic schools in terms of their drain on financial resources on the grounds that schools did not provide the best value for money in the educational arena.

> The Church in England puts too much money into schools and not nearly enough into parish Churches and parish facilities where real education must happen (priest aged between 45 and 49).

Another priest criticized Catholic schools in terms of their drain on his own energy and time. His view was as follows:

> School takes up far too much time (priest aged between 45 and 49).

A third priest identified the major problem with Catholic schools to concern their lack of focus on admissions policies. This priest argued that Catholic schools could do a better job if they concentrated more exclusively on serving the families of practising Catholics. This priest wanted to see a

> movement away from Catholic schools [with pupils] who are not practising and [are therefore] not working for them (priest aged between 45 and 49).

Priests' attitudes in England and Wales to the Catholic press is one of tolerant indifference. The words of one priest express a generally representative attitude.

> Catholic press in general unimportant. *Tablet* . . . and other special publications, very important (priest aged between 70 and 74).

Shaping the questions

Against this background, the *Catholic Parochial Clergy Survey* framed three main themes relevant to exploring the priests' attitude toward Catholic institutions. The first theme focused on the appointment of bishops and explored the extent to which priests felt empowered or disempowered in this process. To what extent do priests feel that they have a say in the appointment of bishops?

The second theme examined how priests feel about Opus Dei. What proportion of priests feel that Opus Dei is a great force for good in the Catholic Church?

The third theme turned attention to Catholic schools, and to the part played by Catholic schools in the life of the parish. To what extent do priests feel that Catholic schools fulfil their purpose in their parish?

The fourth theme in this section examined how the priests evaluated the role of the Catholic press. How important do they feel that the Catholic press is to the life of their parish?

Interpreting the statistics

Table 15.1 demonstrates that the majority of priests have a low regard for many Catholic institutions. They feel disempowered over the appointment of bishops. They feel that Opus Dei is far from being a great force for good in the Catholic Church. They feel that the Catholic press is of little importance for the life of their parish. Against this general lack of confidence in Catholic institutions, Catholic schools fare comparatively well, with more priests feeling that Catholic schools fulfil their purpose in their parish than feel that they do not fulfil their purpose in the parish.

Over three-quarters of Catholic priests (77%) felt that they have no say in the appointment of bishops, compared with only 14% who felt that they might have some say, and another 10% who felt uncertain about the matter. The episcopacy is clearly a Catholic institution over which the priests feel they have little say.

Only three out of every twenty priests (15%) felt that Opus Dei is a great force for good in the Catholic Church. Three times that number (48%) took the opposite view. The remaining 37% preferred to remain non-committal about Opus Dei. What is clear from these statistics is that only a small proportion of priests are willing to speak positively about Opus Dei as a Catholic institution.

Once again only three out of every twenty priests (15%) felt that the Catholic press is important to the life of their parish. Four times that number (63%) took the opposite view. The remaining 22% preferred to remain non-committal about the Catholic press. What is clear from these statistics is that only a small proportion of priests are willing to speak positively about the Catholic press as a Catholic institution that is important to the life of their parish.

Overall the priests are considerably more positive about the Catholic school as a Catholic institution that may bring positive benefit to the local Church. Two-fifths of priests (43%) considered that Catholic schools fulfil their purpose in the parish, compared with one-third (32%) who considered that Catholic schools failed to fulfil their purpose in the parish. This leaves a quarter of the priests (25%) who still remained to be convinced over the value of Catholic schools.

Regular and secular

Table 15.2 demonstrates that there are no significant differences between regular priests and secular priests concerning the ways in which they evaluate Opus Dei or Catholic schools. Thus, 17% of the regular priests and 14% of the secular priests felt that Opus Dei is a great force for good in the Catholic Church. Catholic schools were felt to fulfil their purpose in the parish by 45% of the regular priests and by 43% of the secular priests.

There were significant differences, however, in the ways in which regular priests and secular priests evaluated the Catholic press. Regular priests were more likely than secular priests to feel that the Catholic press is important to the life of their parish (20% compared with 14%).

There were also significant differences in the ways in which regular priests and secular priests felt about their say in the appointment of bishops. Unsurprisingly, the regular priests were more likely than the secular priests to feel that they have no say in the appointment of bishops (82% compared with 75%). The fact that three-quarters of the secular priests felt this way is indicative of the gap between diocesan priests and the episcopacy that deploys them.

Generational differences

Table 15.3 demonstrates that there were no significant differences between the three cohorts of priests in terms of the way they view their influence in the appointment of bishops, or in terms of the way they view the effectiveness of Catholic schools in their parish. The sense of powerlessness in the appointment of bishops stood between 76% and 77% among all three age groups. The sense that Catholic schools fulfil their purpose in the parish stood between 41% and 45% among all three age groups.

On the other hand, there are significant differences in the evaluation of Opus Dei and in the evaluation of the Catholic press between priests under the age of 60 and priests aged 60 and over. Priests aged 60 and over showed greater regard for Opus Dei, in comparison with their younger colleagues. While 20% of priests aged 60 and over valued Opus Dei as a great force for good in the Catholic Church, the proportions fell to 11% among both the 45–59-year-olds and those aged under 45.

Priests aged 60 and over also showed greater regard for the Catholic press, in comparison with their younger colleagues. While 22% of priests aged 60 and over valued the Catholic press as important to the life of their parish, the proportions fell to 10% among both the 45–59-year-olds and those aged under 45.

CHAPTER SIXTEEN

Ecumenism and Intercommunion

In every age the Spirit nudges the collective consciousness of the Church to see ever more clearly the radical new order of the gospel message. I thought of this point when I came across a letter, written over two hundred years ago, from Bishop John Carroll of Baltimore to the prioress of the Carmelite Sisters. The letter announced a gift from the bishop intended to ease the hardship of the sisters' demanding life in the new world. The gift consisted of two slaves, a mother and her daughter . . . Two hundred years from now, our descendants will be puzzled at the blind spots of our present church. They were good and wise people, it will be reasoned, why couldn't they see what we are able to see from this point in history (Cozzens, 2000, p. 92).

This chapter is concerned with *ecumenism and intercommunion*. Starting with an appreciation of the wider ecumenical movement at the beginning of the twentieth century, attention is given to key Catholic considerations concerning the role of the papacy, the validity of ministry and eucharist outside the Catholic Church and the question of who can receive communion.

Context

In 1898, in Garrison, New York, two Episcopalians, Paul Francis Wattson (1863–1940) and Lurana Mary White (1870–1935) founded The Society of the Atonement, a Franciscan community of friars and nuns dedicated to praying for and fostering ecumenism. In 1908 they initiated eight days of prayer – from 18 to 25 January – for Church unity. The community was corporately received into the Catholic Church on 30 October 1909.

Few Catholics will be aware that it was largely the Protestant churches that first appreciated the need to do something positive to correct the doleful impression given by Christian disunity. The word ecumenical re-entered popular language comparatively recently, in fact after the first World Missionary Council held in Edinburgh, Scotland, 13–23 January 1910. Although Pope Leo XIII in his encyclical *Praeclara* (1894) was the first Pope to speak of the Orthodox and Protestant Christian communities as 'separated brothers', the Catholic Church of the time in its more prevalent opinion saw Protestants as heretics and Orthodox as schismatics who had broken from the true Church. In the last analysis there may be little to choose between attitudes of the saintly Pope Leo XIII (1878–1903) and the expression of Pope Boniface VIII in 1302 that

We are required by faith to believe and hold that there is one holy, Catholic and apostolic church: we firmly believe it and unreservedly profess it; outside it there is neither salvation nor remission of sins (Denzinger and Schoenmetzer, 1965, pp. 468–9).

In rather more than the popular Catholic mind, Protestants were looked upon as little more than a *massa damnata*. It was Catholic opinion that the possibility of the salvation of Protestants could only be ensured if they returned to Rome. In mitigation the possibility was acknowledged that well-meaning but misguided individuals who persisted in their heresy might find themselves (after death and probably to their perplexity and annoyance) within the Roman Catholic pale, since only Catholics were heavenly citizens. It is ironic that in the same year as the World Missionary Council Meeting in Scotland, former-president Theodore Roosevelt of the United States of America, who was lecturing at a Methodist conference in Rome, was refused the request of a papal audience because he was a Protestant (McCarthy, 1998, p. 177). The piety even of saintly Pope Pius X failed to expand his own vision beyond that of the contemporary ingrained prejudice of his fellow Catholics toward those of other Christian opinions.

There had to be a limit to the time the Catholic Church could maintain its closed view to the presence of other great, world religions, to say nothing of its disdain of other Christian churches, denominations and sects. It was as late as 1949 in the encyclical *Ecclesia Sancta* that Pope Pius XII, bravely setting aside the judgement of his predecessors, formally permitted not only Catholic dialogue with other Christians, but even allowed that such meetings could begin and end with shared prayer. The recent world war and the experience of those who had suffered in concentration camps, as well as a growth in communication and travel, had made it untenable for any one religion to claim to exist in a closed society that could ignore other religions.

Catholicism had paid an expensive price for its narrow outlook. 'The breakdown of the Christian missions in the countries of the Asian higher religions – in which a decisive part was played by catastrophic, quasi-infallible, wrong decisions by Rome, shamefacedly corrected centuries too late, but also by the equally long Protestant absenteeism – was cruelly brought home after the Second World War to missionaries of the post colonial age from North Africa to Korea' (Küng, 1978, p. 89). The intended opportunity to convert Eastern religions out of existence had been lost, largely by the recurring intervention of Rome in imposing mistaken decisions in theology and liturgy, which did irreparable missionary damage.

Notwithstanding the ecumenical gesture made by Pope Pius XII, a remarkable volte-face regarding ecumenism among Christian churches was given expression in the Decree on Ecumenism published in 1964 by the Second Vatican Council (Abbott, 1966). The former attitude, embodied in the hope that Protestants would 'return' to the one true Catholic Church, gave way to a vision of a pilgrim church in which believers in Christ are reborn in baptism and are sanctified and saved, not in spite of, but because of their link to God through their own church.

The Council document had continued to claim that, although the Catholic Church has been endowed with all divinely revealed truth and with all means of grace, her members fail to live by them with all the fervour they should (Abbott, 1966, p. 348). Ecumenism had been made possible by an appreciation of the distinction, not hitherto made by the magisterium, between the deposit of faith and the changing linguistic formulation in which such beliefs are articulated. The Second Vatican Council's ecumenical document is couched, however, in very Rome-centred language. One can see from a distance of years not only how far the document had progressed the discussion, but also how inflexible had been the position from which the new ecumenical journey had begun.

The encyclical letter of Pope John Paul II, *Ut Unum Sint* (1995), on commitment to ecumenism acknowledges what practical advances have been made: 'The increase of fellowship in a reform which is continuous and carried out in the light of the Apostolic Tradition is certainly, in the present circumstances of Christians, one of the distinctive and most important aspects of ecumenism' (*Ut Unum Sint*, 1995, p. 22). It might not seem much after thirty years to highlight an 'increase in fellowship', but it is truly significant when measured by how little movement had been made in the four hundred and fifty years since the Protestant reformation. When contrasted with previous animosity, the small achievements of ecumenism have made it possible to think to some extent of a united Christian witness, albeit often only at the level of shared prayer.

An adequately grounded and theologically motivated ecumenism should be one in which members of different churches are led through study and mutual conversation to a deeper understanding of their own and others' traditions. It should mean that previously unacknowledged presuppositions and prejudices are brought to light, deficiencies are made good and distortions corrected. This, however, takes time. There should be no question of any of the parties abandoning special insights, but rather sharing them so that mutual enrichment might follow. Unfortunately, ecumenism is seen by some, not as an invitation to engage in hard and demanding thinking, but as an excuse for abandoning it (Mascall, 1984). Such a view is shared by Pope John Paul II who writes as follows.

> All forms of reductionism or facile 'agreement' must be absolutely avoided. Serious questions must be resolved, for if not, they will reappear at another time, either in the same terms or in different guise (*Ut Unum Sint*, 1995, p. 36).

The report of a study by Ranson, Bryman and Hinings (1977) based upon three Roman Catholic dioceses in England, remarked on the attitude to ecumenism of the priests. First, the priests (in comparison with other Christian ministers taking part in the study) were generally more cautious and guarded in their ecumenical expression. Second, the priests were less willing to compromise the central canons of their theological cosmology. Third, the priests were willing to consider unity and co-operation with churches of other denominations only on Roman Catholic terms. A rereading of the Vatican Council Decree on Ecumenism (Abbott, 1966) cannot help but draw attention to a perception that the official position on ecumenism at that time was more advanced than that expressed by many English priests even three decades later. A similar impression is derived from a review of

Ut Unum Sint (1995), that the adopted position of Pope John Paul II on the theological underpinning of the essentials of ecumenism is well ahead of the opinion of the average United Kingdom Catholic, whereas on the vexed matter of artificial contraception it is quite some way behind.

On the subject of intercommunion, the official Roman Catholic position states that: 'Ecclesial communities derived from the reformation and separated from the Catholic Church have not preserved the proper reality of the eucharist mystery in its fullness, especially because of the absence of the sacrament of Holy Orders. It is for this reason that eucharistic intercommunion is not possible for the Catholic Church' (*Catechism of the Catholic Church*, 1994, p. 1400). One is left to wonder where God is being honoured in this or our fellow Christians being served. One might also question what level of impossibility is being referred to in the Catechism in light of the following distinction made by Pope John Paul II: 'In Catholic teaching there exists an order or "hierarchy" of truths, since they vary in their relationship to the foundation of the Christian faith' (*Ut Unum Sint*, 1995, p. 37).

Proof that the opinion expressed by Pope Leo XIII in his September 1898 encyclical letter *Apostolicae Curae* that Anglican orders 'have been and are absolutely null and utterly void' had not been revoked, was evidenced by the reordination as Catholic priests of those Anglican-ordained ministers, including the former Anglican Bishop of London, Graham Leonard, who had joined the Catholic Church following the decision of the Church of England to ordain women to the priesthood. On the question of intercommunion, the fundamental tension has been expressed in the question whether sharing the eucharist is to be seen as a seal on unity achieved or as a means of creating unity. Seemingly intransigent Catholic attitudes continue to raise barriers that are presented as insurmountable but regrettably unavoidable. 'The official Catholic position enunciates in terms of sacramental discipline an absolute, ahistorical idea of unity present in the Catholic Church (and if the validity/invalidity argument is pursued, it is difficult to see how even partial embodiment is possible elsewhere). In other words, the official position appears to express obliquely the "one true church" claims of pre-Vatican II Catholicism and with them the former one true eucharist claim' (Laishley, 1991, p. 228).

It is understandable that many priests and theologians today would be less confident of the church's wish or ability thus to shorten God's arm.

> We know that some of the greatest missionary saints believed that God would commit to the flames of Hell those who were not baptised into the church, even if they lived in perfectly good faith. They were saints but they were badly mistaken. We also know that Christian missionaries in Asia frequently forced converts to Christianity to renounce all their previous strivings for God as utterly sinful, made them renounce many social and cultural patterns of their own countries, and made them adopt Western ways that had nothing to do with religion. These missionaries were zealous apostles, but they were wrong (Hellwig, 1970, p. 93).

It is painful for some priests to accept that the Catholic Church has often been compelled to acknowledge more tolerant truths that have been gained and developed outside of itself.

The document *One Bread One Body* (Catholic Bishops, 1998) was the teaching document issued by the three Catholic Bishops' Conferences of England and Wales, Ireland, and Scotland, setting down the rare occasions on which non-Catholics could be admitted to communion. In reply, the House of Bishops of the Church of England in 2001 published *The Eucharist: sacrament of unity*, not only setting forth the teaching of the Church of England on the eucharist, but also questioning the Roman Catholic teaching 'that Anglican celebrations of the eucharist lack the fullness of the means of salvation that one claimed for the Roman Catholic Church because they have not retained ... the authentic and full reality of the eucharist mystery' (House of Bishops, 2001, p. 15). The Catholic Church still questions the validity of Anglican orders and therefore the authenticity of Anglican eucharist. No such judgement is made by Anglicans of the Roman Catholic eucharist, which raises the topic of Anglicans receiving communion in a Roman Catholic Church at mass. One particular group receive particular mention. 'We believe that it is vital to do justice to the truth that in the case of a Christian couple, one of whom is a Roman Catholic and the other, say, an Anglican, there is a double bond of unity in Christ – through baptism and through marriage. That twofold sacramental bond seems to be nullified when communion together at the eucharist is forbidden' (House of Bishops, 2001, p. 19).

Listening to the priests

It is only comparatively recently that the Catholic Church has acknowledged that those who follow other religions can certainly be saved, not in spite of but through those religions. There is a particular Christian attitude that is patronizing of other world religions and a particular Catholic attitude that is patronizing of other Christians. The Catholic anti-ecumenical attitude, once official teaching, is now sufficiently unfashionable rarely to be voiced publicly, but it does still exist and was voiced by several priests in the survey. One priest, for example, commented as follows.

> I feel our ministry as RC priests is greatly hampered by ecumenism (which NO priest I know believes in). Local ecumenical projects are a huge drain on our resources and energies and prevent us from evangelising. Catholic parishes should withdraw from all ecumenical covenants (priest aged between 45 and 49).

A number of priests expressed the clear view that the only form of ecumenism that they could envisage was one in which other churches acknowledged the leadership of the Pope. One priest expressed this view very simply.

I feel strongly that unity with the Pope is essential today (priest aged between 45 and 49).

Other priests took a more nuanced approach and recognized that this form of unity would also require some radical changes in the papacy itself. This point was made by one priest in the following way.

I see union as all Christians acknowledging the leadership of the Pope (and hence 'Catholic') but not as exercised by the present one (priest aged between 75 and 79).

For a number of other priests the current reality of local ecumenism proved to be a real source of encouragement, inspiration and support. One priest, for example, singled out how important to his ministry he found the support derived from the clergy serving other denominations, and he criticized the survey for not giving greater prominence to this issue.

You should have asked about support from non-Catholic clergy. A very significant question (priest aged between 45 and 49).

Another priest noted laconically the wider benefits of ecumenical support by writing as follows.

The value of ecumenical support [and family] needs including (priest aged between 40 and 44).

At a practical level many priests noted the real tension they experienced in applying the Catholic teaching on admission to communion. One priest spoke for many when he summed up the issue by talking about his own personal experience.

One big question I wrestle with concerns intercommunion. How can we refuse good practising non-Catholics communion when every year we are giving communion to what are to all intents and purposes baptised pagans at the celebration of First Holy Communion? I refer here to the parents, family and friends of the children making their First Holy Communion. This isn't a judgement on those people. It comes from first hand experience (priest aged between 50 and 54).

Shaping the questions

Against this background, the *Catholic Parochial Clergy Survey* framed four main themes relevant to exploring the priests' perceptions of and attitudes toward ecumenism and intercommunion. The first theme focused on the extent to which priests were committed to the ecumenical movement broadly conceived. How many, for example, would take the view that ecumenical co-operation has gone as far as it can go?

The second theme examined the place that Catholic priests would wish to ascribe to the papacy in any ecumenical future which they envisaged. This theme was explored from both a soft and a hard perspective. The soft perspective focused on the place of papal supremacy in ecumenical collaboration. What proportion of priests consider that papal supremacy is essential for any church unity scheme? The hard perspective focused on whether papal supremacy in fact meant a superior role for the Catholic Church. What proportion of priests consider that Christian unity means all should eventually become Roman Catholic?

The third theme examined the priests' attitude toward those ordained in the Anglican Church. What proportion of priests hold to the view that Anglican orders are null and void?

The fourth theme turned attention to the question of intercommunion and approached this question from two perspectives: the perspective of Catholics communicating in non-Catholic churches and the perspective of non-Catholics communicating in Catholic churches. What proportion of priests believe that the Catholic Church should permit Catholics to communicate in non-Catholic churches? What proportion of priests believe that non-Catholic Christians should be permitted to communicate at mass?

Interpreting the statistics

Table 16.1 demonstrates quite a complex and mixed attitude toward ecumenism and intercommunion among Catholic priests. The majority of priests feel that there is still potential for further progress in the ecumenical movement. The weight of opinion is that papal supremacy is essential for church unity, but that this is not paramount to all other Christians becoming Catholics. There is still quite a strong tendency toward regarding Anglican orders as null and void and an even stronger tendency toward discouraging intercommunion.

Clearly the majority of priests are far from turning their back on the ecumenical movement. Although nearly one in every five priests (18%) took the view that ecumenical co-operation has gone as far as it can go, more than three times that number (61%) clearly argued against that position. It is significant, however, that another one in every five priests (22%) remained uncertain about the future of ecumenical co-operation.

For three out of every five priests the kind of ecumenical future which they envisaged clearly includes recognition of papal supremacy. Thus 62% of priests argued that papal supremacy is essential for any church unity scheme, compared with less than a third of that number (18%) who were willing to forgo the place of papal supremacy in the cause of church unity. Another one in every five priests were not confident enough to forgo papal supremacy, but were nonetheless willing to entertain the possibility.

Many priests were willing to distinguish between the case for papal supremacy and the wholesale conversion of other denominations to Catholicism. While only 18% of priests denied that papal supremacy is essential for any church unity scheme, three times that number (53%) denied that Christian unity means all should eventually become Roman Catholic. However, this still leaves almost one priest in every three (31%) who believed that Christian unity means all should eventually become Roman Catholic.

Ecumenical collaboration is not made easier by the official teaching of the Catholic Church regarding the invalidity of Anglican orders. The statistics demonstrate that between two-fifths and a half of priests (44%) accepted the official position, as pronounced by Pope Leo XIII, that Anglican orders are 'null and void'. Nonetheless, the fact that one in four priests (25%) now rejected this official line and a further one in three priests (31%) now at least held reservations about accepting this official line shows considerably more good-will for collaboration with Anglican clergy at the local level than represented in church teaching.

At the local level, however, the issue of intercommunion provides a very real index of the vitality of the ecumenical movement. At the local level the sacrament of unity can become the most visible sign of disunity. Overall the priests have very little enthusiasm for extending the opportunities for intercommunion. Thus, only 25% of priests believed that non-Catholics should be permitted to communicate at mass, compared with 58% who stood firmly against this principle. Moreover, the priests were even more strongly opposed to permitting Catholics to communicate in non-Catholic churches. While 25% of priests considered that non-Catholics should be permitted to communicate at mass, the proportion fell to 17% of priests who considered that the Catholic Church should permit Catholics to communicate in non-Catholic churches. While 58% of priests were firmly against permitting non-Catholics to communicate at mass, the proportion rose to 71% of priests who were firmly against permitting Catholics to communicate in non-Catholic churches. There were also fewer priests willing to waiver over the issue of permitting Catholics to communicate in non-Catholic churches (13%) than were willing to waiver over the issue of permitting non-Catholics to communicate at mass (17%).

Regular and secular

Table 16.2 demonstrates that there are no significant differences between the views of regular priests and secular priests in respect of their broad support for ecumenical co-operation, their views on Anglican orders, or their approach to intercommunion. There is, however, a significant difference between these two groups of priests concerning the position in which they would place the Catholic Church within the ecumenical future. While 30% of the secular priests argued that Christian unity means all should eventually become Roman Catholic, the proportion rose to 37% among the regular priests who took this view.

Generational differences

Table 16.3 demonstrates that overall priests under the age of 60 hold a more open view to ecumenism than is the case among priests aged 60 and over. There is a tendency, however, for the youngest cohort of priests, those under the age of 45, to revert to a more conservative position, especially over the issue of intercommunion.

Nearly one in every four of the priests aged 60 and over (23%) felt that ecumenical co-operation has gone as far as it can go. The proportion dropped significantly to 14% among the priests aged between 45 and 59 and remained at that level (14%) among the priests under the age of 45.

Over three-quarters of the priests aged 60 and over (79%) held to the view that papal supremacy is essential for any church unity scheme. The proportion dropped dramatically to 51% among the priests aged between 45 and 59 and remained at the level of 52% among the priests under the age of 45.

For two out of every five priests aged 60 or over (40%) Christian unity meant all should eventually become Roman Catholic. The proportion dropped significantly to 24% among the priests aged between 45 and 59 and rose only slightly to 27% among the priests under the age of 45.

Over half of the priests aged 60 or over (55%) believed, as Pope Leo XIII had said, that Anglican orders are 'null and void'. Among the priests aged between 45 and 59 belief in the invalidity of Anglican orders fell to 35% and then rose slightly to 39% among the priests under the age of 45.

Although never at a high level, enthusiasm for facilitating intercommunion was considerably higher among priests in the 45–59 age cohort than among priests aged 60 and over. While 23% of priests aged 60 and over supported the view that non-Catholic Christians should be permitted to communicate at mass, the proportion rose to 30% among the 45–59 age cohort. While 14% of priests aged 60 and over supported the view that Catholics should be permitted to communicate in non-Catholic churches, the proportion rose to 21% among the 45–59 age cohort. Among the priests under the age of 45, however, the figures returned to the levels espoused by the priests aged 60 and over. Among the priests under the age of 45, just 14% wanted to see Catholics communicate in non-Catholic churches, and just 20% wanted to see non-Catholics communicate at mass.

CHAPTER SEVENTEEN

Changes in the Catholic Church

Sister Arvonne is a reverent woman like Sister Brunhilde, but is much smaller and lighter on her feet, so her reverence takes other forms than kneeling, such as reform for example ... when the new edict came down on nun dress she put her wimple on the bust of Newman and developed the taste for pants suits. Some old *Catholische* thought it was the end of the world, but looking at her, they could see it wasn't, she zipped around like it was eight o'clock in the morning. Around the same time, the new liturgy was greeted with a long low moan by the faithful and even from the unfaithful – Arvonne's sister Rosalie who had not uttered a *Pater Noster* since the early days of the Eisenhower administration nevertheless mourned the Latin mass as if it were her dear departed mother – but Arvonne didn't pause for a moment. 'English', she told Rosalie, 'is an excellent language. Look at Shakespeare. Look at Milton – hell, if a Congregationalist could write like that, think what you could do if you actually knew something' (Keillor, 1986, p. 228).

When you went before Canon Cooney in the confessional it felt like going on trial for your life (Cornwell, 2001, p. 66).

This chapter is concerned with recent changes in the Catholic Church. Particular attention is given to the climate of change initiated by the Second Vatican Council, to the growth of feminism in the Catholic Church, to decline in the sacrament of reconciliation and the reordination of convert Anglican clergymen following the decision of the Church of England to ordain women to the priesthood.

Context

Conservative Catholics, who derived a deep sense of contentment and reassurance from the seeming dependability and unchanging nature of Catholic doctrine and practice stretching back hundreds of years, felt and feel acutely uneasy about the plethora of changes introduced into the Catholic Church in the last forty years. 'The intellectual attraction of strongly presented, theoretically closed systems of thought such as pre-1960s Catholicism or communism has frequently been commented upon' (Berger, 1988, p. 63). Unfortunately the long period in history without substantial change only accentuated the fortress model of the

Catholic Church as a perfect society complete in itself, beleaguered by formidable enemies. The impression felt was one of the Catholic Church as a bastion of religious truth in a world of needless uncertainty. As Sister Arvonne herself might have said, the Church has all the answers if people would only listen.

Few could have anticipated or did in fact foresee the level of upheaval occasioned in the life of the average practising Catholic by the Second Vatican Council. Arbuckle (1996) has described the upheaval that Catholics experienced by the technical word 'chaos', which describes confrontation with the inevitability of change and the necessity of adopting alternative or radically different ways of seeing and doing things. The Second Vatican Council had asked fundamental questions about what in faith and practice is substantial and essential and therefore to be retained, and what is accidental and can be let go. An initial stage of unease that came with the prospect of change was occasioned by a fear that what was essential might be lost with what was dispensable. This stage was followed by one of ambiguity, during which questions arose concerning the very identity and purpose of the church, and old patterns of religious reality were confronted by new ways of looking at the world.

Lack of any anticipatory preparation for the decisions of the Council gave rise to an impression summed up by the ironic Catholic dictum of the time that 'everything was forbidden until it became compulsory'. One cause of the confusion was the low level of theological awareness among most of the laity. In general an insufficient distinction had been made in popular Catholicism between the trivial and the important, between the novena and the nativity. Popular Catholic belief inculcated by generations of well-intentioned but theologically deprived teachers emphasized what was in effect the need for Catholic certainty; the need always to be right and to try to show those poor benighted Protestants how wrong they were.

There is now a far greater readiness by many Catholics to acknowledge the possibility that the Catholic Church does not have all of the answers. It was observed that 'The ancient dikes showed punctures. Not that there were no little boys ready and willing to stick their fingers into all the holes; the conservatives were, and did. And now, when all the furniture seems to be swimming out to sea, they can say with some justice, "We told you so"' (Berger, 1969). Catholics in general were more buoyant than anxious. Closer to those times it was perceptively observed that 'Some priests appear to share the feeling that it is humiliating and undignified for the church to admit that it had or has anything to learn from anyone' (Hebblethwaite, 1975). Priests holding such opinions have not entirely disappeared even in the twenty-first century.

Perhaps the most embarrassing statement made during the distinguished episcopacy of the late Basil Hume, Cardinal Archbishop of Westminster (1976–2000), was his description of the transfer of allegiance of a hundred or so Anglican clergy from Canterbury to Rome, occasioned by the ordination of women to the priesthood of the Church of England. His declaration that it could herald the conversion of England for which Roman Catholics had been praying for so long, struck a discordant, distant note harking back to an earlier theology that still saw in Anglicanism ordinations that were 'absolutely null and utterly void' and a church that contained little more than valueless spectacle.

Whatever else was at issue, the Cardinal's retrogressive statement had been occasioned by the inability of some Anglican clergymen (who represented the failure of a substantial number of their fellow Christians) to integrate the female into their experience of the sacred. An exclusively male priesthood in a male-centred and male-controlled church had been supported by a traditional male-authored theology, intrinsically structured, even if not intentionally, to relegate women to subservient roles.

Mary Daly, Elizabeth Schüssler Fiorenza, Ute Ranke Heinemann, Monika Hellwig, Sallie McFague and Rosemary Radford Ruether are but a few of the better known feminist theologians who have seen it as one of their tasks to critique the whole historical cultural tradition, shared by Judaism and Christianity, that has misunderstood and misrepresented aspects of scripture to the detriment and oppression of women. Cultural prejudice absorbed in everyday communication found its way by tradition and theology into the weft and weave of Christian reflection. This had become so integral to a Roman Catholic thought pattern that it had been all but rendered invisible until the advent and access of women to the study of theology. No generally acceptable reason can any longer be offered by the Church authorities to exclude women from the major processes and decisions relating as much to women as to men (Hellwig, 1992). That such exclusion still persists is a measure more of the tenacity of male vested interest dressed in theological motley than any real respectable theological robes.

Not for nothing did the line spoken by the irreverent Scottish comedian Billy Connolly thirty years ago strike a chord when he first said, 'I am a Catholic; I have an A-level in guilt.' Older priests and laypeople can remember not only the Latin mass conducted with the priests' back to the congregation but can recall the detailed rubrics governing its celebration that turned a sacred activity into a minefield of petty rubrical ordinances. According to the moralists, priests could damn themselves at the altar just as easily as they and the laity could court damnation on a Friday by failing to conform to the regulations concerning abstinence from meat. Sin was to the fore and was seen more as the breaking of formal laws than as damaging a personal relationship with a God who loves us.

Of all the traditional practices formerly associated with Catholicism, none has experienced such a falling off as the sacrament of reconciliation, or penance, or confession as it has been variously called. For millions of Catholics worldwide the 'confessional box' had been a symbol and location of forgiveness, in which sinfulness and a need for repentance and penance was acknowledged. In confessing their violation of the commandments to the priest, Catholics acknowledged personal guilt before God and the Church (O'Keefe, 1990). Confession to a priest was an acknowledgement of the social effects of personal sin, the priest being the representative of the community in the sacrament. As a regular Catholic practice, it has all but ceased in many Western countries, yet a remarkable characteristic of this phenomenon has been the near total silence of the Catholic Church on the matter. This is more noticeable considering the importance and encouragement formerly given to the practice of regular confession, making the silence concerning its near abandonment doubly puzzling.

The dramatic decline in those availing themselves of the sacrament of reconciliation is seen by some as proof of liberation from an unhealthy guilt that had formerly burdened many Catholics. Whatever the theory, the actual experience by hundreds of millions of the sacrament of confession could scarcely be categorized as a 'celebration' of God's healing forgiveness. 'It was more a sign of the Church's tight grip on the intimate lives of Catholics and of the fear that characterised many people's notion of God' (Gillis, 1999, p. 171). A rare acknowledgement of the decline in the use of the sacrament of reconciliation was made in a recent annual Holy Thursday letter to priests by Pope John Paul II. This included a reminder of the need for 'renewed boldness in re-proposing the meaning and practice of this sacrament' (*The Tablet*, 7 April 2001, p. 496).

The rediscovery that forgiveness was not exclusively restricted to that sacrament has led to a greater awareness of other aspects of sin and reconciliation. The reality of social sin has been vividly depicted by the image of a 'slave owner of good conscience who could quite conceivably recognise his or her cruelty to an individual slave but remain completely inattentive to the evil in the institution of slavery itself' (O'Keefe, 1990, pp. 10–11). Whether a restored appreciation of the reality of social sin provides an adequate explanation for the abandonment of the individual rite of the sacrament, the wholesale disregard of what was until recently an insisted-upon sacrament, cannot but be on reflection a source of considerable anxiety to Church authorities.

Listening to the priests

Clearly some of the priests responding to the survey had felt very disorientated and disturbed by the many changes they had witnessed in the Catholic Church, and some considerable emotion came through their responses. For example, one priest made his point felt as follows.

> Priests are now irrelevant, as bishops ignore us in favour of dissidents and feminists. Bishops have no interest in maintaining soundness and unity of teaching. They have reneged on their pastoral office. The main function of an ordained priest in today's church is to be a rubber stamp for institutional hypocrisy. We have failed Christ's command to teach his gospel. We baptise for the sake of counting numbers and confirm and marry for [the] same reasons (priest aged between 60 and 64).

Other priests were themselves more than willing and eager to embrace the potential for change that they saw in the Catholic Church, but felt ill-equipped and poorly guided to promote the change that they so much wanted to see. One priest put the situation like this:

> We are in a changing church and I don't feel very well equipped for that, though pray that I may be open and able for those future demands (priest aged between 30 and 34).

Another priest made a similar point by emphasizing how he actually felt disabled in promoting change by the structure of the Catholic Church.

> The church needs to get real. It is out of touch. Its set-up is out of date. We need bishops who will speak the truth directly, listen to the needs of people, including priests, and set up systems that work (priest aged between 45 and 49).

Underlying many of these comments was the practical outworking of the great change that has taken place in the dominant models that underpin our under-standing of the Church. The metaphor for the experience changes from emphasis on the institution – a perfect society – to a rather less stable image concentrating on the people who find themselves on a pilgrim journey on which the road to follow is not as obviously well-signposted as was once believed. As did the Israelites who followed Moses into the desert, so also might the leaders of the twenty-first century pilgrim people express understandable unease about the 'journey' they are on and learn to put more reliance in religious faith concerning the direction they are taking than making inappropriate claims to objective certainty that theirs is invariably the right road to follow. The alternative to retreating to past securities is to move forward into an uncertain future with more risk but full of hope (Arbuckle, 1993).

A clear oversight in the survey was the failure to ask priests how they were responding to the opportunities and challenges of information technology. Some priests drew the omission to our attention, as exampled by the following senti-ment.

> Something should have been asked about the use made of computer technol-ogy in our work (priest aged between 60 and 64).

Comments received on information technology were quite evenly balanced between those who saw this innovation as offering great support to ministry and those who regarded it as a further unnecessary burdensome complication within their already overstretched lives.

Shaping the questions

Against this background, the *Catholic Parochial Clergy Survey* formed four main themes relevant to exploring the priests' perspectives and experiences of changes in the Catholic Church. The first theme focused on the view that would be taken by reactionary priests who might consider that changes in the Church had already gone too far in pursuit of a liberal agenda. What proportion of priests feel that the Catholic Church has become too liberal?

The second theme examined the priests' reactions to trends concerning the sacrament of reconciliation. How much are priests concerned that so few receive the sacrament of reconciliation, or are they content to accept this major change in the practice of the laity?

The third theme examined the priests' responses to feminism within the Catholic Church and did so from two perspectives. The first perspective was concerned with the respect in which they might hold feminist theology. For example, how many priests would go as far as to condemn feminist theology as a travesty of theology? The second perspective was concerned with the integration of female images into hymns and prayers. How many priests believe that hymns and prayers should use female as well as male images for God?

The fourth theme returned to the significant integration of convert Anglican clergymen into the Catholic Church by means of reordination. How many priests were content with the reordination of convert Anglican clergymen into the Catholic Church?

Interpreting the statistics

Table 17.1 demonstrates that it is only a small proportion of priests who feel that the Catholic Church has become too liberal. Nevertheless, there is widespread concern over the neglect of the sacrament of reconciliation. The jury is still largely out on the influence of feminism in the Catholic Church. Overall the reordination of convert Anglican clergymen was met with approval.

The proportion of priests who sided with those who feel that the Catholic Church has become too liberal was really quite small. Just three out of every twenty priests (15%) felt that the Catholic Church has become too liberal, compared with five times that number (75%) who felt that the Catholic Church has not become liberal enough. Quite a small proportion (11%) sat on the fence, not wanting to side with those who feel that the Catholic Church has become too liberal, and at the same time not wanting to deny it.

The fall in the response of the laity to the sacrament of reconciliation was looked on with concern by a large number of priests. Three-quarters of the priests (74%) expressed concern that so few receive the sacrament of reconciliation. By way of comparison, only 14% of the priests said that they felt no concern over this issue, and the remaining 12% were uncertain about their reaction.

The feminist agenda has been met by a mixed reception among the clergy. The vitriolic view that feminist theology is a travesty of theology was endorsed by 28% of the priests, but rejected by a considerably larger proportion (41%). While not wanting to side with the view, the remaining 31% were not willing to reject it either. Nearly two out of every five priests (37%) agreed that hymns and prayers should use female as well as male images of God, but a slightly larger proportion (41%) disagreed with this view. The remaining 22% of priests appeared to be acknowledging that there is a case for the use of female as well as male images of God, but were not yet willing to sign up to that case.

Two-thirds of the priests (68%) were happy with the reordination of convert Anglican clergy, compared with 12% who were unhappy with this and 19% who were not too clear where they stood on the issue.

Regular and secular

Table 17.2 demonstrates that there are no significant differences between the views of regular priests and secular priests concerning changes in the Catholic Church. Thus, 14% of the regular priests considered that the Catholic Church has become too liberal and so did 15% of the secular priests. Three-quarters of the regular priests (73%) were concerned that so few receive the sacrament of reconciliation and so were 74% of the secular priests. A third of the regular priests (32%) believed feminist theology is a travesty of theology and so did 28% of the secular priests. Two-fifths of the regular priests (41%) agreed that hymns and prayers should use female as well as male images of God and so did 36% of the secular priests. Finally, 71% of the regular priests and 68% of the secular priests were happy with the reordination of convert Anglican clergymen into the Catholic Church.

Generational differences

Table 17.3 demonstrates that priests aged 60 and over are more likely than their younger colleagues to feel that the Catholic Church has become too liberal, are more likely to be scathing about feminist theology and are more likely to lament the eclipse of the sacrament of reconciliation. These older priests are also less likely to welcome the use of female images for God in hymns and prayers. They are, however, more likely to be happy with the reordination of convert Anglican clergymen into the Catholic Church.

The statistics show that one in every five of the priests aged 60 and over (20%) considered that the Catholic Church has become too liberal. The proportion of priests who felt this way declined to 11% among the 45–59 year age cohort and to 12% among the priests under the age of 45. Discontent with any liberalization that the Catholic Church has experienced is, therefore, twice as prevalent among priests aged 60 and over than among their younger colleagues.

Concern that so few receive the sacrament of reconciliation stood at 79% among the priests aged 60 and over, but declined somewhat to 70% both among the priests aged between 45–59 and among the priests under the age of 45. Although a little less pronounced than among their older colleagues, at 70% the level of concern expressed by the younger priests is nonetheless considerable.

More than two out of every five priests aged 60 and over (43%) dismissed feminist theology as a travesty of theology. The proportion halved among the 45–59 age group to 21% and fell further to 16% among those under the age of 45. Another indication of the growing acceptance of the case argued from the feminist position is seen in a growing acceptance of female imagery for God. While a quarter of the priests aged 60 and over (25%) accepted that hymns and prayers should use female as well as male images for God, the proportion grew to 44% among the 45–59-year-olds, and almost doubled to 48% among those under the age of 45.

Contentment with the reordination of convert Anglican clergymen into the Catholic Church clearly declined across the age cohort. While 79% of priests aged 60 and over were happy with the reordination of convert Anglican clergymen into the Catholic Church, the proportions fell to 66% among the 45–59-year-olds and to 55% among those under the age of 45.

CHAPTER EIGHTEEN

Ordination of Women

In November 1992, the Church of England approved (by only a two-vote margin) the ordination of women priests. Two months earlier the Anglican Church of South Africa had voted to ordain women. As recently as 1976 the Episcopal Church in the United States voted to recognise the ordination of women priests. The first woman rabbi in the United States was ordained in 1972. Although the African Methodist Churches have a long tradition of women clergy, only in the 1950s did white Methodists allow women to be ordained. Presbyterians first began ordaining women in the 1950s and Lutherans began in the 1970s (Torjiesen, 1993).

This chapter is concerned with examining the attitude of the Catholic Church toward the ordination of women. Attention is given to the official teaching of the Catholic Church and to the arguments against the ordination of women based on scripture and based on tradition.

Context

There was a time in Catholic affairs when employment of the assertion that Protestant churches had done this or that would have been considered a totally counterproductive argument. In the present-day debate, however, concerning whether the Catholic Church should contemplate ordaining women to the priesthood, it now carries an undeniable relevance. The question can be asked whether God is calling the Catholic Church in the twenty-first century to a form of priesthood that does not necessarily depend on the premise of maleness. Shocking though this may sound to some, and in spite of the papal embargo upon its discussion, Jesus himself rebuked the Pharisees and Sadducees for remaining ignorant of that which really mattered, in spite of their ability to interpret the inessentials (Matthew 16:3).

According to the Vatican statement issued in 1976, 'The Declaration on the Question of the Admission of Women to the Ministerial Priesthood', the primary argument against the admission of women to priestly ordination was the allegedly unbroken tradition of restricting priesthood to men. Its conclusion declared that the Catholic Church, in fidelity to the example of the Lord, does not consider herself authorized to admit women to priestly ordination. Some have argued that it is one thing to make the debatable assertion that there is no biblical evidence for women even having shared in priestly ministry, but another to argue that Jesus intended thereby to exclude women from the priesthood. Pope John Paul II in his 1993 statement 'On Priestly Ordination' reiterated the view of his predecessor Pope Paul VI that the Catholic Church does not have the authority to ordain women, adding that he, John Paul II, was speaking 'definitively' and embargoing further discussion of the subject. Here, Pope John Paul II appears in effect to have stated that a theological decision was made since New Testament times to exclude women from priestly ministry. If women can definitively be excluded on scriptural grounds then that would be the end of the matter, but such finality does not appear to be the case at all. Less reliance is now placed on the final word of scripture merely quoted, as, by mainstream theological consent, even scripture has to be interpreted by the living Church. It is now, therefore, the weight of accumulated tradition that is used in the official tenet of the Catholic Church to support the ongoing exclusion of women from ministerial priesthood.

In the ongoing struggle to justify the ordination of women to the priesthood by countering arguments based on both scripture and tradition, it is significant that the scriptural argument appears to have been won. One factor above all others influencing the women's ordination debate has been the use made of critical biblical scholarship to cast doubt upon the use hitherto made of the interpretation of scripture to confound even the proposal of women in priestly ministry (Nesbitt, 1997). But there are levels, it has been argued, at which the debate ought no longer be conducted.

> The argument that a male is needed to represent the word made flesh is really just a laughable failure of third class theologians to understand either the classical theology of the incarnation and redemption or anthropology, the structures and limitations of religious symbolism and, even, the history of western linguistics (Hastings, 1990, p. 97).

If it is conceded that arguments from scripture may no longer be used to justify the exclusion of women from priesthood (because there does not appear to be any), the argument from tradition deserves further scrutiny. By definition, tradition refers to what is handed down, handed on. Such special features, traditions, are what differentiate one group or community from another. St Paul himself commended the eucharistic tradition he was passing on, specifically by emphasizing that in turn it had been handed on to him (1 Corinthians 11). Because humans change and collective traditions only exist within human perception, traditions change with them. Take for instance 1 Timothy, in which it is stated that a bishop should have a wife and children, yet the Church felt able subsequently to appoint celibate men as bishops. The Catholic Church went further and reversed the original traditions, insisting that only unmarried men could become bishops. It is clear, therefore, that the Catholic Church then and always has felt able to establish tradition.

With a confidence born of the conviction that the Catholic Church collectively possesses the gift of the Holy Spirit, new decisions have been made through history regarding what was necessary for ministry in ways more in keeping with the needs of changed social and human circumstances. The determining factor, far from a readiness to jettison tradition, was to encapsulate the core of the tradition within the new cultural context. Slavish adherence to all tradition as an immutable 'given' has never been a viable option for the Catholic Church as the transformation carried out by the Second Vatican Council re-emphasized.

The growing shortage of priests in 'first world' countries has obliged the Catholic Church increasingly to rely on the engagement of women to help keep parishes operating, particularly in the United States of America. Though the Catholic Church denies access to priesthood and the clerical state to women, many women are functioning as lay pastors sometimes alongside a priest, sometimes as sole administrator of parishes that have no priest. 'Since all but one of the laity heading parishes are women . . . this means that approximately 74% of parishes are headed by women' (Wallace, 1993).

A Vatican document entitled 'Instructions on Certain Questions Regarding the Collaboration of the non-Ordained Faithful in the Sacred Ministry of the Priest', released 13 November 1997, warns against abuses of lay ministry and emphasizes the unique position of ordained ministry based on apostolic succession, which it says is 'an essential part of Catholic ecclesiological doctrine'. Though supporting the involvement of the laity, and therefore of women in the pastoral ministry of clerics in parishes, the document insists that this should be allowed only where there is a shortage of priests. The document gives an impression, difficult to avoid in spite of assurance to the contrary, that though ostensibly supported, lay participation and particularly women's participation is accepted 'without enthusiasm', as an emergency albeit long-term, non-optimum solution, constrained only because of the shortage of priests (*The Tablet*, 22 November 1997, p. 1524).

It appears increasingly doubtful that as long as the supply of qualified men is sufficient to meet the demand for priests, however depleted in numbers in comparison with the recent past, any alternative organizational response will be tried before that of ordaining women to the priesthood. The phenomenon of the revival of the ordained permanent diaconate, open only to males, but including even married men, may be cited to highlight this. Whether that development would have been embraced with any enthusiasm if recruitment to the priesthood had held up is open to charges of cynicism but is exposed to serious doubt. What applies to lay ministers and to deacons appears to apply in stronger measure to women's ministry. If Roman Catholic past precedent and practice is anything to go by it would appear difficult to gainsay the following statement.

> The deprofessionalisation of the priests' role, particularly as parish pastor, to a series of parish administrative and pastoral roles that can be filled by lay or religious women and men has served greatly to reduce clericalism and at the same time open the way for new professional opportunities for women. Yet because of the denomination's tight sacramental control by men, including the maintenance of a priestly class as set apart through ordination, which is the basis of both occupational and organisational authority, women's participation remains peripheral and ultimately expendable should clergy supply problems ever be resolved (Nesbitt, 1997, p. 154).

Few readers would correctly guess in advance the author of a quotation cited, not simply because of its relevance to the subject of the ordination of women to the priesthood, but because it is a reminder of the absolute need not to forget that the Catholic Church and therefore priesthood is essentially rooted in humanity.

> Surely, our own sense of humour is, in some way, a small reflection of the great humour of God . . . As to the question of validity [of women's ordination] from a biological perspective, some men have more female than male elements in their genetic code (DNA); externally, however, they appear to be male. If, according to Vatican teaching, women cannot validly be ordained, how then do we explain the ordination of priests and bishops with genetic codes that reveal them to be more like women? . . . The moral of the story is this: when we begin with wrong premises, reasonable and sensible solutions can never be achieved. Illusory, ill-informed, and contrived arguments might best be overcome, at least in part by a good sense of humour (Häring, 1996, p. 91).

There is always the temptation to believe that arguments which lead to conclusions that we reject must be wrong. The foregoing discussion has concentrated on arguments for and against ordination of women to the priesthood. It might be worth rehearsing briefly one of the arguments concerning the ordination of women to the episcopate. It has been called the endangered succession argument.

Christians would generally agree that a central component of faith is that Jesus is both human and divine and that his incarnation has saving consequences for the whole human race. There is no doubt that Jesus was a man, not a woman, but the theological point of the incarnation is that God became a man to save all human beings both male and female. It was sharing in the common lot of humanity, not just manhood (*pace* the wording of John Henry Newman's 'Dream of Gerontius') that was crucial. To argue otherwise could lead to the implication that female humanity was not included in Christ's saving work, which is a novel Christian heresy that has, fortunately, yet to make its mark (Dowell and Williams, 1994).

The traditional debate over the ordination of women, both to the priesthood and to the episcopate, centres on the theological significance of maleness and it may be summed up as follows. Men, it is generally conceded, have occupied the offices of deacon, priest and bishop for the past nineteen hundred years, but of late the question has been raised whether maleness is theologically essential to Christian priesthood. To state this to be the case leads to what has been called an astonishingly perplexing idea that female humanity is the wrong stuff for validity in one of the sacraments. Just as in the textbook terms of yesteryear, water is the matter of baptism, not oil or wine, so the matter of priestly, and *a fortiori* episcopal ordination, is male humanity, not female (Mason, 1998). It follows from this viewpoint that the attempted ordination of a woman as a priest would cast in doubt the sacraments she ministered, but if a woman were to become a bishop, according to this argument 'the security of the whole sacramental system and its dependence on the ministry of bishops will be cast into jeopardy. Since a minister of a sacrament must mean to do what the Church does, the intention to ordain a woman or suffer a woman to act as a minister, which the Church never does, is exposed as impossible from the outset' (Mason, 1998, pp. 10–11).

Whatever one's belief in the strength of such an argument, so long as Rome stands firm in its resolve to disbar women from ordination to the priesthood, assertions by the Catholic Church of the fundamental equality of men and women fail to sound convincing, especially when it is acknowledged that there can and must be seven sacraments for men but only six for women.

That both laywomen and religious women have made inroads into non-ordained ministries and positions of responsibility closed to them before the Second Vatican Council is undeniable. The argument most used in the Catholic Church is that lack of ordination is no bar to effective ministry, but the church has a perennial tendency to undervalue ministries that are not part of the hierarchy. It should also be of no surprise that the place of women in the Catholic Church should reflect the place of women in society as a whole. In other words, the lesser value placed on women in society as a whole is precisely mirrored by the Catholic Church.

Listening to the priests

It is perhaps unsurprising in a church in which there is an official embargo on debating even the possibility of women being priests in the church, that even priests who took part in the survey indicated their understandable concurrence by making no reference to the matter of ordination of women to the priesthood in any comments they made.

Shaping the questions

Against this background, the *Catholic Parochial Clergy Survey* framed three main themes relevant to exploring the priests' attitude toward the ordination of women. The first theme examined the priests' views on the permanence of the Catholic Church's current pronouncement on the ordination of women. What proportion of priests consider that Rome's pronouncement against ordained women as priests should never change?

The second theme turned attention to the priests' attitude toward those churches that had already taken the decision to ordain women to the priesthood and how that decision might affect the relationship between those churches and the Catholic Church. For example, how many priests consider that by ordaining women Anglicans have made unity with Rome impossible?

The third theme focused on the priests' understanding of whether women could validly be ordained and distinguished between the three orders of deacon, priest and bishop. What proportion of priests believe a woman could validly be ordained deacon? What proportion of priests believe a woman could validly be ordained priest? What proportion of priests believe a woman could validly be ordained bishop?

Interpreting the statistics

Table 18.1 demonstrates that priests are quite divided over their views on the ordination of women. Two-fifths feel that Rome's pronouncement against ordained women as priests should never change, another two-fifths feel that things should change and the remaining fifth are not willing to give a view. Speaking for themselves, half the priests believe that women could validly be ordained deacon, a third believe that women could validly be ordained priest and a quarter believe that women could validly be ordained bishop.

The statistics show that two out of every five priests (39%) believed that Rome's pronouncement against ordained women as priests should never change. In this sense the decisions of the Catholic Church should be true and immutable. An equal number of priests (40%), however, took the opposite view and argued that Rome's pronouncement should change. In this sense the decisions of the Catholic Church should be flexible and open to revision in light of the guidance of the Holy Spirit and changed circumstances. The remaining 21% of priests may still be struggling to resolve this issue for themselves.

A very similar split is found in respect of the way in which the priests evaluate the implications of the Anglican Church's decision to ordain women to the priesthood. Two out of every five priests (38%) took the view that, by ordaining women, Anglicans have made unity with Rome impossible. An equal number of priests (38%), however, took the opposite view and argued that the decision to ordain women did not necessarily render unity between the Anglican Church and Rome impossible. The remaining 24% of priests may still be struggling to resolve this issue for themselves.

The priests make a clear distinction between the threefold orders of ministry and are twice as likely to welcome women as deacons than as bishops. Half of the priests (49%) believe a woman could validly be ordained deacon. The proportions then fell to a third of the priests (34%) who believe a woman would validly be ordained priest and to a quarter of the priests (25%) who believe a woman could validly be ordained bishop. These figures are mirrored closely by the proportions of priests who denied the validity of orders to women. While only 28% of the priests denied that women could validly be ordained deacon, the proportions rose to 46% of the priests who denied that women could validly be ordained priest and to 57% of the priests who denied that women could validly be ordained bishop. Around one in five of the priests (between 19% and 23%) were not willing to pass a judgement on the validity of the ordination of women to any of the three orders of bishop, priest and deacon.

Regular and secular

Table 18.2 demonstrates that there are no significant differences between the views of regular priests and secular priests on the issue of the ordination of women. Thus, 42% of the regular priests felt that Rome's pronouncement against ordained women as priests should never change, and so did 38% of the secular priests. Similarly, 42% of the regular priests believed that by ordaining women

Anglicans have made unity with Rome impossible, and so did 38% of the secular priests. The valid ordination of women as deacons was upheld by 52% of the regular priests and 48% of the secular priests. The valid ordination of women as priests was upheld by 32% of the regular priests and 35% of the secular priests. The valid ordination of women as bishops was upheld by 23% of the regular priests and 25% of the secular priests.

Generational differences

Table 18.3 demonstrates that there is much more support for the ordination of women among priests in the 45–59 age cohort than among priests aged 60 and over. Priests under the age of 45 show less support for the ordination of women than priests in the 45–59 age cohort.

While half of the priests aged 60 and over (50%) maintained that Rome's pronouncement against ordained women as priests should never change, the proportions maintaining this view dropped to 30% among the 45–59-year-olds and to 33% among those under the age of 45. Clearly there has been a marked move toward greater openness to change among the younger priests.

While nearly half of the priests aged 60 and over (47%) maintained that by ordaining women Anglicans have made unity with Rome impossible, the proportions maintaining this view dropped to 31% among the 45–59-year-olds and to 34% among those under the age of 45. Clearly there has been a marked move against seeing the ordination of women in the Anglican Church as a specific barrier to church unity.

On the issue of the validity of the ordination of women to the diaconate, there was a significant increase in the proportion of priests in favour from 43% among those aged 60 and over to 59% among those in the 45–59 age cohort. Among those under the age of 45, however, the proportion reverted to 45%. The ground won in favour of the ordination of women as deacons has been entirely lost.

On the issue of the validity of the ordination of women to the priesthood, there was a significant increase in the proportion of priests in favour from 24% among those aged 60 and over to 45% among those in the 45–59 age cohort. Among those under the age of 45, however, the proportions dropped to 35%. Half of the ground won in favour of the ordination of women as priests has been lost.

On the issue of the validity of the ordination of women to the episcopacy, there was a significant increase in the proportion of priests in favour from 14% among those aged 60 and over to 35% among those in the 45–59 age cohort. Among those under the age of 45, however, the proportion dropped back to 27%. Less than half of the ground won in favour of the ordination of women as bishops has been lost.

CHAPTER NINETEEN

Emotional Exhaustion

It became clear that emotional experiences played an important role in the provision of health care. Some of these experiences were enormously rewarding and uplifting, as when patients recovered because of the practitioner's efforts. However, other experiences were emotionally stressful for the practitioner, such as working with difficult or unpleasant patients, having to give 'bad news' to patients or their families, dealing with patient deaths or having conflicts with co-workers or supervisors. Such emotional strains were sometimes overwhelming and practitioners talked about being emotionally exhausted and drained of all feeling (Maslach, 1993, p. 22).

This chapter is concerned with the concept of *emotional exhaustion* and the extent to which clergy in the Catholic Church may be subject to or experience emotional exhaustion as a consequence of their work in ministry. In this context emotional exhaustion is explored as the first of three central defining characteristics of psychological burnout.

Context

Strictly defined, burnout should be understood as a syndrome as distinct from a disease. The word 'syndrome' describes a group of symptoms occurring together constituting a recognizable condition, whereas a disease tends to have familiar, uniform symptoms and a generally predictable treatment and outcome. Over the past twenty-five years attempts have been made to develop more precise definitions of burnout and to develop standardized measures of it. Through psychometric research, one of the best-known instruments developed to measure burnout is the Maslach Burnout Inventory (Maslach and Jackson, 1981). The Maslach Burnout Inventory consists of 22 items that are divided into the three subscales of emotional exhaustion, depersonalization and reduced personal accomplishment. The items are written in the form of personal statements about personal feelings or attitudes and are answered on a seven-point scale in terms of the frequency with which the respondent experiences them. The items on the emotional exhaustion subscale of the Maslach Burnout Inventory describe feelings of being emotionally overextended and exhausted by one's work (Maslach and Jackson, 1981, p. 7).

Burnout, far from being a new phenomenon, is a long-established human affliction that has been given a new name. The condition has been described as 'insidious' in that it does not occur as a result of one or two traumatic events, but unpredictably emerges over time through a general erosion of spirit. Burnout is said to develop in a way that is so gradual that the individual may be unaware it is happening and refuses to believe that anything is wrong (Dolan, 1987). It seems particularly to strike those working in what in the United States of America are called the caring professions, and the manner by which people are affected tends to operate along the following lines. There is an expectation that professionals are generally highly trained, compassionate, caring, competent, autonomous people, enjoying job satisfaction, working in an adequately resourced environment along-side supportive and collegial co-workers with co-operative, responsive and grateful clients. Such an attractive, idealistic perspective may be reinforced by the education of young professionals, leading to highly unrealistic expectations that all too often clash with the tedious reality of day-to-day work experience (Cherniss, 1980). Hence one definition of burnout describes it as 'a state of fatigue or frustration brought about by devotion to a cause, way of life or relationship that failed to produce the expected reward' (Freudenberger and Richelson, 1980, p. 13). Such a definition may serve to highlight the importance during seminary training of fostering realistic expectations of what is entailed by service in the priestly role.

Priesthood par excellence implies devotion to a cause that involves a way of life over and above what in fact a priest may be seen to do. Reference to priest-hood as a vocation, a calling, or a ministry-for-others, implies a personal commitment to a role. Consequently self-perceived failure in such a role is poten-tially more personally threatening than to those in jobs with no such role identification, for the precise reason that it menaces the priest's value system, self-esteem and self-image. If this is so, it makes priests, in theory at least, potentially vulnerable to burnout.

Although the burnout syndrome lacks a universally accepted definition, deple-tion of energy or exhaustion, both emotional and physical, is commonly recognized as the core of all definitions of burnout. In the context of priesthood, a progressive loss of idealism is inherent in the burnout concept. However defined, the syndrome describes the end result of a process in which highly moti-vated and committed individuals lose their spirit and lose the desire to continue in the role.

Time is another important dimension of the burnout syndrome. The evidence shows that people do not suddenly become burned out. Rather people move either toward increased professional efficacy or toward burnout as a function of their personal reaction to persistent aspects of their work environment (Leiter, 1993). The term efficacy in this context may be described as a sense of mastery that may be present in one role or situation but not necessarily in another. So a crucial distinction clarifying the difference between burnout and stress is that, while stress is characterized by over-engagement with activities, burnout is char-acterized by disengagement from activities (Hart, 1984).

At the core of Christian religious ministry lies the gospel imperative to 'Go out to the whole world; proclaim the gospel to all creation' (Matthew 16:15). It is nothing less than belief in a divine mandate to effect a profound influence on people's lives. It appears to be significant that a set of beliefs to guide one's work can be helpful in alleviating stress and burnout (Cherniss, 1993). An inherent belief in the significance of what they are doing would imply to those so engaged that, because their work is important, they themselves matter. Such a perception is at the heart of an affirmation of self. Such perception of affirmation enables people to flourish in stressful and demanding jobs so long as they retain the feeling that their work is significant and they are appreciated. According to Pines and Caspi (1993) the root cause of burnout lies in the incongruity between belief in the essential meaningfulness of our lives and the significance of our work and a failure to find that meaningfulness and significance. Work becomes more than a vehicle for self-maintenance, a provider of economic security; it becomes additionally a vehicle for self-fulfilment, particularly for those who perceive what they do as in some sense a divine calling. 'If it is true that people who choose this path are trying to derive from their work a sense of meaning for their entire existence, a belief that they have failed may lead to burnout' (Pines, 1993b, p. 391).

Awareness of what this means with regard to exercising priestly ministry seems to entail the adoption of a view both that the role of a priest inherently involves caring and commitment and that the person in the role is warm, empathetic and accepting. Failure adequately to identify oneself as a warm empathetic carer can lead to disengagement from the activity that brings this sense of 'failure' to the surface, a form of psychological escape intended to reduce the distress already experienced. Because commitment and idealism are so central to priestly ministry, loss of enthusiasm, optimism and involvement reinforces withdrawal in an ever-increasing downward spiral.

The notion of 'psychological success' is a useful one in the context of what effect emotional exhaustion can have on priestly ministry. Psychological success is the term used to describe a person's feelings of success, rather than success objectively measured. It is encapsulated in the current ethos associated with running a city marathon. Running in one of these marathons is probably the last competitive sport, in the original spirit of the modern Olympiad revived in 1894 by Baron de Coubertin, in which mere taking part rather than coming first, still holds as being equally important for all the participants. Psychological success says that all marathon runners are winners. Lack of such psychological success in the context of professional work would incline a person to withdraw from those areas of endeavour where failure is experienced.

Psychological escape is a major characteristic associated with burnout. In the opinion of Hobfoll and Freedy (1993), Cherniss (1980) saw burnout as a response to stress. His developmental model of burnout suggested that burnout is the last stage of a failed coping process whose final stage is seen as a defensive posture meant to halt more precipitous effects of stress. The so-named 'sacristy priest' might be an example of this. Excessively shy, only reluctantly engaging with parishioners, such a priest might prefer to keep his distance from unpredictable, discouraging people-work and concentrate instead upon activities in which appreciation is received or satisfaction gained from involvement in the environment of the sacred space of church-based liturgical service that involves less immediate contact with disagreeable humanity.

The higher the regard in which the priest is held within a given community and the better this is communicated to the priest himself, the more this will contribute to warding off burnout, as social status appears to be a notable environmental factor affecting self-efficacy (Bandura, 1982). Left to their own resources, however, priests are often found to be very bad at caring for their own psychological health, as suggested by Coate in her book on *Clergy Stress*.

> Ministers of religion are notoriously bad at caring for themselves in their response to a 'received' dictum of total availability and a merging of personal and professional such as would not be tolerated by many other people ... Blurring the boundaries between work and personal life may be a way of staving off loneliness in terms of time and can make sense of personal worthlessness and emptiness. 'If I stay in the role, people will want me; they might not just for myself', goes the inner, often unacknowledged dialogue (Coate, 1989, pp. 94–5).

Shaping the questions

Against this background, the *Catholic Parochial Clergy Survey* wanted to include a set of questions designed to explore emotional exhaustion among the clergy. Copyright reasons would have made it difficult to include items from the Maslach Burnout Inventory itself. Moreover, many items in the published test, designed as they were for use among the caring professionals in general in the United States of America, did not transfer easily to the environment of parochial ministry in England and Wales. Five items were, therefore, framed to gauge emotional exhaustion within the specific context of parish ministry.

The first item focused on the notion of burnout itself in order to determine the extent to which priests would find that word provided an appropriate description of their personal experience. What proportion of priests would actually say that they feel burned out from their parish ministry?

The second item focused on the notion of fatigue and recognized that emotional exhaustion is expressed through overwhelming feelings of fatigue at having to get up to face another day. What proportion of priests would admit to feeling fatigued when they get up in the morning and have to face another day in the parish?

The third item focused on the notion of being emotionally drained by ministry and explores the extent to which priests actually speak of being emotionally drained. What proportion of priests would admit to feeling emotionally drained from their parish ministry?

The fourth item recognized that a clear sign of emotional exhaustion is found in higher levels of frustration. Those who are experiencing emotional exhaustion may find that more aspects of their ministry cause them frustration. What proportion of priests would admit to feeling frustrated by their parish ministry?

The fifth item recognized that a second clear sign of emotional exhaustion is found in the depletion of energy levels. Those who are experiencing emotional exhaustion go to bed drained at the end of the day. What proportion of priests would admit to feeling used up at the end of the day?

Interpreting the statistics

Table 19.1 demonstrates that, by their own self-definition, three out of every twenty priests feel burned out from their parish ministry. While not saying that they feel burned out, just over a third of the priests generally go to bed feeling used up and exhausted at the end of the day in parish ministry.

The fact that three out of every twenty priests (14%) have actually described themselves as suffering from burnout by saying that they felt burned out from their parish ministry might seem to indicate an unacceptable level of emotional exhaustion among a group of men whose vocation it is to extend God's care to others. The fact that another three out of every twenty priests (16%) checked the uncertain response and did not feel confident enough in themselves to deny that they felt burned out from their parish ministry could be interpreted to suggest that burnout affects not three in twenty priests (14%), but three in every ten priests (30%). What is clear is that just 70% of the priests said that this statement did not apply to them and that they did not feel burned out from their parish ministry.

The feeling of fatigue was also very real to three out of every twenty priests (16%) who said that they felt fatigued when they get up in the morning and have to face another day in the parish. When the uncertain responses were added in as well, the proportion rose to 27% who did not deny that they were familiar with the feeling of fatigue when they get up in the morning.

The proportion of priests who actually said that they felt emotionally drained from their parish ministry rose to four in every twenty (19%). When the uncertain responses were added in as well, the proportion rose to 33% who did not deny that they were familiar with the feeling of being emotionally drained from their parish ministry.

Frustration was slightly more widespread than fatigue, with a quarter of the priests (23%) actually saying that they felt frustrated in their parish ministry. When the uncertain responses were added in as well, the proportion rose to 34% who did not deny that they were frustrated by their parish ministry.

Just under half the priests (47%) said that they go to bed not feeling used up at the end of the day in parish ministry. As many as 36% openly admitted that this is their general experience, while another 17% could not really deny it. If going to bed feeling used up at the end of the day in parish ministry really is a sign of emotional exhaustion, then the psychological health of the Catholic parochial clergy may well be worth closer investigation and deserve greater pastoral care.

Regular and secular

Table 19.2 demonstrates that there are some ways in which the secular priests report higher levels of emotional exhaustion than is the case among the regular priests. On the one hand, the same proportions of both groups of priests described themselves as feeling burned out from their parish ministry (14%). The same proportions of both groups of priests described themselves as feeling fatigued when they get up in the morning and have to face another day in the parish (16%).

There was no significant difference between the proportions of the regular priests (16%) and the secular priests (20%) who reported that they felt emotionally drained from their parish ministry.

On the other hand, the secular priests were more likely than the regular priests to feel frustrated by their parish ministry and to feel used up at the end of the day. While 16% of the regular priests reported that they felt frustrated by their parish ministry, the proportion rose to 24% among the secular priests. While 30% of the regular priests reported that they felt used up at the end of the day in parish ministry, the proportion rose to 38% among the secular priests.

Generational differences

Table 19.3 demonstrates that emotional exhaustion is highest among the priests under the age of 45 and lowest among the priests aged 60 and over.

The clearest indicator regarding this age trend in emotional exhaustion is provided by the two items concerning frustration and being emotionally drained. While just 12% of the priests aged 60 and over felt frustrated by their parish ministry, the proportions rose to 27% among those aged between 45 and 59 and to 34% among those aged under 45. While just 14% of the priests aged 60 and over felt emotionally drained from their parish ministry, the proportions rose to 20% among those aged between 45 and 59 and to 26% among those aged under 45.

In respect of two other items, those aged under 45 and those in the 45–59 year age group reported responses that were very similar to each other but were significantly different from the responses of those aged 60 and over. While 32% of the priests aged 60 and over felt used up at the end of the day in parish ministry, the proportions rose to 39% among the 45–59-year-olds and to 40% among those under the age of 45. While 11% of the priests aged 60 and over felt burned out from their parish ministry, the proportions rose to 17% among the 45–59-year-olds and to 15% among those under the age of 45.

The final item in this set revealed a similar age trend, although this did not reach statistical significance. The feeling of fatigue when they get up in the morning and have to face another day was reported by 14% of priests aged 60 and over, by 16% of priests aged between 45 and 59, and by 19% of priests under the age of 45.

The finding that higher levels of emotional exhaustion are experienced by younger priests is not entirely surprising. There are two reasons which may account for lower levels of emotional exhaustion among the older priests. First, it needs to be remembered that the data are derived from priests actively engaged in parochial ministry. Older priests who were suffering from higher levels of burnout may already have exited from parochial ministry, leaving their fitter colleagues still serving the parishes. Second, those who have survived parochial ministry for a number of years are likely to have developed the coping mechanisms to deal with problems like emotional exhaustion.

CHAPTER TWENTY

Depersonalization

When the individual has no belief in his own act and no ultimate concern with the beliefs of his audience, we may call him cynical, reserving the term 'sincere' for individuals who believe in the impression fostered by their own performance. It should be understood that the cynic, with all his professional disinvolvement, may obtain unprofessional pleasures from his masquerade, experiencing a kind of spiritual aggression from the fact that he can toy at will with something his audience must take seriously (Goffman, 1990, pp. 28–9).

This chapter is concerned with the concept of *depersonalization* and the extent to which clergy in the Catholic Church may be subject to or experience depersonalization as a consequence of their work in ministry. In this context depersonalization is explored as the second of three central defining characteristics of psychological burnout. The broader notion of psychological burnout itself is distinguished from the related but distinct notion of stress.

Context

In the context of life looked at as a performance, whether dramatic or mundane, Goffman is describing the consequence of a failure to believe in the part one is playing. Though referring to a somewhat different concept, the Goffman quotation contains elements illustrating the burnout characteristic known as depersonalization. Depersonalization occurs when professional people begin to treat those among whom they work as impersonal objects, devoid of proper feeling and unworthy of proper respect.

Depersonalization was identified by Maslach and Jackson (1981) as one of the three defining characteristics of psychological burnout, alongside emotional exhaustion and reduced personal accomplishment. The basic conceptual framework on which this model of burnout is based concerns the fragmentation of the social relationship between provider and recipient, which is most clearly observed among individuals who do 'people work of some kind' (Maslach, 1982). Of course, the work of priests falls into this category. Burnout appears, then, to be a defensive coping strategy leading to psychological detachment from job stress (Cherniss, 1980). Depersonalization is core to this defensive coping strategy employed by the caring professionals who need, under pressures of burnout, to keep the people for whom they are supposed to care at a safe emotional distance. The items on the depersonalization subscale of the Maslach Burnout Inventory describe an unfeeling and impersonal response toward the individuals in one's care.

Burnout is said to occur when demands are made over time in a way that tax individuals without proper rewards or resources for addressing demands (Hobfoll and Freedy, 1993). Emergency medical teams, police officers and fire fighters have on occasion to function calmly and efficiently in situations characterized by crisis, danger and chaos. The notion of 'detached concern' (Lief and Fox, 1963) refers to the medical ideal of combining compassion with emotional distance from the object of one's professional concern. The aim is one of detached objectivity. An allied concept is that of dehumanization of the recipient of one's service in self-defence (Zimbardo, 1970). This is the process by which emotional or sympathetic feelings are not allowed to interfere with the provision of appropriate practical care by responding to people more as objects than as persons. Both of these concepts assisted Christina Maslach in conceptualizing the depersonalization component of the burnout syndrome.

Attainment of an appropriate level of detached concern, a distancing and detachment from sources of emotional strain proves impossible for some priests, and over time perceptions and feelings about parishioners, in extreme cases, turns into dislike and despisal. Such depersonalization 'refers to a negative, callous or excessively detached response to other people who are usually the recipients of one's services or care' (Maslach, 1993, p. 21). The depersonalization component of burnout emphasizes the effect of how a particular individual relates to other individuals whereas the component called 'reduced personal accomplishment' refers to the effect that burnout has upon the efforts of that individual herself or himself.

Collectively, priests might be regarded as sharing in the motivation to do those things for others that create a difference in people's lives. Such behaviour has been given the name 'dedicatory ethic'. Yet at one time or another all professionals have negative feelings about those with whom they deal, whether they are referred to as clients, parishioners or patients. Clergy are not immune from feelings of antipathy toward some of those whom they are called to serve. Most priests will admit to having harboured feelings from time to time that the parish would be fine if it were not for one, most, or even all of the parishioners. It is the frequency and magnitude of such negative feelings that are the crucial element in burnout.

Clergy, however, because of their espousal of the dedicatory ethic, are more likely to blame themselves when things go wrong by assuming personal short-comings than to suggest, for instance, a flaw in the organization; the priest is the problem rather than the parish or the Church (Baum, 1975). Because the organization has effectively been divinized, since after all the Church is the body of Christ, the fault must obviously lie with the individual, not with the Church, or so the argument goes. This phenomenon reflects the notion of 'structured punishment', defined by Lauer (1973, p. 189) as 'punitive relations that are "built into" a particular organisation, that inhere in the structure of that organisation'. The notion of structured punishment can assist in an understanding of concepts underlying the depersonalization component of burnout.

Priestly ministry is demanding, among other things, of compassion, sympathy and pity. It entails carrying out tasks such as giving bad news, attending the dying, conducting funerals and public speaking, which for the average person are situations generally perceived as frightening, distasteful and where possible to be avoided. Priests are expected to keep going, however inequitable the structures in which they work. The underlying assumption is that the dedicatory ethic must never be contradicted; that priests are not supposed to be affected by lack of equity. If they show themselves to be, the fault is theirs, not that of the structures. Structured punishment, therefore, becomes a painful reality in the absence of equitable reward.

Some recognition, some perception of reward in exchange for the care and concern shown is not a supplementary bonus demanded by weakling priests over and above the assured promise of heavenly reward. It is a psychological necessity in normal human interchange. It was Mark Twain who is first reported to have said, 'I can live for a month on a compliment.' That is not to say that on occasion, or even regularly, altruistic behaviour is not possible, but it is equally normal ordinarily to expect some rewarding exchange, a thank you, for our efforts. Over familiarity with the scriptures might give priests the impression that Jesus, like an actor, was speaking a given text when he asked, 'Were not all ten made clean? The other nine, where are they?' (Luke 17:11–19). It has to be that Jesus is giving expression to a profoundly felt human disappointment at the failure of the nine to respond to the gift of healing God had given to them through him. 'We believe that social exchange theory can provide a useful conceptual framework to understand the dynamics of this particular social relationship that is critical for the development of burnout' (Buunk and Schaufeli, 1993, p. 68).

Brockman (1978) drew attention to what he called the perils of a false conscience, and asserted that the religious leader must place realistic limits on the time it is possible to devote to ministry. The notion of exhausting oneself in God's work, though little heard of today, has not entirely disappeared. It persists in the potentially dangerous myth that the Pope cannot retire and that diocesan priests work a regular eighteen-hour day. As in any other walk of life, human endurance finally dictates that common sense prevails. It would appear essential during seminary training to emphasize a realistic awareness of what an individual priest is capable of providing, and in parishes of fostering realistic expectations in parishioners of what may reasonably be provided by priests.

Further clarification regarding this notion of psychological burnout can be provided by contrasting burnout with stress. While burnout is always regarded as a negative and damaging phenomenon, stress, in the wider psychological usage of the term, can be regarded as either positive or negative, depending on its practical implications. In one sense, stress appears to be both unavoidable and normal. There seem to be optimal levels or states of stimulation at which human beings best function. In other words, a certain level of stress seems necessary in order to function well.

In the main, people are not aware of the stress they initially felt when faced with what they do for a living. Theatre actors, dancers, musicians, sportsmen and sportswomen, and all those whose occupation includes an element of personal performance, have frequently alluded to the presence of a level of stress, 'butter-flies', which enervates them before a performance. If asked, most people could effortlessly walk along the length of a twelve-inch wide plank laid along the ground. Securely suspend the plank fifty feet above the ground and the same assignment turns legs to jelly and becomes for most a terrifying, near impossible challenge. In this instance too much stress leads to physical incoherence. With-drawal of sensory stimulation as in noiseless, lightless confinement or deprivation of social stimuli, is equally capable of leading to the fragmentation of thought process. Too little sensory stimulation often leads to mental incoherence. The effects of the stress suffered by an individual who had been 'sent to Coventry', though not necessarily conceptually known for the same length of time, have been broadly understood universally for centuries.

It is a modern anthropological assumption that those reactions of mind and body made in response to excessive demands of any kind are residual behaviour from an evolutionary heritage where such a mobilization of resources, exempli-fied in the so-called 'fight or flight response', was essential for survival in a world in which external dangers were more frequent but more difficult to anticipate or prepare for. In the twenty-first century bodily defence is mobilized by most people in response to psychological rather than physical danger. We are unlikely nowadays to be stalked by a lion but few of us feel wholly free of pursuit by nameless demons. In short, psychological stress has much to do with cognitive appraisal, with the individual's perception of a situation and how its distressing features might be reduced or avoided and its anxieties anticipated. Modern life, it seems, tricks the body into believing there is a constant crisis, with the result that an excessive amount of adrenaline is produced to cope with this persistent illusion.

Stress as disease or distress occurs when the internal responses to a stressful situation are unsuccessful or are over-prolonged, so that instead of being dis-charged in removal of the stressor, they recoil upon the body they were originally designed to protect.

> A potential for stress exists when an environmental situation is perceived as presenting a demand which threatens to exceed a person's capabilities and resources for meeting it under conditions where he expects a substantial dif-ferential in the rewards and costs from meeting the demand and not meeting it (McGrath, 1976, p. 1352).

Priests enjoy immunity from few, if any, of those tensions and pressures that afflict other normal human beings at work and at home. Though excessive stress as such cannot be said to cause burnout, for people are able to flourish in stress-ful and demanding jobs, burnout appears to result in some individuals from particular stressful demands that arise in circumstances involving interaction with people (Pines, 1993a).

Shaping the questions

Against this background, the *Catholic Parochial Clergy Survey* wanted to include a set of questions designed to explore depersonalization among the clergy. Once again, copyright reasons would have made it difficult to include items from the Maslach Burnout Inventory itself, while the origin of the instrument in the United States of America for use among caring professionals in general meant that the items did not transfer easily to the environment of parochial ministry in England and Wales. Five items were, therefore, framed to gauge depersonalization within the specific context of parish ministry.

One of the first signs of the tendency toward depersonalization is a growing loss of patience with people. Priests who once seemed to possess inexhaustible supplies of patience now begin to find themselves losing patience with people more readily. What proportion of priests recognize in themselves a tendency to be less patient with parishioners than they used to be?

A second early sign of the tendency toward depersonalization is a growing difficulty in listening to what others are trying to say. Priests who used to try to listen carefully to others now begin to find that proper listening takes time and energy that they cannot really afford. What proportion of priests recognize in themselves a tendency to find it difficult to listen to what some parishioners are really saying to them?

At a more advanced stage depersonalization is reflected in a tendency to become callous toward others. Priests who used to be able to project an image of being soft-hearted, now begin to find themselves projecting a much more hard-hearted image. What proportion of priests recognize in themselves a tendency to have become more callous toward people since working in parish ministry?

Callousness goes hand in hand with ceasing to really care what happens to people. Priests who used to take pastoral problems to heart and really care about the outcomes of their interactions in other people's lives now begin to find themselves not really caring how those pastoral problems get resolved. What proportion of priests recognize in themselves a tendency no longer to really care what happens to some parishioners?

Depersonalization at its worst wants simply to give up on people and to be left alone. Priests who began with an idealism determined to work alongside others now begin to sigh each time they are approached in the street or after a service. They simply want people to go away. What proportion of priests recognize in themselves a tendency to wish that parishioners would leave them alone?

Interpreting the statistics

Table 20.1 demonstrates that one out of every four priests admit to the first signs of depersonalization beginning to affect their ministry, while at least one in every ten have reached a more advanced stage of experiencing depersonalization.

Indications of the early signs of depersonalization are provided by the proportions of priests who find their patience wearing thin and who find it difficult to listen to people. A quarter of the priests (27%) readily admitted to the fact that they were less patient with parishioners than they used to be and a further 12% were not confident that they could deny this. In other words, just 61% of the priests were confident that their level of patience had continued to hold firm, leaving two out of every five (39%) who were at least aware of the possibility of danger signals in this area.

Similarly, a quarter of the priests (26%) readily admitted to the fact that they find it difficult to listen to what some parishioners are really saying to them, and a further 15% were not confident that they could deny this. In other words, just 58% of the priests were confident that they did not find it difficult to listen to what some parishioners were really saying to them.

Indications of the more advanced signs of depersonalization are provided by the proportions of priests who admit to becoming more callous, who do not really care what happens to some parishioners, and who really wish that parishioners would just leave them alone. About one in every ten priests fall unequivocally into this category as indicated by the following statistics, although the proportion might more realistically be approaching one in every five. For example, one in every ten priests (9%) readily admitted to the fact that they have become more callous toward people since working in parish ministry, but an additional 10% were not willing to deny that this was the case. Thus, only four out of every five priests (81%) felt completely free from this first sure indicator of depersonalization.

Similarly, one in every ten priests (11%) readily admitted that they do not really care about what happened to some parishioners, but an additional 9% were not willing to deny that this was the case. Thus, only four out of every five priests (80%) felt completely free from this second sure indicator of depersonalization.

At the same time, one in every thirteen priests (7%) readily admitted that they wished parishioners would leave them alone, but an additional 10% were not willing to deny that this was the case. Thus, only four out of every five priests (83%) felt completely free from this third sure indicator of depersonalization.

Regular and secular

Table 20.2 demonstrates that there are some ways in which secular priests report higher levels of depersonalization than is the case among regular priests. On the one hand, the same proportions of both groups of priests described themselves as not really caring what happens to some parishioners (11%). There was no significant differences between the proportions of the regular priests (25%) and the secular priests (27%) who found it difficult to listen to what some parishioners are really saying to them. Similarly, there was no significant difference between the proportions of the regular priests (6%) and the secular priests (7%) who wished that parishioners would leave them alone.

On the other hand, the secular priests were more likely than the regular priests to recognize within themselves tendencies to be less patient and more callous to others. While 22% of the regular priests admitted to being less patient with parishioners than they used to be, the proportion rose to 28% among the secular priests. While 6% of the regular priests admitted to having become more callous toward people since working in parish ministry, the proportion rose to 10% among the secular priests.

Generational differences

Table 20.3 demonstrates that depersonalization is highest among priests under the age of 45 and lowest among priests aged 60 and over.

The clearest indicator regarding their age trend in depersonalization is provided by the two items concerned with callousness and with not really caring what happens to some parishioners. While just 5% of priests aged 60 and over felt that they had become more callous toward people since working in parish ministry, the proportions rose to 11% among those aged between 45 and 59, and to 14% among those under 45. While 9% of priests aged 60 and over felt that they did not really care what happens to some parishioners, the proportions rose to 11% among those aged between 45 and 59, and to 16% among those aged under 45.

In respect of two other items, those under the age of 45 and those in the 45–59 year age group reported responses which were quite similar, but were significantly different from the responses of those aged 60 and over. While 23% of priests aged 60 and over admitted that they find it difficult to listen to what some parishioners are really saying to them, the proportions rose to 30% among the 45–59 age group and then dropped to 26% among those under the age of 45. While 22% of priests aged 60 and over admitted that they were less patient with parishioners than they used to be, the proportions rose to 31% among those aged between 45 and 59 and then dropped slightly to 29% among those under the age of 45.

The final item in the set revealed a similar age trend, although this did not reach statistical significance. The desire that parishioners would leave them alone was reported by 6% of priests over the age of 60, 7% of priests between the ages of 45 and 59, and 10% of priests under the age of 45.

The finding that higher levels of depersonalization are expressed by younger priests is totally consistent with the findings of the previous chapter that higher levels of emotional exhaustion were also reported by younger priests. The two explanations offered in the previous chapter are also relevant here to account for the finding that lower levels of depersonalization are reported among the older cohort of parochial clergy. First, older priests who were suffering from higher levels of burnout may already have exited from parochial ministry, leaving their fitter colleagues still serving the parishes. Second, those who have survived parochial ministry for a number of years are likely to have developed the effective coping mechanisms necessary to deal with problems like depersonalization.

CHAPTER TWENTY-ONE

Personal Accomplishment

In arguing, too, the parson owned his skill
For even though vanquished he could argue still
While words of learned length and thundering sound
Amazed the gazing rustics ranged around.
And still they gazed and still their wonder grew
How one small head could carry all he knew.
But past is all his fame. The very spot
Where many a time he triumphed, is forgot.
(Oliver Goldsmith, 'The Deserted Village')

This chapter is concerned with the concept of *reduced personal accomplishment* and the extent to which clergy in the Catholic Church may be subject to or experience an absence of personal accomplishment in their ministry. In this context reduced personal accomplishment is explored as the third of three central defining characteristics of psychological burnout.

Context

In 'The Deserted Village' by Oliver Goldsmith (1728–74), the village schoolmaster exemplifies the extreme difficulty of experienced professionals to admit to feelings of inadequacy, a phenomenon analysed less concisely but with more precision more than two centuries later by Cherniss (1993). In the three-component model of burnout developed by Maslach and Jackson (1981), the psychological syndrome has been characterized as involving emotional exhaustion, depersonalization and reduced personal accomplishment. The last component, reduced personal accomplishment, as stated in the previous chapter, refers to the effect that burnout has upon the efforts of that individual himself or herself. It represents a decline in one's feelings of competence and successful achievement in one's work.

This three-component model of burnout comprises two indices of negative affect (emotional exhaustion and depersonalization) and one index of positive affect (personal accomplishment). In order to function as an index of psychological pathology the index of positive affect, personal accomplishment, has to be reverse coded so that it becomes in effect a measure of reduced personal accomplishment. In other words, those who record high scores on this index reveal *low* levels of personal accomplishment. Nevertheless, the psychological dynamics remain between the tensions of positive affect and negative affect. Psychological burnout is associated with *high* levels of negative affect (emotional exhaustion and depersonalization) and *low* levels of positive affect (personal accomplishment).

It was Bradburn's (1969) classic study on psychological well-being as 'balanced-affect' which clearly established the view that positive affect and negative affect are not simply the opposite ends of one continuum. In fact the two domains can often function independently. For example, high levels of negative work-related affect (depersonalization and emotional exhaustion) can be found going hand-in-hand with high levels of positive work-related affect (job satisfaction). At one and the same time, clergy may feel emotionally exhausted from their work and nonetheless benefit from the sense that they are achieving a great deal of good in their ministry. According to this three-component model of burnout, the real danger comes when high levels of negative affect are coupled with low levels of positive affect, when priests who experience high levels of emotional exhaustion and high levels of depersonalization *also* experience low levels of personal accomplishment.

Achievement of a sense of competence in their work, noted Cherniss (1993), was a particularly important concern among new professionals. It appears that when young social workers, doctors and the like were confronted by clients who were resistant to their efforts to assist, or who did not improve, the distress experienced by the professionals seemed to arise primarily because these client behaviours prevented them from feeling competent and successful. 'All too often, the experience of emotional turmoil was interpreted as a failure to "be professional" (non-emotional, cool, objective) and led people to question their ability to work in a health career. Many practitioners felt that their formal training had not prepared them for the emotional reality of their work and its subsequent impact on their personal functioning' (Maslach, 1993, p. 23).

The question arises whether priests who are increasingly confronted by religious, ethical, and moral versions of resistant client behaviours, for example, in the form of religious or moral indifference or in the form of lapsation by parishioners, are thereby deprived of feelings of competence or success and in a similar way suffer feelings of incompetence or failure. Something of this malaise is described in the 1988 document *Reflections on the Morale of Priests*, published in the United States of America by the Committee on Priestly Life and Ministry of the National Conference of Catholic bishops.

Among some priests there are a significant number who have settled for a part-time presence to their priesthood. Many feel they have worked hard and long to implement, or at least adjust to, the practical consequences of Vatican II. They sense that much of that effort is now being blunted or even betrayed and they elect to drop out quietly. This is particularly true of those in the 45 to 60 age group who are willing to go through the necessary minimum of motions but whose hearts and energies are elsewhere. Many more of our priests believed in renewal, were willing to adapt, worked hard and now are just plain tired (Cozzens, 2000, pp. 17–18).

Some readers might understandably bridle at what may be construed as an over-simplistic analysis that attempts to reduce priestly ministry to a commercial transaction, as if some simple numerical yardstick can measure success and failure in religious ministry. It is readily acknowledged that success in a religious context is notoriously difficult to gauge, as may be understood had any of Jesus' disciples been asked immediately following the crucifixion about their leader's success. Nonetheless, few would deny the importance of trying to determine whether this or that course of action leads to the building up or breaking down of the Christian community. To that extent, therefore, some attempt to appraise whether one practice rather than another is more successful in achieving a desired objective appears to be legitimate, if only on the principle that some theory is better than no theory.

In a notable Australian study, Gross (1989) discovered that pastors on the road to burnout appeared to feel badly about themselves unless they were achieving certain 'ideal' results. Although subscribing to the view that an individual's worth is not dependent upon his ability or efficiency, 'pastors of all persuasions appear as ready as others to assume that "success" in their lives depends upon the achievement of visible results and that their self worth is conditional upon such "success"' (Gross, 1989, p. 29). However defined, notions of success and failure in one's work are quite natural self-evaluations. Perceptions of reduced personal accomplishment reflect a dimension of self-evaluation that is closely related to a negative self-image (Schaufeli and Van Dierendonck, 1993). Reduced personal accomplishment can weaken one's ambition and motivation to do well, one's ability to cope with anxiety, even raising the level of anxiety when faced with a problem (Gentry, Foster and Froehling, 1972) as well as raising an individual's level of neuroticism (Noworol, Zarczynski, Fafrowicz and Marek, 1993).

The term 'cognitive dissonance' describes a situation where there is a discrepancy between cognition and behaviour, between what a person thinks and how a person behaves. Dissonance is a state that when aroused elicits actions designed to return a person to a state of equilibrium. In other words when a person is in a state of cognitive dissonance, an attempt is made to harmonize discordant perceptions, to rationalize inconsistent behaviour. Personal accomplishment is related to a tolerance of cognitive dissonance in that lower personal accomplishment causes lower tolerance for discrepancies. Thus the person with low tolerance of cognitive dissonance will have more difficulties in handling the conflicting demands of different job roles (Lazarus and Folkman, 1984). Roles commonly falling to the priest are celebrant of the sacraments, evangelist, preacher, visitor to the sick and housebound, moderator, problem solver, financial manager, youth worker and school governor. Role conflict occurs in the gap between expectation and reality, often arising as a consequence of parishioners' expectations of the priest.

'It is through a free decision that individuals have joined the community of faith and remain in it' (Küng, 1972, p. 31). In contemporary society the church is a voluntary associational organization, one of the many forms of organized leisure. It is more and more a community of the like-minded, choosing to associate, not by coercion, as was for long the case, but out of shared conviction about a transcendental belief system. In the developed countries, status and prestige generally go to those whose skill and expertise is considered socially useful and valuable. In first world countries the priest as a representative of his church has increasingly become a marginalized figure with an expertise in matters that appear to concern the average citizen less and less. What is worse, many older priests are left bemused at having to accept the current orthodoxy that much of their work, until so recently and categorically asserted to be uniquely priestly, had not been so at all. It is little wonder, therefore, if priests are led to experience something of the marginality of their role and are left wondering at times what precisely it is that they are uniquely expected to accomplish within it. Lack of certainty regarding the objectives of the role necessarily leads to a lack in the sense of personal accomplishment that would be derived from fulfilling those objectives.

Shaping the questions

Against this background, the *Catholic Parochial Clergy Survey* wanted to include a set of questions designed to explore the positive affect associated with the sense of personal accomplishment among the clergy. Once again, copyright reasons would have made it difficult to include items from the Maslach Burnout Inventory itself, while the origin of the instrument in the United States of America for use among caring professionals in general meant that the items did not transfer easily to the environment of parochial ministry in England and Wales. Five items were, therefore, framed to gauge personal accomplishment within the specific context of parish ministry.

One of the most visible characteristics of parochial ministry, as distinguishable from other forms of ministry, concerns the emphasis on working with people. Parochial ministry is defined by its relationship to parishioners. A clear indicator of personal accomplishment, therefore, in parochial ministry comes from the level of satisfaction derived from working with people. What proportion of priests feel that they actually gain a lot of personal satisfaction from working with people?

There are, of course, a number of specific ways in which this overall sense of satisfaction in working with people can be experienced and expressed. The survey identified three specific markers, relating to the sense of having a positive influence on people, to the sense of understanding how people feel, and to the sense of dealing well with the problems people present. What proportion of priests feel that they are positively influencing other people's lives through their parish ministry? What proportion of priests feel that they can easily understand how their parishioners feel about things? What proportion of priests feel that they deal very effectively with the problems of their parishioners? Positive responses to such questions are indicative of personal accomplishment.

A different approach to assessing personal accomplishment is achieved by taking a broader view of parish ministry in general and by asking about the priests' overall sense of how things have gone for them in their parish ministry. What proportion of priests feel that they have accomplished many worthwhile things in their parish ministry?

Interpreting the statistics

Table 21.1 demonstrates that the majority of priests feel very positive about their experience of parish ministry. Nine out of every ten continue to gain a lot of satisfaction from working with people and only a handful feel that they have not accomplished many worthwhile things in their parish ministry.

Only 3% of priests were clear that they do not gain a lot of personal satisfaction from working with people, while an additional 6% were possibly tempted to take that position as well. This means that 91% positively endorsed the sentiment that they gain a lot of personal satisfaction from working with people.

Only 4% of priests were clear that they were not positively influencing other people's lives through their parish ministry, although an additional 25% were not so clear about what they were actually achieving in this area. Nonetheless, this still means that 71% endorsed the sentiment that they were positively influencing other people's lives through their parish ministry.

Only 7% of priests were clear that they could not easily understand how their parishioners felt about things, although an additional 33% were not so clear about how easily they really understood what was going on in their parishioners' lives. Nevertheless, this still means that 60% positively endorsed the sentiment that they could easily understand how their parishioners felt about things.

Only 9% of priests were clear that they do not deal very effectively with the problems of their parishioners, although an additional 59% were not so clear about how to evaluate the effectiveness of this aspect of their ministry. This left one in three of the priests (32%) who felt that they deal very effectively with the problems of their parishioners.

Taking a different perspective on the overall assessment of levels of personal accomplishment, three-quarters of the priests (75%) felt that they had accomplished many worthwhile things in their parish ministry, compared with just 4% who felt that they had accomplished little that was worthwhile and 21% who appeared to feel ambivalent about what they had accomplished in their parish ministry.

Regular and secular

Table 21.2 demonstrates that there are few significant differences between the levels of personal accomplishment in ministry reported by regular priests and by secular priests. For example, the same high proportions of both groups of priests reported that they gain a lot of personal satisfaction from working with people (91%). Similar proportions of both groups felt that they have accomplished many worthwhile things in their ministry (72% among the regular priests and 76% among the secular priests). Similar proportions of both groups felt that they can easily understand how their parishioners feel about things (58% of the regular priests and 60% of the secular priests). Similar proportions of both groups felt that they deal very effectively with the problems of their parishioners (33% of the regular priests and 31% of the secular priests).

On the other hand, the regular priests rated significantly higher on their positive influence on people's lives. Thus, 76% of the regular priests felt that they were positively influencing other people's lives, compared with 70% of the secular priests.

Generational differences

Table 21.3 demonstrates that, in some ways although not in all, priests aged 60 and over are likely to record a lower level of personal accomplishment in their parish ministry. A more nuanced interpretation of the statistics suggests that, while retaining a sense of personal satisfaction from their ministry, the older priests feel that they are achieving less.

The proportion of priests who felt that they gained a lot of personal satisfaction from working with people remained high across the three age cohorts, fluctuating only between 90% and 91%. Priests aged 60 and over retained the same sense of personal satisfaction from working with people as their younger colleagues. On the other hand, looking back over the span of their whole ministry to date, the older priests were less likely than their younger colleagues to appraise highly their overall achievements in parish ministry. While 77% of the priests under the age of 45 and 78% of the priests aged between 45 and 59 felt that they had accomplished many worthwhile things in their parish ministry, the proportion fell to 71% among the priests aged 60 and over. It is likely that a lower sense of personal accomplishment in the recent past, as a consequence of the ageing process, has coloured their perception of accomplishments earlier in their ministry.

Two of the other items suggest that the highest levels of personal accomplishment are to be found among the youngest cohort of priests, those under the age of 45. For example, 37% of the priests under the age of 45 felt that they deal very effectively with the problems of their parishioners, compared with 32% of the priests aged between 45 and 59 and 29% of the priests aged 60 and over. Similarly, 76% of the priests under the age of 45 felt that they were positively influencing other people's lives through their parish ministry, compared with 71% of the priests aged between 45 and 59 and 68% of the priests aged 60 and over.

The remaining item in the set provides an anomalous finding which shows the priests in the 45–59 age group least confident in their powers of empathy. While 63% of the priests under the age of 45 and 63% of the priests aged 60 and over reported that they can easily understand how their parishioners felt about things, the proportion dropped to 54% of the priests in the 45–59 age group.

The overall finding that the lowest overall levels of personal accomplishment were recorded by the priests aged 60 and over must be placed alongside the findings of the previous two chapters which reported that priests aged 60 and over also recorded the lowest levels of emotional exhaustion and the lowest levels of depersonalization. Two comments need to be made on the juxtaposition of these findings.

First, the findings fully accord with the theory that positive affect (personal accomplishment) and negative affect (emotional exhaustion and depersonalization) are not simply opposite ends of the same continuum. The older priests are able to display both lower emotional exhaustion and lower depersonalizations (both signs of lower vulnerability to burnout) *and* lower personal accomplishment (a sign of higher vulnerability to burnout).

Second, the lower sense of personal accomplishment recorded by the priests aged 60 and over accords with the view that, as age erodes energy levels, the demands of parochial ministry became that much harder to meet. The older priests may well be working harder than ever to keep the parish structures in good shape and yet lack the very physical energy and resources needed to do so with any sense of accomplishing anything that is really worthwhile. As increasing demands are placed by the Catholic Church on a decreasing and ageing group of priests, life is likely to become harder not easier for these senior clergy. These are men who would, in any other walk of life, be by now enjoying a well-earned period of retirement, during which they could look back with a sense of personal satisfaction on the worthwhile things they had achieved during their younger working lives.

CHAPTER TWENTY-TWO

A Future in Priesthood

Adrian Hastings, himself one of the many distinguished priests who separated themselves from the formal structures of the Church [wrote] 'It was a tragedy of a whole generation of able priests – perhaps the ablest the Catholic Church in England ever had – who went down leaderless between Rome and their people (Longley, 2000, p. 271).

This final chapter reporting on the results of the survey is concerned with the extent to which those priests currently engaged in parochial ministry in the Catholic Church continue to see for themselves *a future in priesthood*. Are they happy with their original intention to become ordained and, if they had their time all over again, would they still choose to be priests?

Context

It is not without significance that the Catholic Church settled upon an ordained, lengthily trained, centrally regulated group of celibate males to oversee its organization. It is equally significant:

> how the minister comes to be devoted to serving a distant, all powerful master who is brought close by the power of his own mind. He speaks for this master and in doing so, takes on some of this authority without, however, replacing him (Barry and Bordin, 1967, p. 399).

Psychological studies conducted over the past fifty years hypothesized that the possession of a particular personality might predispose those with strong personality determinants to be attracted to particular professions, including the priesthood. It is not a question that because there were unconscious motivations prompting a man to seek priestly ordination or that being a priest may be a means used to resolve psychological conflicts that there was anything wrong or unusual about this (Bloom, 1971). Those who become priests as much as those who are attracted to any other profession are swayed in their life choices by complicated, mixed motives. This is quite normal. It should not be surprising, therefore, given someone with a particular personality profile who has found equanimity in the priesthood, to declare satisfaction with his choice and to state that were the option possible he would make the same choice over again. The conviction that one has answered God's personal call and spent a life specifically

181

in God's service doing God's work could be expected to bring with it a predictable claim to contentment. If it is true that everyone is looking for approval from those known as significant others, then belief in divine approval for those of a religious inclination will be the ultimate level of approbation.

The previous three chapters, however, have indicated that things are not quite as straightforward as all that. On the one hand, the majority of priests indicate a high level of personal accomplishment and satisfaction in ministry. On the other hand, an unacceptably high level of priests show the classic signs of burnout as revealed through emotional exhaustion and depersonalization. It cannot be taken for granted, therefore, that all of those priests currently engaged in parochial ministry would really want to remain there or that, if they could have their time all over again they would still wish to become ordained.

Recruitment and retention of personnel in many professions would appear to be closely linked yet empirical studies of the reciprocal effects of recruitment and retention of priests are non-existent principally because the data are hard to get and techniques for testing hypotheses are extremely complex. Nevertheless the logical interconnection between a decision to be ordained and a decision to remain in the priesthood makes it reasonable to assume that ordination trends have an impact on resignations and vice versa (Schoenherr and Young, 1993, p. 204). Dramatic priest losses over the past forty years coupled with a failure to recruit replacements is a major concern for first world hierarchies.

In the two and a half decades prior to the Second Vatican Council the annual voluntary resignation rate for diocesan priests in the United States of America was approximately one-tenth of one per cent. By 1974 the Roman Catholic priest defection in the United States had risen to a startling cumulative loss of ten thousand of its clergy in eight years. It is estimated that between 12.5% and 13.5% of all diocesan priests active in 1970 resigned in the following ten years and that 15% to 17% of all regular priests active in 1970 had resigned by 1980. Most priests who resigned were under 45 years of age (Schoenherr and Young, 1993).

The decline in priest numbers was equally dramatic in England and Wales. Evidence from the *National Catholic Directory of England and Wales* between 1963 and 1995 presents a profile of numerical decline. Of the 22 dioceses in England and Wales, four were formed in this period. Arundel and Brighton was formed in 1965 by a division of the diocese of Southwark; East Anglia in 1976 by a division of the diocese of Northampton; Hallam in 1980 from areas of the dioceses of Leeds and Nottingham; and Wrexham in 1987 from territory taken from the diocese of Minevia. The overall decline in priest numbers from the five provinces in England and Wales was as follows. In the Birmingham province there was a decline of 30% from 1289 to 905 priests; in the Cardiff province there was a decline of 33% from 427 to 288 priests; in the Liverpool province there was a decline of 29% from 2720 to 1933 priests; in the Southwark province there was a decline of 29% from 1542 to 1098 priests; and in the Westminster province there was a decline of 24% from 1809 to 1376 priests.

The unprecedented acceleration in the number of priests resigning, an unmistakable sign of a fundamental problem in any organization, only slowly triggered changes. Vocal or direct criticism had failed to produce change. The basic reaction of bishops and superiors was to 'let the troublemakers go'. Priest resignations were often represented as the perfidy of disloyal clergy. Bishops appeared to watch the most dissatisfied clergy depart, while considering neither protest nor departure a legitimate form of criticism of the Catholic Church. Bishops of that era behaved in the manner of senior executives of lazy monopolies (Seidler, 1979) allowing disgruntled members and officials to retreat from the organization rather than dealing with difficult but fundamental issues. One impression gained is that Roman Catholicism is content to be rid of troublemakers. Significantly the only acceptable reason for petition for release from vows or solemn promises, as many priests discovered, defined the applicant as deviant. The definition of deviancy was broadened to cope with increased voluntary requests for resignation.

Assistance given by the diocese to any priest who resigns from active ministry varies from case to case, but is minimal. Such a lack of assistance is constrained as much by want of diocesan funds as by a prevailing attitude of scant responsibility towards those no longer willing to serve as priests. Though no longer demonized, Davis, Hebblethwaite, Kenny, Lash, Wijngaards and McTernan are but high-profile examples of the many hundred priests who have resigned.

When the Fathers of the Second Vatican Council recommended resignation at a certain age for bishops and priests, they were motivated by concern for the welfare of the Catholic Church and its pastors. They had no premonition of the exodus of priests and the dearth of vocations, with the consequence that this recommendation would make the situation worse. No one could have foreseen the drastic decline in seminarians or the vast exodus of young clergy from the Catholic priesthood (Fichter, 1985). Though retirement was not unheard of among Catholic priests in England and Wales prior to the 1960s it was a relatively new avenue of exit bestowed by the Second Vatican Council. Hitherto the majority of parish priests continued to work until ill-health constrained or death intervened, but now retirement was an option made respectable and freed from any associated stigma of inconstancy.

Although bankers, college professors, dentists, engineers, executives, physicians, school counsellors, social scientists, social workers and teachers have been studied, research on retirement in clergy is so scanty that Chen and Goodwin (1991) reported that a review of the literature revealed only three studies of retirement among Catholic priests had been conducted since the 1970s.

The phenomenon of reluctant retirement of priests might be viewed as a throwback to pre-industrial societies where there was no real retirement. Whereas in industrial societies there is no demand for what the elderly can do for others, in the Catholic Church elderly priests were still viewed as serving an important function rather than condemned to social obsolescence. That they did less, often much less than formerly, did not appear particularly important. Theirs became a service of relative privilege and freedom compared to the earlier stages of their priesthood. Although parishes tended to be sympathetic to the diminished activity of elderly priests, the numerous assistant priests of the time saw the old men as impeding their progress. Elderly religious, because they were not seen as barriers to the promotion of their younger confrères, were encouraged to remain in active ministry for as long as they were able or inclined.

There is a real sense in which those priests who exit the active ministry and the dearth of would-be seminarians are generating a pressure for change upon the Catholic Church worldwide. Hoge (1987) reported that the vast majority of young Catholic males in the United States of America declare that for them compulsory celibacy is not a meaningful requirement for priesthood.

Over the past forty years in England and Wales, priest resignation rates have peaked and declined, and retirement rates have increased substantially. What is paradoxically of greater significance is that 'recruitment' is more critical than retention. According to Schoenherr and Young (1993, p. 332) 'the impact of ordination on overall decline is three to four times greater than that of the next most powerful transitions, namely resignation and retirement'. It was their belief in 1993 that low ordination rates would continue into the foreseeable future. Reporting in *The Times*, 25 May 2002, the Religion Correspondent Ruth Gledhill reported a record low in seminarian numbers in Britain, about which the hierarchy had called a special meeting to discuss the potential closure of some of the seven seminaries.

What is inevitable is that priestly ranks are getting smaller and many in the ranks are the wrong side of the age they would like to be. The Catholic Church must admit to the gravity of the vocation crisis. Although some may see a solution in the ordination of married men and even in the ordination of women, certain transitional decisions have already been taken that have helped ward off some of the serious repercussions of the priest shortage, namely the growth of lay ministry and the restoration of the diaconate. The longer the inadequate supply of male celibate priests, the more likely clergy control will be weakened and lay leadership will gain legitimation. The preservation of the eucharistic tradition, an essential element of Catholicism, might eventually involve the elimination of non-essentials such as compulsory celibacy and male exclusivity.

Listening to the priests

The prospects of ageing plus near-compulsory retirement for diocesan priests lead many priests if they are typical of their age cohort, to prefer to ignore its inevitable arrival than attempt to negotiate advanced provision. Anxieties are evident from a number of respondents' comments.

For example, one priest commented as follows.

> You could have included questions about my plans, fears, anxieties about retirement, e.g. At what age? What financial means? Accommodation, diocesan schemes? (priest aged between 60 and 64).

Another priest wrote in the following terms.

> Something should have been asked about . . . how priests face ageing and retirement, their preparation for this and the provision that will be made for them (priest aged between 60 and 64).

Two other priests expressed their anxieties.

> I am worried about retired support from the diocese (priest aged between 60 and 64).

> I have endured [surgery] but provisions made for retirement are not enticing (priest aged between 65 and 69).

Those clergy who will confront retirement soonest are most likely to have been influenced and unsettled by that older philosophy which saw retirement as syn-onymous with sickness, with those who have outlived productive usefulness and ought to be relegated to some sort of ghetto because they are unwelcome symbols of death. Priests are as likely as others to believe unwelcome things happen to others not to them, sharing in the common misconception about ageing and retirement of older people as poor, sick and helpless (Gulledge, 1992).

Shaping the questions

Against this background, the *Catholic Parochial Clergy Survey* framed three main themes relevant to exploring the priests' views on the future that they saw in priesthood. The first theme focused on whether the individual priests saw them-selves rooted in ministry for the rest of their lives and explored this issue from two directions. On the positive side, how many priests consider that they will remain in active priesthood for the rest of their lives? On the negative side, how many priests consider that they would feel a lot better if they could get out of parish ministry?

The second theme focused on how the experience of priesthood has shaped the direction of the priests' spiritual lives, and again this issue was explored from two directions. On the positive side, how many priests consider that their faith is stronger now than when they were first ordained? On the negative side, how many priests consider that they are more disillusioned with the Church now than when they were first ordained?

The third theme focused on what the priests would do if they could go back and start again from the beginning. How many of them would still choose to be a priest if they could have their time over again?

Interpreting the statistics

Table 22.1 demonstrates that the majority of priests are content in ministry. Since ordination their faith has grown stronger rather than weaker. Given their time over again, the majority are clear that they would choose the same path and become ordained into the Catholic Church.

Only a very small proportion of priests, one in every twenty-five (4%) were clear that they do not expect to remain in active priesthood for the rest of their lives, although a considerably larger proportion (13%) have kept open the possi-bility of moving out of the priesthood. This still leaves a very high proportion

(83%) who believed that they would remain in active priesthood for the rest of their lives.

By way of contrast, almost one in every ten priests (8%) said that they would feel a lot better if they could get out of parish ministry, and an additional 11% thought that this might be the case. This still leaves a very high proportion (81%) who do not appear to want to get out of parish ministry.

So far a very positive interpretation has been given to these statistics, emphasizing that at least four-fifths of the workforce are content in their vocation and have every intention of staying put. The same statistics also suggest, of course, that up to one-fifth of the workforce is feeling unsettled, restless and discontent. Given the already severe shortage of parish priests and the difficulty of generating new vocations into the priesthood this is an alarming statistic.

Two-thirds of the priests (68%) claimed that their faith had strengthened since working in the Catholic Church: their faith was stronger now than when they were first ordained. Just 11% took the opposite view and 21% were not so sure.

Three-fifths of the priests (59%) claimed that working for the Catholic Church had not undermined their confidence in the institution: they were not now more disillusioned with the Church than when they were first ordained. Between a quarter and a third of the priests (29%), however, took the opposite view and said that they were more disillusioned with the Church now than when they were first ordained, and 12% were not so sure.

A major test of contentment into the future is provided by the proportion of priests who said that if they had their time over again, they would still choose to be a priest. Faced with this question, 84% said they would, 4% said they would not and 12% said that they were not really sure. It is these three priests in every twenty (16%), who are not willing to say that, given the chance again, they would still decide to be ordained, who are the most likely to seek a way out of ministry.

Regular and secular

Overall there is a slight tendency for regular priests to be more content in ministry than is the case among secular priests.

There are two items on which the regular priests record a significantly more positive response in comparison with the secular priests. First, 87% of the regular priests considered that they would remain in active priesthood for the rest of their lives, compared with 81% of the secular priests. Second, only 24% of the regular priests said that they were more disillusioned with the Church than when they were first ordained, compared with 31% of the secular priests.

Although not reaching statistical significance, two of the other items pointed in the same direction. Nearly three-quarters of the regular priests (73%) said that their faith was stronger now than when they were first ordained, compared with two-thirds of the secular priests (67%). Similarly, 87% of the regular priests said that, if they had their time over again, they would still choose to be a priest, compared with 83% of the secular priests.

Finally, 7% of the regular priests and 8% of the secular priests said that they would feel a lot better if they could get out of parish ministry.

Generational differences

Table 22.3 demonstrates that the older priests who have stayed in ministry to the age of 60 and over show the highest level of commitment in ministry. Only three-quarters of the young priests under the age of 45 see themselves as being really committed to ministry for life.

By the time that they have reached the age of 60 priests who have remained in ministry must be really quite committed to that way of life. Almost nine out of every ten priests aged 60 and over (88%) said that they would remain in active priesthood for the rest of their lives. The proportion, however, dropped to 81% among the 45–59-year-olds, and to 75% among those under the age of 45.

The statistics do not imply that there is likely to be an immediate exodus from ministry of many of the younger priests. Rather it means that their eyes may be open to other possibilities in the future. At present just 8% or 9% from each of the three age cohorts claimed that they would feel a lot better if they could get out of parish ministry.

Priests under the age of 60 showed greater discontent with the Church than their older colleagues. While a third of the priests under the age of 45 (32%) and between the ages of 45 and 59 (32%) said that they were more disillusioned with the Church than when they were first ordained, the proportion dropped to 25% among those aged 60 and over.

A similar picture is provided by the statistics relating to the development of faith. While 72% of the priests aged 60 and over claimed that their faith was stronger than when they were first ordained, the proportions dropped to 70% among the 45–59 year age group and to 56% among those under the age of 45.

While 89% of the priests aged 60 and over said that, if they had their time all over again, they would still choose to be a priest, the proportion fell to 81% among those under the age of 60. Given that it is the younger priests who have the greater opportunity to reshape their future outside the priesthood, these statistics alert us again to the fact that we may need to expect as many as one in five of the priests under the age of 60 currently serving in parochial ministry to seek ways to exit the priesthood.

Conclusion

The present study has provided a unique window into hearts, minds and souls of regular and secular priests serving in parochial ministry in England and Wales. Each of the 22 core chapters has focused on one specific topic. The first aim of this brief concluding chapter is to distil and highlight the main findings from each chapter to generate an overview of the main beliefs, values and attitudes so often so successfully concealed behind the Roman collar and behind the clerical persona. Here is a résumé of what is seen when the Catholic priest is stripped bare. The second aim of this concluding chapter is to draw attention to the importance of the age group to which the priest belongs for shaping his worldview. Today it is the young priests who sometimes provide the greatest level of support for the conservatism of the Catholic Church. The third aim of this concluding chapter is to suggest an agenda for future research.

The Naked Parish Priest

Chapter 1 on *training for public ministry* demonstrates that more priests are appreciative than critical of the way they were prepared for public ministry by their seminary. According to their view, seminaries made a better job of preparing them for conducting the liturgy than for preaching, and really failed to equip them for participating in interfaith dialogue.

Chapter 2 on *training for pastoral ministry* demonstrates that overall the priests felt much less well prepared by their seminaries for pastoral ministry than for public ministry as discussed in chapter 1. While fewer than half felt properly prepared for any area of pastoral ministry, only a handful felt prepared for the ministry of marriage counselling.

Chapter 3 on *training for work with people* demonstrates that priests are very discontent with the way in which their seminary training prepared them for ministry to young people. Fewer than one in five priests felt well prepared for ministry among children, teenagers and women. No more than two in five priests felt well prepared for any other area of work with people.

Chapter 4 on *training for the priestly life* demonstrates that seminary training is rated much more highly for preparing priests to develop a spiritual life than for living in their parish, than for living with their sexuality, and than for knowing how to make good use of their time off. Seminary training equipped them for living in the sanctuary much better than for living in the presbytery. Seminary training equipped them better for relating to God than for relating to their parishioners.

Chapter 5 on *theology of priesthood* demonstrates that the majority of priests have a clear theology of priesthood and that the majority remain faithful to the traditional discipline of the daily office and of the daily mass.

Chapter 6 on the practicalities and realities of *experiencing priesthood* demonstrates that the majority of priests felt properly rewarded for their role, although a sizeable minority raised warning signs about isolation and overwork.

Chapter 7 on the outward signs of priesthood, characterized as *dress and deference*, demonstrates that the balance of opinion remains in favour of clerical dress and the continuing use of the title Father, although a considerable minority of priests express dissatisfaction with both. Only a minority of priests feel that parishioners treat them with too much deference.

Chapter 8 on the way in which priests *relate to the laity* demonstrates that the majority of priests feel confident about their ability to relate to the laypeople in their parish, to men, women and children. The majority of priests feel really positive about the greater involvement of the laity in parish life.

Chapter 9 on the relationship between *celibacy and priesthood* demonstrates that, among priests currently engaged in parish ministry in the Catholic Church, there is a high regard for the principles of chastity and celibacy and a balance of opinion in favour of retaining celibacy as the norm for entry into the priesthood. Comparatively few serving parochial priests would wish to get married. On the other hand, there is general acceptance of the view that married men could be ordained priest.

Chapter 10 which concentrates on *fallen priests* demonstrates how sharply the priests distinguish between the differing levels of importance that should be ascribed to different ways of falling from the high standards that may be expected from the priesthood. Paedophilia is to be taken very seriously and homosexual activity is to be taken quite seriously too. Sex with women is to be treated much more lightly. Alcoholism is regarded as a matter of little significance. Many priests feel demoralized by reports of child sex-abuse by clergy.

Chapter 11, which is concerned with the issue of *doctrinal orthodoxy*, demonstrates the very high levels of orthodox belief professed by Catholic parochial clergy. Only a very small minority dissent from the doctrinal teaching of the Catholic Church, even on matters like the assumption of Mary.

Chapter 12, which is concerned with issues of *moral orthodoxy*, demonstrates that priests exercise a considerable degree of discretion regarding the support that they give to different aspects of the moral teachings of the Catholic Church. While there is almost unanimous support for the Catholic Church's teaching on abortion and euthanasia, there is much less support for the Catholic Church's teaching on artificial contraception. There is also significant support for a major overhaul of the Catholic Church's teaching on divorce and remarriage.

Chapter 13, which is concerned with *ecclesial orthodoxy*, demonstrates that Catholic clergy have a well-nuanced understanding concerning their commitment to the doctrines about the nature of the Church. Generally they accept the view that the Catholic Church is uniquely the one true Church founded by Jesus. They are less concerned about the hierarchical structure of the Catholic Church being divinely ordained. They are generally unconvinced by the doctrine that outside the Catholic Church there is no salvation. Belief in the real presence of Christ in the eucharist is very high.

Chapter 14, which is concerned with attitudes toward *Rome and the Vatican*, demonstrates that the vast majority of priests remain thoroughly behind the Second Vatican Council, and that only a very small minority would want to turn the clock back to the days of the pre-Vatican II Church. Many more priests are against the way Pope John Paul II has re-centralized the authority of the Catholic Church in Rome than are in support of it, although there is an equal balance of opinion over the role of Rome in appointing bishops.

Chapter 15, which is concerned with attitudes toward *Catholic institutions*, demonstrates that the majority of priests have a low regard for many Catholic institutions. They feel disempowered over the appointment of bishops. They feel that Opus Dei is far from being a great force for good in the Catholic Church. They feel that the Catholic press is of little importance for the life of their parish. Against this general lack of confidence in Catholic institutions, Catholic schools fare comparatively well, with more priests feeling that Catholic schools do a good job in their parish than feel that they do a poor job.

Chapter 16 on the subject of *ecumenism* demonstrates quite a complex and mixed attitude toward ecumenism and intercommunion among Catholic priests. The majority of priests feel that there is still potential for further progress in the ecumenical movement. The weight of opinion is that papal supremacy is essential for church unity. There is still quite a strong tendency toward regarding Anglican orders as null and void, and an even stronger tendency toward discouraging inter-communion.

Chapter 17, which is concerned with *changes in the Catholic Church*, demonstrates that it is only a small proportion of priests who feel that the Catholic Church has become too liberal. Nevertheless, there is widespread concern over the neglect of the sacrament of reconciliation. The jury is still largely out on the influence of feminism in the Catholic Church. Overall the reordination of convert Anglican clergymen was met with approval.

Chapter 18, which turns attention to the *ordination of women*, demonstrates that priests are quite divided over their views on the ordination of women. Two-fifths feel that Rome's pronouncement against ordained women to the priesthood should never change, another two-fifths feel that things will change, and the remaining fifth are not willing to give a view. Speaking for themselves, half the priests believe that women could validly be ordained to the diaconate, a third believe that women could validly be ordained priests, and a quarter believe that women could validly be ordained bishops.

Chapter 19, which turns attention to *emotional exhaustion*, demonstrates that, by their own self-definition, three out of every twenty priests feel burned out from their parish ministry. While not saying that they feel burned out, just over a third of the priests generally go to bed feeling used up and exhausted at the end of the day in parish ministry.

Chapter 20, which is concerned with *depersonalization* as a sign of burnout, demonstrates that up to two out of every five priests recognize the first signs of depersonalization beginning to affect their ministry, while at least one in every ten have reached a more advanced stage of experiencing depersonalization.

Chapter 21 on the sense of *personal accomplishment* demonstrates that the majority of priests feel very positive about their experience of parish ministry. Nine out of every ten continue to gain a lot of satisfaction from working with people, and only a handful feel that they have accomplished nothing worthwhile in their parish ministry.

Chapter 22, which examines a *future in priesthood*, demonstrates that the majority of priests are content in ministry. Since ordination their faith has grown stronger rather than weaker. Given their time over again, the majority are clear that they would choose the same path and become ordained into the Catholic Church.

Priests for the future

One of the key analyses undertaken on the present database provides a comparison between three cohorts of priests: those aged 60 and over, those between the ages of 45 and 59, and those under the age of 45.

Chapter 1 on *training for public ministry* demonstrates important shifts in the perceptions of seminary training for aspects of public ministry across different generations of priests. Generally speaking the younger priests rated their seminary training for the public aspects of ministry more highly than the older priests. All five issues included in this section of the survey deserve comment.

Chapter 2 on *training for pastoral ministry* demonstrates that priorities in seminary training for pastoral ministry have changed across the generations. In some areas of pastoral ministry, younger priests felt better equipped by their seminaries than was the case among their older colleagues. In other areas of pastoral ministry, younger priests felt less well equipped by their seminaries than was the case among their older colleagues. In yet other areas of pastoral ministry, no significant differences emerged between the generations.

Chapter 3 on *training for work with people* demonstrates that it is the oldest cohort of priests who felt best trained by their seminary for work with people. Overall the middle cohort felt less well prepared than the oldest cohort. Then the youngest cohort felt better prepared than the middle cohort, but less well prepared than the oldest cohort.

Chapter 4 on *training for the priestly life* demonstrates some very significant generational differences in the perception of the value of seminary training in preparation for the priestly life. The oldest cohort rated their seminary training more highly in this area than the two younger groups. At the same time, there are some areas in which the youngest cohort rated their seminary experience more highly than is the case among the middle cohort, but other areas in which the youngest cohort rated their seminary experience less highly than is the case among the middle cohort.

Chapter 5 on *theology of priesthood* demonstrates that younger Catholic priests are less likely to maintain the discipline of the daily mass and the discipline of the daily office espoused by their older colleagues.

Chapter 6 on the practicalities and realities of *experiencing priesthood* demonstrates that younger priests are reporting a less positive view of the priesthood than is the case among their older colleagues. They are less content with their stipend, more isolated and more oppressed by the job.

Chapter 7 on the outward signs of priesthood demonstrates some interesting age trends in the attitudes of Catholic priests toward issues of clerical dress and deference. It is, overall, the priests in the 45–59 age category who are the most liberal in their attitudes on these issues.

Chapter 8 on the way in which priests *relate to the laity* demonstrates that there is no significant relationship between age and attitude toward the involvement of the laity in parish life, although there is a significant association between age and the priests' perception of their ability to relate to some sectors of the laity.

Chapter 9 on the relationship between *celibacy and priesthood* demonstrates that, overall, priests in the 45–59 age category take a more liberal view on the issues surrounding celibacy in comparison with the position adopted by priests aged 60 and over. Priests in the youngest age cohort, under the age of 45, however, are less liberal on issues regarding celibacy than those aged between 45 and 59.

Chapter 10 on the subject of *fallen priests* demonstrates that there are some key differences in the attitudes espoused by the three age cohorts. The most interesting, and possibly the most disturbing, of these differences concerns the profile of the youngest cohort, the priests under the age of 45. While these young priests adopted a more severe attitude in comparison with the 45–59 age cohort in respect of heterosexual activity, they are more accepting of paedophilia, homosexual activity and alcoholism.

Chapter 11 on the issue of *doctrinal orthodoxy* demonstrates a slight tendency among the younger cohorts of clergy to depart from the very high levels of orthodoxy maintained by the oldest cohort of clergy on the two doctrines of the virginal conception of Jesus and the assumption of Mary.

Chapter 12 on the issue of *moral orthodoxy* demonstrates that parishioners served by priests under the age of 60 can expect a more liberal attitude among their clergy to issues like contraception, euthanasia, and remarriage after divorce, compared with parishioners served by priests aged 60 or over. On the issue of abortion, however, the priests under the age of 60 held almost as tightly to the traditional teaching of their Church as the priests aged 60 and over.

Chapter 13, which is concerned with *ecclesial orthodoxy*, demonstrates that it is the priests aged 60 and over who are most likely to espouse a traditional theology concerning the nature of the Catholic Church, while it is the priests in the 45–59 age category who are most likely to take a radical approach. The youngest priests under the age of 45 are reverting more in favour of the traditional beliefs.

Chapter 14, which is concerned with attitudes toward *Rome and the Vatican*, demonstrates that there are no significant differences in the levels of support given to the Second Vatican Council across the three age cohorts. On the other hand, the three age cohorts do behave differently in respect of the central power of Rome. Both the priests under the age of 45 and the priests aged 60 and over show more support for centralizing power in Rome than is the case among the priests in the 45–59 year age group.

Chapter 15 on *Catholic institutions* demonstrates that there were no significant differences between the three cohorts of priests in terms of the way they view their influence in the appointment of bishops, or in terms of the way they view the effectiveness of Catholic schools in their parish.

Chapter 16 on *ecumenism* demonstrates that overall priests under the age of 60 hold a more open view to ecumenism than is the case among priests aged 60 and over. There is a tendency, however, for the youngest cohort of priests, those under the age of 45, to revert to a more conservative position, especially over the issue of intercommunion.

Chapter 17 on *changes in the Catholic Church* demonstrates that priests aged 60 and over are more likely than their younger colleagues to feel that the Catholic Church has become too liberal, are more likely to be scathing about feminist theology and are more likely to lament the eclipse of the sacrament of reconciliation. These older priests are also less likely to welcome the use of female images for God in hymns and prayers. They are, however, more likely to be happy with the reordination of convert Anglican clergymen into the Catholic Church.

Chapter 18 on the *ordination of women* demonstrates that there is much more support for the ordination of women among priests in the 45–59 age cohort than among priests aged 60 and over. Priests under the age of 45 show less support for the ordination of women than priests in the 45–59 age cohort.

Chapter 19, which examines *emotional exhaustion* as a component of burnout, demonstrates that emotional exhaustion is highest among the priests under the age of 45 and lowest among the priests aged 60 and over.

Chapter 20, which examines *depersonalization* as a second component of burnout, demonstrates that depersonalization is highest among priests under the age of 45 and lowest among priests aged 60 and over.

Chapter 21, which examines low levels of *personal accomplishment* as a third component of burnout, demonstrates that, in some ways although not in all, priests aged 60 and over are likely to record a lower level of personal accomplishment in their parish ministry. A more nuanced interpretation of the statistics suggests that, while retaining a sense of personal satisfaction from their ministry, the older priests feel that they are achieving less.

Chapter 22, which is concerned with *a future in ministry*, demonstrates that the older priests who have stayed in ministry to the age of 60 and over show the highest level of commitment in ministry. Only three-quarters of the young priests under the age of 45 see themselves as being really committed to ministry for life.

Setting the agenda

This book has been set up as an innovative exercise in empirical theology. Two theologically informed authors have employed the professional tools of the social sciences to hold up a mirror to the Catholic Church. With a great deal of openness and honesty over 1400 priests serving in parochial ministry have laid bare their hearts, their minds and their souls.

The job of the authors has been to ensure that the voices of these Catholic clergy can be heard with clarity and with precision. It is not our task to evaluate or to interpret. That is a task to be undertaken by the Catholic Church, by the hierarchy, by the Catholic press and most of all by the priests themselves. The findings need to be discussed, reflected on, interpreted and criticized. Here is the raw material to inform working seminars and conferences.

The first major criticism to be faced is that these data are already five years old at the time of publication. There are three responses to this criticism. The first response is that major government planning remains informed by a decadal census. It is almost inevitable that valuable data are already ageing by the time they are ready to be applied. The second response is that a slightly ageing map is a great deal better than no map at all. The third response is that the most useful form of social data is often a form that allows change over time to be monitored. Here in the late 1990s we have established a fully professional and thoroughly reliable benchmark against which trends can be measured. This study is ripe for replication.

When Bryman (1989) tried to replicate the earlier study *Clergy, Ministers and Priests* by Ranson, Bryman and Hinings (1977) the opportunity was lost through lack of funding and through lack of co-operation. Here is a study with more potential to benefit the Catholic Church through replication than even that provided by Bryman's research. The authors are keen to serve the Catholic Church by securing funding to enable such a replication to take place.

APPENDIX

Statistical Tables

Table 1.1 Training for public ministry

	yes	?	no
	%	%	%
My seminary training prepared me well for conducting the liturgy	66	12	22
My seminary training prepared me well for public speaking	59	15	26
My seminary training prepared me well for preaching	57	17	26
My seminary training prepared me well for changes in the Church	49	18	33
My seminary training prepared me well for interfaith dialogue	25	20	56

Table 1.2 Training for public ministry by canonical status

	regular	secular	X^2	$P<$
	%	%		
My seminary training prepared me well for conducting the liturgy	63	67	1.50	NS
My seminary training prepared me well for public speaking	57	59	0.34	NS
My seminary training prepared me well for preaching	57	57	0.01	NS
My seminary training prepared me well for changes in the Church	52	48	1.13	NS
My seminary training prepared me well for interfaith dialogue	26	25	0.16	NS

Table 1.3 Training for public ministry by age

	under 45	45–59	60+	X^2	$P<$
	%	%	%		
My seminary training prepared me well for conducting the liturgy	70	64	66	2.94	NS
My seminary training prepared me well for public speaking	69	60	51	28.05	.001
My seminary training prepared me well for preaching	66	55	54	15.00	.001
My seminary training prepared me well for changes in the Church	59	59	33	96.84	.001
My seminary training prepared me well for interfaith dialogue	37	27	15	56.48	.001

Table 2.1 Training for pastoral ministry

	yes %	? %	no %
My seminary training prepared me well for ministry to the sick	46	15	39
My seminary training prepared me well for pastoral visiting	43	17	40
My seminary training prepared me well for hospital visiting	37	18	45
My seminary training prepared me well for pre-marriage instruction	22	19	59
My seminary training prepared me well for marriage counselling	14	20	66

Table 2.2 Training for pastoral ministry by canonical status

	regular %	secular %	X^2	$P<$
My seminary training prepared me well for ministry to the sick	39	48	6.87	.01
My seminary training prepared me well for pastoral visiting	37	45	6.01	.05
My seminary training prepared me well for hospital visiting	27	39	15.10	.001
My seminary training prepared me well for pre-marriage instruction	22	22	0.08	NS
My seminary training prepared me well for marriage counselling	16	14	0.87	NS

Table 2.3 Training for pastoral ministry by age

	under 45 %	45–59 %	60+ %	X^2	$P<$
My seminary training prepared me well for ministry to the sick	41	41	53	19.67	.001
My seminary training prepared me well for pastoral visiting	50	39	43	10.61	.01
My seminary training prepared me well for hospital visiting	47	37	30	24.83	.001
My seminary training prepared me well for pre-marriage instruction	19	20	25	7.29	.05
My seminary training prepared me well for marriage counselling	17	14	12	4.12	NS

Table 3.1 Training for work with people

	yes	?	no
	%	%	%
My seminary training prepared me well for ministry to children	18	19	63
My seminary training prepared me well for ministry to teenagers	13	19	68
My seminary training prepared me well for relating to women	18	22	60
My seminary training prepared me well for relating to men	40	24	36
My seminary training prepared me well for ministry to the elderly	39	18	43
My seminary training prepared me well for ministry to the bereaved	25	22	53

Table 3.2 Training for work with people by canonical status

	regular	secular	X^2	P<
	%	%		
My seminary training prepared me well for ministry to children	22	17	4.99	.05
My seminary training prepared me well for ministry to teenagers	17	12	5.40	.05
My seminary training prepared me well for relating to women	26	17	12.97	.001
My seminary training prepared me well for relating to men	46	39	5.06	.05
My seminary training prepared me well for ministry to the elderly	36	40	2.95	NS
My seminary training prepared me well for ministry to the bereaved	25	25	0.04	NS

Table 3.3 Training for work with people by age

	under 45	45–59	60+	X^2	P<
	%	%	%		
My seminary training prepared me well for ministry to children	19	15	19	3.66	NS
My seminary training prepared me well for ministry to teenagers	14	11	15	4.39	NS
My seminary training prepared me well for relating to women	21	15	21	8.77	.05
My seminary training prepared me well for relating to men	41	36	45	10.91	.01
My seminary training prepared me well for ministry to the elderly	38	36	43	6.15	.05
My seminary training prepared me well for ministry to the bereaved	24	21	29	8.93	.05

Table 4.1 Training for the priestly life

	yes %	? %	no %
My seminary training prepared me well for living on limited means	55	15	30
My seminary training prepared me well for looking after myself	34	20	46
My seminary training prepared me well for accepting my sexuality	29	22	49
My seminary training prepared me well for living as a single man	32	21	47
My seminary training prepared me well for the life of celibacy	38	21	41
My seminary training prepared me well for creative use of free time	33	25	43
My seminary training prepared me well for developing a spiritual life	68	15	17

Table 4.2 Training for the priestly life by canonical status

	regular %	secular %	X^2	$P<$
My seminary training prepared me well for living on limited means	65	53	15.66	.001
My seminary training prepared me well for looking after myself	43	32	14.81	.001
My seminary training prepared me well for accepting my sexuality	38	27	13.17	.001
My seminary training prepared me well for living as a single man	43	29	21.85	.001
My seminary training prepared me well for the life of celibacy	48	35	16.69	.001
My seminary training prepared me well for creative use of free time	39	31	7.45	.01
My seminary training prepared me well for developing a spiritual life	76	65	13.27	.001

Table 4.3 Training for the priestly life by age

	under 45 %	45–9 %	60+ %	X^2	$P<$
My seminary training prepared me well for living on limited means	40	52	68	71.18	.001
My seminary training prepared me well for looking after myself	30	29	40	17.79	.01
My seminary training prepared me well for accepting my sexuality	28	20	38	44.84	.001
My seminary training prepared me well for living as a single man	21	24	46	82.70	.001
My seminary training prepared me well for the life of celibacy	25	29	53	101.32	.001
My seminary training prepared me well for creative use of free time	33	25	39	24.35	.001
My seminary training prepared me well for developing a spiritual life	59	63	76	35.74	.001

Table 5.1 Theology and priesthood

	yes	?	no
	%	%	%
I have a clear theology of priesthood	73	20	6
As a priest I value highly saying a daily mass	83	8	10
As a priest I value highly saying the daily office	73	10	17
Most days I do not find time to pray all the daily office	41	3	56

Table 5.2 Theology and priesthood by canonical status

	regular	secular	X^2	P<
	%	%		
I have a clear theology of priesthood	76	73	0.85	NS
As a priest I value highly saying a daily mass	85	82	1.24	NS
As a priest I value highly saying the daily office	79	72	5.92	.05
Most days I do not find time to pray all the daily office	33	43	9.22	.01

Table 5.3 Theology and priesthood by age

	under 45	45–59	60+	X^2	P<
	%	%	%		
I have a clear theology of priesthood	74	69	77	10.20	.01
As a priest I value highly saying a daily mass	75	79	91	51.68	.001
As a priest I value highly saying the daily office	60	68	86	83.86	.001
Most days I do not find time to pray all the daily office	55	46	28	75.41	.001

Table 6.1 Experiencing priesthood

	yes %	? %	no %
As a priest I receive enough money to live comfortably	79	7	14
As a priest I feel I am underpaid	20	13	68
I am largely irrelevant to the lives of my parishioners	16	20	63
As a priest I often feel lonely and isolated	34	8	58
As a priest I feel that my workload is excessive	43	15	42
As a priest my major source of relaxation is watching television	23	10	67

Table 6.2 Experiencing priesthood by canonical status

	regular %	secular %	X^2	$P<$
As a priest I receive enough money to live comfortably	80	79	0.24	NS
As a priest I feel I am underpaid	15	21	5.51	.05
I am largely irrelevant to the lives of my parishioners	13	17	2.11	NS
As a priest I often feel lonely and isolated	23	37	21.63	.001
As a priest I feel that my workload is excessive	30	46	27.57	.001
As a priest my major source of relaxation is watching television	16	25	11.15	.001

Table 6.3 Experiencing priesthood by age

	under 45 %	45–59 %	60+ %	X^2	$P<$
As a priest I receive enough money to live comfortably	70	77	86	34.23	.001
As a priest I feel I am underpaid	28	20	15	24.04	.001
I am largely irrelevant to the lives of my parishioners	19	19	11	16.02	.001
As a priest I often feel lonely and isolated	41	40	25	39.00	.001
As a priest I feel that my workload is excessive	52	48	33	41.42	.001
As a priest my major source of relaxation is watching television	27	23	20	5.29	NS

Table 7.1 Dress and deference

	yes %	? %	no %
It is important that priests should wear distinctive dress	48	18	34
Priests should wear a 'clerical collar' when on duty	58	15	27
I prefer parishioners to call me Father	47	20	33
Parishioners treat me with too much deference	16	23	61

Table 7.2 Dress and deference by canonical status

	regular %	secular %	X^2	$P<$
It is important that priests should wear distinctive dress	45	49	1.23	NS
Priests should wear a 'clerical collar' when on duty	59	58	0.06	NS
I prefer parishioners to call me Father	47	47	0.00	NS
Parishioners treat me with too much deference	18	16	1.07	NS

Table 7.3 Dress and deference by age

	under 45 %	45–59 %	60+ %	X^2	$P<$
It is important that priests should wear distinctive dress	48	37	60	61.08	.001
Priests should wear a 'clerical collar' when on duty	56	48	70	54.64	.001
I prefer parishioners to call me Father	36	36	64	108.93	.001
Parishioners treat me with too much deference	16	17	15	0.56	NS

Table 8.1 Relating to the laity

	yes %	? %	no %
I welcome the greater involvement of the laity in parish life	98	2	0
Increasing influence of laity in the Catholic Church makes me anxious	7	6	87
Lay people have too much power and influence in my parish	3	7	90
As a priest I relate well to children	84	13	3
As a priest I relate well to women	88	10	2
As a priest I relate well to men	90	9	1

Table 8.2 Relating to the laity by canonical status

	regular %	secular %	X^2	$P<$
I welcome the greater involvement of the laity in parish life	99	98	0.66	NS
Increasing influence of laity in the Catholic Church makes me anxious	5	7	2.76	NS
Lay people have too much power and influence in my parish	5	3	6.39	.05
As a priest I relate well to children	84	84	0.90	NS
As a priest I relate well to women	91	88	3.43	NS
As a priest I relate well to men	93	89	4.55	.05

Table 8.3 Relating to the laity by age

	under 4 %	45–59 %	60+ %	X^2	$P<$
I welcome the greater involvement of the laity in parish life	98	99	98	3.10	NS
Increasing influence of laity in the Catholic Church makes me anxious	7	5	8	2.75	NS
Lay people have too much power and influence in my parish	4	2	3	2.87	NS
As a priest I relate well to children	87	83	84	2.34	NS
As a priest I relate well to women	93	86	88	10.55	.01
As a priest I relate well to men	93	88	91	6.65	.05

Table 9.1 Celibacy and priesthood

	yes	?	no
	%	%	%
Chastity is essential for a Catholic priest	73	10	17
Most priests are faithful to their commitment to celibacy	72	23	6
Celibacy should remain the norm for entry to the priesthood	46	20	34
I believe a married man could validly be ordained priest	91	5	5
Catholic priests who left and married should be readmitted to ministry	45	26	29
The Catholic Church has too readily ordained married convert Anglican clergymen	32	22	46
If it were permitted, I would get married and stay in priestly ministry	18	24	58

Table 9.2 Celibacy and priesthood by canonical status

	regular	secular	X^2	P<
	%	%		
Chastity is essential for a Catholic priest	74	73	0.20	NS
Most priests are faithful to their commitment to celibacy	71	72	0.11	NS
Celibacy should remain the norm for entry to the priesthood	51	45	3.61	NS
I believe a married man could validly be ordained priest	89	91	1.54	NS
Catholic priests who left and married should be readmitted to ministry	45	45	0.05	NS
The Catholic Church has too readily ordained married convert Anglican clergymen	29	33	2.14	NS
If it were permitted, I would get married and stay in priestly ministry	12	20	10.19	.001

Table 9.3 Celibacy and priesthood by age

	under 45	45–59	60+	X^2	P<
	%	%	%		
Chastity is essential for a Catholic priest	66	69	79	22.71	.001
Most priests are faithful to their commitment to celibacy	68	66	79	23.68	.001
Celibacy should remain the norm for entry to the priesthood	41	35	59	71.06	.001
I believe a married man could validly be ordained priest	90	95	88	16.24	.001
Catholic priests who left and married should be readmitted to ministry	45	57	35	54.97	.001
The Catholic Church has too readily ordained married convert Anglican clergymen	43	35	24	37.87	.001
If it were permitted, I would get married and stay in priestly ministry	18	24	12	27.53	.001

Table 10.1 Fallen priests

	yes %	? %	no %
A priest who practises paedophilia should be barred from ministry	90	6	4
A priest who practises homosexuality should be barred from ministry	65	14	21
A priest who has sex with a married woman should be barred from ministry	19	20	61
A priest who has sex with an unmarried woman should be barred from ministry	14	19	67
A priest who becomes alcoholic should be barred from ministry	7	14	79
I feel demoralized by reports of child sex-abuse by clergy	68	10	22

Table 10.2 Fallen priests by canonical status

	regular %	secular %	X^2	$P<$
A priest who practises paedophilia should be barred from ministry	91	90	0.33	NS
A priest who practises homosexuality should be barred from ministry	72	63	8.98	.01
A priest who has sex with a married woman should be barred from ministry	18	19	0.13	NS
A priest who has sex with an unmarried woman should be barred from ministry	14	14	0.00	NS
A priest who becomes alcoholic should be barred from ministry	9	7	1.69	NS
I feel demoralized by reports of child sex-abuse by clergy	69	68	0.14	NS

Table 10.3 Fallen priests by age

	under 45 %	45–59 %	60+ %	X^2	$P<$
A priest who practises paedophilia should be barred from ministry	85	90	92	12.08	.01
A priest who practises homosexuality should be barred from ministry	47	61	79	100.94	.001
A priest who has sex with a married woman should be barred from ministry	20	13	24	25.23	.001
A priest who has sex with an unmarried woman should be barred from ministry	15	8	19	28.16	.001
A priest who becomes alcoholic should be barred from ministry	4	6	10	13.26	.01
I feel demoralized by reports of child sex-abuse by clergy	67	68	69	0.34	NS

Table 11.1 Jesus and Mary

	yes	?	no
	%	%	%
I believe that Jesus is fully human	98	1	1
I believe that Jesus is fully God	98	1	1
I believe in the bodily resurrection of Jesus	97	2	1
Jesus was conceived in the womb of a virgin without a human father	94	5	2
Our Lady was taken up body and soul into heavenly glory	91	7	2

Table 11.2 Jesus and Mary by canonical status

	regular	secular	X^2	$P<$
	%	%		
I believe that Jesus is fully human	99	98	0.66	NS
I believe that Jesus is fully God	99	98	0.55	NS
I believe in the bodily resurrection of Jesus	97	97	0.00	NS
Jesus was conceived in the womb of a virgin without a human father	97	93	5.79	.05
Our Lady was taken up body and soul into heavenly glory	91	91	0.03	NS

Table 11.3 Jesus and Mary by age

	under 45	45–59	60+	X^2	$P<$
	%	%	%		
I believe that Jesus is fully human	99	98	99	0.69	NS
I believe that Jesus is fully God	98	98	99	2.61	NS
I believe in the bodily resurrection of Jesus	97	96	98	4.79	NS
Jesus was conceived in the womb of a virgin without a human father	93	91	97	14.40	.001
Our Lady was taken up body and soul into heavenly glory	87	88	95	23.59	.001

Table 12.1 Marriage, sex and death

	yes %	? %	no %
I support the Catholic Church's total ban on abortion	92	5	3
Direct euthanasia is morally unjustifiable	85	5	10
I support the Catholic Church's total ban on artificial contraception	39	19	43
The Catholic Church's teaching on divorce and remarriage should be liberalized	43	17	40
The divorced and remarried should be admitted to communion	49	28	23
In the Catholic Church annulment is too easy	7	15	79

Table 12.2 Marriage, sex and death by canonical status

	regular %	secular %	X^2	$P<$
I support the Catholic Church's total ban on abortion	91	92	0.21	NS
Direct euthanasia is morally unjustifiable	84	85	0.30	NS
I support the Catholic Church's total ban on artificial contraception	42	38	1.52	NS
The Catholic Church's teaching on divorce and remarriage should be liberalized	41	43	0.42	NS
The divorced and remarried should be admitted to communion	47	49	0.83	NS
In the Catholic Church annulment is too easy	5	7	0.91	NS

Table 12.3 Marriage, sex and death by age

	under 45 %	45–59 %	60+ %	X^2	$P<$
I support the Catholic Church's total ban on abortion	91	90	94	7.08	.05
Direct euthanasia is morally unjustifiable	83	81	89	15.42	.001
I support the Catholic Church's total ban on artificial contraception	33	28	52	71.30	.001
The Catholic Church's teaching on divorce and remarriage should be liberalized	48	52	31	54.70	.001
The divorced and remarried should be admitted to communion	50	59	39	44.38	.001
In the Catholic Church annulment is too easy	4	4	10	19.37	.001

Table 13.1 Church and sacrament

	yes	?	no
	%	%	%
The Catholic Church is uniquely the one true church founded by Jesus	85	6	9
Outside the Catholic Church there is no salvation	12	6	81
The hierarchical structure of the Catholic Church is divinely ordained	57	19	25
I believe in the real presence of Christ under the species of bread and wine	99	1	0

Table 13.2 Church and sacrament by canonical status

	regular	secular	X^2	$P<$
	%	%		
The Catholic Church is uniquely the one true church founded by Jesus	86	84	0.50	NS
Outside the Catholic Church there is no salvation	12	12	0.00	NS
The hierarchical structure of the Catholic Church is divinely ordained	58	57	0.20	NS
I believe in the real presence of Christ under the species of bread and wine	99	99	0.63	NS

Table 13.3 Church and sacrament by age

	under 45	45–59	60+	X^2	$P<$
	%	%	%		
The Catholic Church is uniquely the one true church founded by Jesus	80	78	92	46.89	.001
Outside the Catholic Church there is no salvation	12	8	16	18.65	.001
The hierarchical structure of the Catholic Church is divinely ordained	56	46	67	50.68	.001
I believe in the real presence of Christ under the species of bread and wine	99	99	99	0.05	NS

Table 14.1 Rome and the Vatican

	yes	?	no
	%	%	%
If it were possible, I would prefer a return to the pre-Vatican II Church	4	4	92
The Second Vatican Council was a disaster for the Catholic Church	2	3	95
I welcome the way John Paul II has recentralized in Rome			
the authority of the Catholic Church	24	22	55
Rome should not have decisive say in appointing diocesan bishops	42	20	38

Table 14.2 Rome and the Vatican by canonical status

	regular	secular	X^2	P<
	%	%		
If it were possible, I would prefer a return to the pre-Vatican II Church	4	3	0.81	NS
The Second Vatican Council was a disaster for the Catholic Church	2	2	0.30	NS
I welcome the way John Paul II has recentralized in Rome				
the authority of the Catholic Church	27	23	2.64	NS
Rome should not have decisive say in appointing diocesan bishops	41	42	0.12	NS

Table 14.3 Rome and the Vatican by age

	under 45	45–59	60+	X^2	P<
	%	%	%		
If it were possible, I would prefer a return to the pre-Vatican II Church	3	3	5	4.39	NS
The Second Vatican Council was a disaster for the Catholic Church	2	1	2	1.13	NS
I welcome the way John Paul II has recentralized in Rome					
the authority of the Catholic Church	23	15	32	47.69	.001
Rome should not have decisive say in appointing diocesan bishops	34	49	39	22.98	.001

Table 15.1 Catholic institutions

	yes	?	no
	%	%	%
I feel I have no say in the appointment of bishops	77	10	14
Opus Dei is a great force for good in the Catholic Church	15	37	48
Catholic schools fulfil their purpose in my parish	43	25	32
The Catholic press is important to the life of my parish	15	22	63

Table 15.2 Catholic institutions by canonical status

	regular	secular	X^2	$P<$
	%	%		
I feel I have no say in the appointment of bishops	82	75	4.96	.05
Opus Dei is a great force for good in the Catholic Church	17	14	1.30	NS
Catholic schools fulfil their purpose in my parish	45	43	0.41	NS
The Catholic press is important to the life of my parish	20	14	7.34	.01

Table 15.3 Catholic institutions by age

	under 45	45–59	60+	X^2	$P<$
	%	%	%		
I feel I have no say in the appointment of bishops	77	77	76	0.16	NS
Opus Dei is a great force for good in the Catholic Church	11	11	20	24.95	.001
Catholic schools fulfil their purpose in my parish	44	41	45	1.53	NS
The Catholic press is important to the life of my parish	10	10	22	38.24	.001

Table 16.1 Ecumenism and intercommunion

	yes %	? %	no %
Ecumenical co-operation has gone as far as it can go	18	22	61
Papal supremacy is essential for any church unity scheme	62	20	18
Christian unity means all should eventually become Roman Catholic	31	16	53
I believe as Pope Leo XIII said, Anglican orders are 'null and void'	44	31	25
Non-Catholic Christians should be permitted to communicate at Mass	25	17	58
The church should permit Catholics to communicate in non-Catholic churches	17	13	71

Table 16.2 Ecumenism and intercommunion by canonical status

	regular %	secular %	X^2	$P<$
Ecumenical co-operation has gone as far as it can go	15	18	2.48	NS
Papal supremacy is essential for any church unity scheme	66	61	1.82	NS
Christian unity means all should eventually become Roman Catholic	37	30	5.39	.05
I believe as Pope Leo XIII said, Anglican orders are 'null and void'	44	44	0.03	NS
Non-Catholic Christians should be permitted to communicate at Mass	28	24	2.14	NS
The church should permit Catholics to communicate in non-Catholic churches	19	16	1.64	NS

Table 16.3 Ecumenism and intercommunion by age

	under 45 %	45–59 %	60+ %	X^2	$P<$
Ecumenical co-operation has gone as far as it can go	14	14	23	21.89	.001
Papal supremacy is essential for any church unity scheme	52	51	79	111.04	.001
Christian unity means all should eventually become Roman Catholic	27	24	40	37.14	.001
I believe as Pope Leo XIII said, Anglican orders are 'null and void'	39	35	55	50.50	.001
Non-Catholic Christians should be permitted to communicate at Mass	20	30	23	14.07	.001
The church should permit Catholics to communicate in non-Catholic churches	14	21	14	12.55	.01

Table 17.1 Changes in the Catholic Church

	yes	?	no
	%	%	%
The Catholic Church has become too liberal	15	11	75
I am concerned that so few receive the sacrament of reconciliation	74	12	14
I believe feminist theology is a travesty of theology	28	31	41
Hymns and prayers should use female as well as male images for God	37	22	41
I am happy with the reordination of convert Anglican clergymen	68	19	12

Table 17.2 Changes in the Catholic Church by canonical status

	regular	secular	X^2	$P<$
	%	%		
The Catholic Church has become too liberal	14	15	0.45	NS
I am concerned that so few receive the sacrament of reconciliation	73	74	0.20	NS
I believe feminist theology is a travesty of theology	32	28	1.74	NS
Hymns and prayers should use female as well as male images for God	41	36	2.27	NS
I am happy with the reordination of convert Anglican clergymen	71	68	1.38	NS

Table 17.3 Changes in the Catholic Church by age

	under 45	45–59	60+	X^2	$P<$
	%	%	%		
The Catholic Church has become too liberal	12	11	20	19.25	.001
I am concerned that so few receive the sacrament of reconciliation	70	70	79	16.10	.001
I believe feminist theology is a travesty of theology	16	21	43	105.43	.001
Hymns and prayers should use female as well as male images for God	48	44	25	68.81	.001
I am happy with the reordination of convert Anglican clergymen	55	66	79	60.01	.001

Table 18.1 Ordination of women

	yes %	? %	no %
Rome's pronouncement against ordained women as priests should never change	39	21	40
Ordaining women, Anglicans have made unity with Rome impossible	38	24	38
I believe a woman could validly be ordained deacon	49	23	28
I believe a woman could validly be ordained priest	34	20	46
I believe a woman could validly be ordained bishop	25	19	57

Table 18.2 Ordination of women by canonical status

	regular %	secular %	X^2	$P<$
Rome's pronouncement against ordained women as priests should never change	42	38	1.72	NS
Ordaining women, Anglicans have made unity with Rome impossible	42	38	2.37	NS
I believe a woman could validly be ordained deacon	52	48	1.11	NS
I believe a woman could validly be ordained priest	32	35	0.96	NS
I believe a woman could validly be ordained bishop	23	25	0.38	NS

Table 18.3 Ordination of women by age

	under 45 %	45–59 %	60+ %	X^2	$P<$
Rome's pronouncement against ordained women as priests should never change	33	30	50	53.90	.001
Ordaining women, Anglicans have made unity with Rome impossible	34	31	47	32.86	.001
I believe a woman could validly be ordained deacon	45	59	43	33.56	.001
I believe a woman could validly be ordained priest	35	45	24	58.57	.001
I believe a woman could validly be ordained bishop	27	35	14	65.85	.001

Table 19.1 Emotional exhaustion

	yes %	? %	no %
I feel burned out from my parish ministry	14	16	70
I feel fatigued when I get up in the morning and have to face another day in the parish	16	11	73
I feel emotionally drained from my parish ministry	19	14	67
I feel frustrated by my parish ministry	23	11	66
I feel used up at the end of the day in parish ministry	36	17	47

Table 19.2 Emotional exhaustion by canonical status

	regular %	secular %	X^2	P<
I feel burned out from my parish ministry	14	14	0.00	NS
I feel fatigued when I get up in the morning and have to face another day in the parish	16	16	0.09	NS
I feel emotionally drained from my parish ministry	16	20	3.09	NS
I feel frustrated by my parish ministry	16	24	8.11	.01
I feel used up at the end of the day in parish ministry	30	38	5.87	.05

Table 19.3 Emotional exhaustion by age

	under 45 %	45–59 %	60+ %	X^2	P<
I feel burned out from my parish ministry	15	17	11	9.00	.05
I feel fatigued when I get up in the morning and have to face another day in the parish	19	16	14	3.78	NS
I feel emotionally drained from my parish ministry	26	20	14	20.62	.001
I feel frustrated by my parish ministry	34	27	12	63.37	.001
I feel used up at the end of the day in parish ministry	40	39	32	8.60	.05

Table 20.1 Depersonalization

	yes %	? %	no %
I am less patient with parishioners than I used to be	27	12	61
I find it difficult to listen to what some parishioners are really saying to me	26	15	58
I have become more callous toward people since working in parish ministry	9	10	81
I don't really care what happens to some parishioners	11	9	80
I wish parishioners would leave me alone	7	10	83

Table 20.2 Depersonalization by canonical status

	regular %	secular %	X^2	$P<$
I am less patient with parishioners than I used to be	22	28	5.38	.05
I find it difficult to listen to what some parishioners are really saying to me	25	27	0.31	NS
I have become more callous toward people since working in parish ministry	6	10	5.31	.05
I don't really care what happens to some parishioners	11	11	0.01	NS
I wish parishioners would leave me alone	6	7	0.73	NS

Table 20.3 Depersonalization by age

	under 45 %	45–59 %	60+ %	X^2	$P<$
I am less patient with parishioners than I used to be	29	31	22	9.57	.01
I find it difficult to listen to what some parishioners are really saying to me	26	30	23	6.72	.05
I have become more callous toward people since working in parish ministry	14	11	5	22.58	.001
I don't really care what happens to some parishioners	16	11	9	12.21	.01
I wish parishioners would leave me alone	10	7	6	3.59	NS

Table 21.1 Personal accomplishment

	yes %	? %	no %
I gain a lot of personal satisfaction from working with people	91	6	3
I feel I am positively influencing other people's lives through my parish ministry	71	25	4
I can easily understand how my parishioners feel about things	60	33	7
I deal very effectively with the problems of my parishioners	32	59	9
I have accomplished many worthwhile things in my parish ministry	75	21	4

Table 21.2 Personal accomplishment by canonical status

	regular %	secular %	X^2	$P<$
I gain a lot of personal satisfaction from working with people	91	91	0.00	NS
I feel I am positively influencing other people's lives through my parish ministry	76	70	5.07	.05
I can easily understand how my parishioners feel about things	58	60	0.41	NS
I deal very effectively with the problems of my parishioners	33	31	0.32	NS
I have accomplished many worthwhile things in my parish ministry	72	76	2.04	NS

Table 21.3 Personal accomplishment by age

	under 45 %	45–59 %	60+ %	X^2	$P<$
I gain a lot of personal satisfaction from working with people	91	90	90	0.37	NS
I feel I am positively influencing other people's lives through my parish ministry	76	71	68	6.80	.05
I can easily understand how my parishioners feel about things	63	54	63	9.90	.01
I deal very effectively with the problems of my parishioners	37	32	29	6.92	.05
I have accomplished many worthwhile things in my parish ministry	77	78	71	7.52	.05

Table 22.1 A future in priesthood

	yes	?	no
	%	%	%
I will remain in the active priesthood for the rest of my life	83	13	4
I would feel a lot better if I could get out of parish ministry	8	11	81
My faith is stronger than when I was first ordained	68	21	11
I am more disillusioned with the Church than when I was first ordained	29	12	59
If I had my time over again, I would choose to be a priest	84	12	4

Table 22.2 A future in priesthood by canonical status

	regular	secular	X^2	P<
	%	%		
I will remain in the active priesthood for the rest of my life	87	81	5.19	.05
I would feel a lot better if I could get out of parish ministry	7	8	0.16	NS
My faith is stronger than when I was first ordained	73	67	3.79	NS
I am more disillusioned with the Church than when I was first ordained	24	31	5.33	.05
If I had my time over again, I would choose to be a priest	87	83	2.89	NS

Table 22.3 A future in priesthood by age

	under 45	45–59	60+	X^2	P<
	%	%	%		
I will remain in the active priesthood for the rest of my life	75	81	88	26.35	.001
I would feel a lot better if I could get out of parish ministry	9	8	8	0.37	NS
My faith is stronger than when I was first ordained	56	70	72	27.24	.001
I am more disillusioned with the Church than when I was first ordained	32	32	25	7.60	.05
If I had my time over again, I would choose to be a priest	81	81	89	20.11	.001

Bibliography

Abbott, W. M. (ed.) (1966). *The Documents of Vatican II*. London, Geoffrey Chapman.

Alcoholics Anonymous (1986). *Alcoholics Anonymous*. New York, Alcoholics Anonymous World Service.

Arbuckle, G. A. (1993). *Refounding the Church: dissent for leadership*. London, Geoffrey Chapman.

Arbuckle, G. A. (1996). *From Chaos to Mission: refounding religious life formation*. London, Geoffrey Chapman.

Bandura, A. (1982). Self-efficacy mechanism in human agency. *American Psychologist*, 37, 122–47.

Barr, B. G. (1993). Charts, circles and diagrams. In T. Unsworth (ed.), *The Last Priests in America*, pp. 8–12, New York, Crossroad.

Barron, R. (2000). Beyond beige Catholicism. *Church*, 16 (2), 5–10.

Barry, W. A. and Bordin, E. S. (1967). Personality development and the vocational choice of the ministry. *Journal of Counselling Psychology*, 14, 395–403.

Baum, G. (1975). *Religion and Alienation: a theological reading of sociology*. Mahwah, New Jersey, Paulist Press.

Beit-Hallahmi, B. and Argyle, M. (1997). *The Psychology of Religious Behaviour, Belief and Experience*. London, Routledge.

Bennett, A. (1991). *Talking Heads*. London, BBC Books.

Berger, P. L. (1969). *A Rumour of Angels: modern society and the rediscovery of the supernatural*. Harmondsworth, Penguin.

Berger, P. L. (1988). *Invitation to Sociology: a humanistic perspective*. Harmondsworth, Penguin.

Bier, W. C. (1948). A comparative study of a seminary group and four other groups on the Minnesota Multiphasic Personality Inventory. *Studies in Psychology and Psychiatry*, 7 (3), 1–107.

Bier, W. C. (ed.) (1970). *Psychological Testing for Ministerial Selection*. New York, Fordham University Press.

Bier, W. C. (1971). A modified form of the Minnesota Multiphasic Personality Inventory for religious personnel. *Theological Education*, 7 (2), 121–34.

Bigelow, E. D., Fitzgerald, R., Busk, P., Girault, E. and Avis, J. (1988). Psychological characteristics of Catholic sisters: relationships between the MBTI and other measures. *Journal of Psychological Type*, 14, 32–6.

Bloom, J. H. (1971). Who become clergymen? *Journal of Religion and Health*, 10, 50–76.

Boff, L. (1985). *Church, Charism and Power*. New York, Crossroads.

Bradburn, N. M. (1969). *The Structure of Psychological Well-being*. Chicago, Illinois, Aldine.

Brockman, N. (1978). Burnout in superiors. *Review for Religious*, 37, 809–16.

Brothers, J. (1963). Social change and the role of the priest. *Social Compass*, 10, 477–89.

Brown, R. E. (1973). *The Virginal Conception and Bodily Resurrection of Jesus*. New York, Paulist Press.

Bryman, A. (1989). The value of re-studies in sociology: the case of clergy and ministers, 1971 to 1985. *Sociology*, 23, 31–53.

Buunk, B. P. and Schaufeli, W. B. (1993). Burnout: a perspective from social comparison theory. In W. B. Schaufeli, C. Maslach and T. Marek (eds), *Professional Burnout*, pp. 53–69. London, Taylor and Francis.

Cabral, G. (1984). Psychological types in a Catholic convent: applications to community living and congregational data. *Journal of Psychological Type*, 8, 16–22.

Campagna, W. D. and O'Toole, J. J. (1981). A comparison of the personality profiles of Roman Catholic and male Protestant seminarians. *Counselling and Values*, 26, 62–7.

Carroll, J. W. (1992). Towards 2000: some futures for religious leadership. *Review of Religious Research*, 33, 289–305.

Catechism of the Catholic Church (1994). London, Geoffrey Chapman.

Catholic Bishops (1998). Conferences of England and Wales, Ireland and Scotland. *One Bread One Body*. London, Catholic Truth Society.

Cattell, R. B., Eber, H. W. and Tatsuoka, M. M. (1970). *Handbook for the Sixteen Personality Factor Questionnaire (16PF)*. Champaign, Illinois, Institute for Personality and Ability Testing.

Chen, M. Y. T. and Goodwin, J. L. (1991). The continuity perspective of aging and retirement applied to Protestant clergy: an analysis of theory. *Journal of Religious Gerontology*, 7, 55–67.

Cherniss, C. (1980). *Staff Burnout: job stress in the human services*. London, Sage.

Cherniss, C. (1993). Role of professional self-efficacy in the etiology and amelioration of burnout. In W. Schaufeli, C. Maslach and T. Marek (eds), *Professional Burnout*, pp. 135–50. London, Taylor and Francis.

Clark, K. (1986). *Being Sexual and Celibate*. Notre Dame, Indiana, Ave Maria Press.

Coate, M. A. (1989). *Clergy Stress: the hidden conflicts of ministry*. London, SPCK.

Code of Canon Law (1983). London, Collins.

Cornwell, J. (1995). *The Sunday Times Magazine*, 17 September.

Cornwell, J. (2001). *Breaking Faith: the Pope, the people and the state of Catholicism*. London, Penguin Viking.

Cozzens, D. B. (2000). *The Changing Face of the Priesthood*. Collegeville, Minnesota, Liturgical Press.

Davis, C. (1967). *A Question of Conscience*. London, Hodder & Stoughton.

De Jong, J. A. and Donovan, D. C. (1988). Age-related differences in beliefs, attitudes and practices of priests. *Journal for the Scientific Study of Religion*, 27, 128–36.

Denzinger, H. and Schoenmetzer, A. (eds) (1965). *Enchiridion Symbolorum, Definitionum et Declarationum Rebus Fidei et Morum*, Editio 33. Freiburg, Herder.

Dolan, N. (1987). The relationship between burnout and job satisfaction in nurses. *Journal of Advanced Nursing*, 12, 3–12.

Dominian, J. (1991). A Kinsey report on the priesthood. *The Tablet*, 19 January, 69–70.

Dowell, S. and Williams, J. (1994). *Bread, Wine and Women: the ordination debate in the Church of England*. London, Virago Press.

Drewett, A. L. (1966). The social status of the ordained minister in the nineteenth and twentieth centuries. *Modern Churchman*, 9, 127–34.

Dubi, L. A. (1993). Recovering alcoholic. In T. Unsworth (ed.), *The Last Priests in America*, pp. 60–7. New York, Crossroad.

Duffy, E. (1997). Papal authority. *Priest and People*, 2, 301–5.

Dugmore, C. W. (1986). Canonical hours. In J.G. Davies (ed.), *A New Dictionary of Liturgy and Worship*, pp. 140–7, London, SCM.

Dulles, A. (2000). *The Craft of Theology: from symbol to system*. New York, Crossroad.

Dunn, J. (1996). *No Vipers in the Vatican*. Blackrock, County Dublin, Columba.

Dyson, A. (1985). Clericalism, church and laity. In P. Roger (ed.), *All are Called*, pp. 13–17. London, CIO Publishing.

Ellis, J. T. (1993). Church historian. In T. Unsworth (ed.), *The Last Priests in America*, pp. 81–7. New York, Crossroad.

Fichter, J. H. (1961). *Religion as an Occupation: a study in the sociology of professions*. Notre Dame, Indiana, University of Notre Dame Press.

Fichter, J. H. (1965). *Priest and People*. New York, Sheed & Ward.

Bibliography

Fichter, J. H. (1968). *America's Forgotten Priests: what they are saying.* New York, Harper and Row.

Fichter, J. H. (1982). *The Rehabilitation of Clergy Alcoholics: ardent spirits subdued.* New York, Human Sciences Press.

Fichter, J. H. (1985). The dilemma of priest retirement. *Journal for the Scientific Study of Religion,* 24, 101–4.

Fichter, J. H. (1987). Life-style and health status of American Catholic priests. *Social Compass,* 34, 539–48.

Fox, T. C. (1995). *Sexuality and Catholicism.* New York, George Braziller.

Francis, L. J. (2002). Personality theory and empirical theology. *Journal of Empirical Theology* (in press).

Francis, L. J., Jones, S. H., Jackson, C. J. and Robbins, M. (2001). The feminine personality profile of male Anglican clergy in Britain and Ireland: a study employing the Eysenck Personality Profiler. *Review of Religious Research,* 43, 14–23.

Francis, L. J. and Kay, W. K. (1995). *Teenage Religion and Values.* Leominster, Gracewing.

Francis, L. J. and Lankshear, D. W. (1994). Survey response rate as a function of age: a study among clergy. *Psychological Reports,* 75, 1569–70.

Francis, L. J. and Louden, S. H. (2000). Mystical orientation and psychological type: a study among student and adult churchgoers. *Transpersonal Psychological Review,* 4 (1), 36–42.

Francis, L. J. and Louden, S. H. (2001). Parish ministry and Roman Catholic regular clergy: applying Eysenck's dimensional model of personality. *International Journal of Practical Theology,* 5, 216–26.

Francis, L. J., Louden, S. H., Robbins, M. and Rutledge, C. F. J. (2000). Unmasking the clerical persona: interpreting the correlation between neuroticism and lie scale scores among Roman Catholic and male and female Anglican clergy. *Mental Health Religion and Culture,* 3, 133–41.

Francis, L. J., Louden, S. H. and Rutledge, C. F. J. (2003). Burnout among Roman Catholic parochial clergy in England and Wales: myth or reality? (in press).

Francis, L. J. and Robbins, M. (1999). *The Long Diaconate: 1987–1994.* Leominster, Gracewing.

Francis, L. J. and Rutledge, C. F. J. (2000). Are rural clergy in the Church of England under greater stress? a study in empirical theology. *Research in the Social Scientific Study of Religion,* 11, 173–91.

Francis, L. J. and Thomas, T. H. (1996a). Are Anglo Catholic priests more feminine? a study among male Anglican clergy. *Pastoral Sciences,* 15, 15–22.

Francis, L. J. and Thomas, T. H. (1996b). Mystical orientation and personality among Anglican clergy. *Pastoral Psychology,* 45, 99–105.

Francis, L. J. and Thomas, T. H. (1997). Are charismatic ministers less stable? a study among male Anglican clergy. *Review of Religious Research,* 39, 61–9.

Francis, L. J. and Turton, D. (2002). Are charismatic clergy more satisfied with their ministry? a study among male parochial clergy in the Church of England. *Mental Health, Religion and Culture,* 5, 135–42.

Freudenberger, H. J. and Richelson, G. (1980). *Burnout: the high cost of high achievement.* Garden City, New York, Doubleday.

Gannon, T. M. (1979). The impact of structural differences on the Catholic clergy. *Journal for the Scientific Study of Religion,* 18, 350–62.

Gentry, W. D., Foster, S. B. and Froehling, S. (1972). Psychological response to situational stress in intensive and non-intensive nursing. *Heart and Lung,* 1, 793–6.

Gillis, C. (1999). *Roman Catholicism in America.* New York, Columbia University Press.

Goffman, E. (1990). *The Presentation of Self in Everyday Life.* Harmondsworth, Penguin.

Goldner, F. H., Ference, T. P. and Ritti, R. R. (1973). Priests and laity: a profession in transition. *Sociological Review Monograph,* 20, 119–37.

Greeley, A. M. (1972). *The Catholic Priest in the United States: sociological investigations.* Washington, DC, United States Catholic Conference.

Gross, P. R. (1989). Stress and burnout in ministry: a multivariate approach. *Lutheran Theological Journal*, 23, 27–31.

Gulledge, J. K. (1992). Gerontological knowledge among clergy: implications for seminary training. *Educational Gerontology*, 18, 637–44.

Hall, D. T. and Schneider, B. (1973). *Organisational Climates and Careers: the work lives of priests*. New York, Seminar Press.

Halsey, A. H. (1989). *Change in British Society*, 3rd edn. Oxford, Oxford University Press.

Häring, B. (1969). Magisterium and natural law. *American Journal of Jurisprudence*, 14, 95.

Häring, B. (1996). *Priesthood Imperiled: a critical examination of ministry in the Catholic Church*. Liguori, Missouri, Triumph Books.

Harper, C. L. and Schulte-Murray, R. K. (1998). Religion and the sociology of culture: exploring the organisational cultures of two Midwestern Roman Catholic dioceses. *Review of Religious Research*, 40, 101–19.

Hart, A. (1984). *Coping with Depression in the Ministry and other Helping Professions*. New York, Word Press.

Hastings, A. (1990). *The Theology of a Protestant Catholic*. London, SCM Press.

Hathaway, S. R. and McKinley, J. C. (1967). *The Minnesota Multiphasic Personality Inventory Manual*. New York, Psychological Corporation.

Hebblethwaite, P. (1975). *The Runaway Church*. London, Collins.

Hellwig, M. K. (1970). *What are the Theologians Saying?* Dayton, Ohio, Pflaum/Standard.

Hellwig, M. K. (1992). *What are the Theologians Saying Now?* Dublin, Gill & Macmillan.

Hemrick, E. F. and Hoge, D. R. (1985). *Seminarians in Theology: a national profile*. Washington, DC, United States Catholic Conference.

Hemrick, E. F. and Hoge, D. R. (1991). *A Survey of Priests Ordained Five to Nine Years*. Washington, DC, National Catholic Educational Association.

Hill, E. (1997). What does the New Testament say? *Priests and People*, 2, 311–15.

Hobfoll, S. E. and Freedy, J. (1993). Conservation of resources: general stress theory applied to burnout. In W. B. Schaufeli, C. Maslach and T. Marek (eds), *Professional Burnout: recent developments in Theory and Research*, pp. 115–29, London, Taylor and Francis.

Hoge, D. R. (1987). *Future of Catholic Leadership: responses to the priest shortage*. Kansas City, Missouri, Sheed and Ward.

Hoge, D. R., Shields, J. J. and Griffin, D. L. (1995). Changes in satisfaction and institutional attitudes of Catholic priests, 1970–1993. *Sociology of Religion*, 56, 195–213.

Hoge, D. R., Shields, J. J. and Soroka, S. (1993). Sources of stress experienced by Catholic priests. *Review of Religious Research*, 35, 3–18.

Hoge, D. R., Shields, J. J. and Verdieck, M. J. (1988). Changing age distribution and theological attitudes of Catholic priests, 1970–1985. *Sociological Analysis*, 49, 264–80.

Holsworth, T. E. (1984). Type preferences among Roman Catholic seminarians. *Journal of Psychological Type*, 8, 33–5.

House of Bishops of the Church of England (2001). *The Eucharist: sacrament of unity*. London, Church House Publishing.

Hovda, R. (1985). Money or gifts for the poor and the church, the amen corner. *Worship*, 59 (1), 70–1.

Hull, J. M. (1985). *What Prevents Christian Adults from Learning?* London, SCM Press.

Huntington, M. J. (1957). The development of a professional self-image. In R. K. Merton (ed.), *The Student Physician*, pp. 179–87. Cambridge, Massachusetts, Harvard University Press.

Hussey, M. E. (1999). The priesthood after the Council. In K. S. Smith (ed.), *Priesthood in the Modern World*, pp. 19–28, Franklin, Wisconsin, Sheed and Ward.

Jansen, D. G., Bonk, E. C. and Garvey, F. J. (1973). MMPI characteristics of clergymen in counselling training and their relationship to supervisors' and peers' ratings of counselling effectiveness. *Psychological Reports*, 33, 695–8.

Jarvis, P. (1975). The Ministry: occupation, profession or status? *The Expository Times*, 86, 264–7.

Jean, G. and Peterson, M. R. (1988). Comparing religious, diocesan alcoholic priests. *The Priest*, May, 2–5.

Jeffries, V. and Tygart, C. E. (1974). The influence of theology, denomination, and values upon the positions of clergy on social issues. *Journal for the Scientific Study of Religion*, 13, 309–24.

John Paul II (1989). *Christifideles Laici*. In *Acta Apostolicae Sedis*, 81, 472–6.

John Paul II (1995). *Ut Unum Sint*. London, Catholic Truth Society.

Jones, S. H. and Francis, L. J. (1997). The fate of the Welsh clergy: an attitude survey among male clerics in the Church in Wales. *Contemporary Wales*, 10, 182–99.

Jones, S. H. and Francis, L. J. (2002). The relationship between religion and anxiety: a study among Anglican clergymen and women. *Journal of Psychology and Theology* (in press).

Jud, G. J., Mills, E. W. and Burch, G. W. (1970). *Ex-pastors: why men leave the parish ministry*. Philadelphia, Pennsylvania, Pilgrim Press.

Kay, W. K. (2000). *Pentecostals in Britain*. Carlisle, Paternoster.

Kay, W. K. and Francis, L. J. (1996). *Drift from the Churches: attitudes towards Christianity during childhood and adolescence*. Cardiff, University of Wales Press.

Keddy, P. J., Erdberg, P. and Sammon, S. D. (1990). The psychological assessment of Catholic clergy and religious referred for residential treatment. *Pastoral Psychology*, 38, 147–59.

Keehan, T. M. (1993). Young priest, old Church. In T. Unsworth (ed.), *The Last Priests in America*, pp. 151–5, New York, Crossroad.

Keillor, G. (1986). *Lake Wobegon Days*. London, Faber & Faber.

Kenneally, W. G. (1993). Valuing the things that really matter. In T. Unsworth (ed.), *The Last Priests in America*, pp. 156–60, New York, Crossroad.

Kennedy, E. C. and Heckler, V. J. (1972). *The Catholic Priest in the United States: psychological investigations*. Washington, DC, United States Catholic Conference.

Klimoski, V. (1999). The priest as parish leader: a contextual analysis. In K. Schuth (ed.), *Seminaries, Theologates and the Future of Church Ministry*, pp. 35–53, Collegeville, Minnesota, The Liturgical Press.

Knights, P. and Murray, A. (2002). *Evangelisation in England and Wales: a report to the Catholic bishops*. London, Catholic Communication Services.

Küng, H. (1972). *Why Priests? a proposal for a new church ministry*. Garden City, New York, Doubleday.

Küng, H. (1978). *On Being a Christian*. Glasgow, Collins, Fount Paperback.

Laishley, F. J. (1991). Unfinished business. In A. Hastings (ed.), *Modern Catholicism: Vatican II and after*, pp. 215–29, London, SPCK.

Lane, D. A. (ed.) (1997). *Reading the Signs of the Times: a survey of priests in Dublin*. Dublin, Veritas.

Lauer, R. H. (1973). Occupational punishment: punitive relations in a voluntary association: a minister in a Protestant church. *Human Relations*, 26, 189–202.

Lawler, M. G. (1990). *A Theology of Ministry*. Kansas City, Missouri, Sheed and Ward.

Lazarus, R. S. and Folkman, S. (1984). *Stress, Appraisal, and Coping*. New York, Springer.

Lee, J. L. (1971). Seminary persisters and leavers. *Counseling and Values*, 16, 39–45.

Leiter, M. P. (1993). Burnout as a developmental process: consideration of models. In W. B. Schaufeli, C. Maslach, and T. Marek (eds), *Professional Burnout: recent developments in theory and research*, pp. 237–50, London, Taylor and Francis.

Lewis, C. S. (1955). *Mere Christianity*. London, Collins, Fontana.

Lief, H. I. and Fox, R. C. (1963). Training for 'detached concern' in medical students. In H. I. Lief and N. R. Lief (eds), *The psychological basis of medical practice*, pp. 12–35, New York, Harper and Row.

Likert, R. (1932). A technique for the measurement of attitudes. *Archives of Psychology*, 140, 1–55.

Longley, C. (2000). *The Worlock Archive*. London, Geoffrey Chapman.

Louden, S. H. and Francis, L. J. (1999). The personality profile of Roman Catholic parochial secular priests in England and Wales. *Review of Religious Research*, 41, 65–79.

Bibliography

Louden, S. H. and Francis, L. J. (2001). Are priests in England and Wales attracted to the charismatic movement emotionally less stable? *British Journal of Theological Education*, 11, 65–76.

Lynch, J. R. (1993). Seminary prof, psychologist. In T. Unsworth (ed.), *The Last Priests in America*, pp. 190–4, New York, Crossroad.

McBrien, R. P. (1987). Homosexuality and the priesthood. *Commonweal*, 114, 380–3.

McBrien, R. P. (1993). Theologian sans ivory tower. In T. Unsworth (ed.). *The Last Priests in America*, pp. 195–201, New York, Crossroad.

McCall, G. J. and Simmons, J. L. (1966). *Identities and Interactions*. New York, Free Press.

McCarthy, T. G. (1998). *The Catholic Tradition: the church in the twentieth century*. Chicago, Illinois, Loyola Press.

McGrath, J. E. (1976). Stress and behaviour in organizations. In M. Dunnette (ed.), *Handbook of Industrial and Organizational Psychology*, pp. 1351–95, Chicago, Illinois, Rand McNally.

McLaughlin, V. (1998). *A Priestless People? A new vision for the Catholic priesthood*. Norwich, Canterbury Press.

Mannix, J. (2000). Lay Formation Study: report commissioned by the Queen's authority and governance project. Birmingham, Queen's College Research Centre.

Mascall, E. L. (1984). *Theology and the Gospel of Christ: an essay in reorientation*, 2nd edn. London, SPCK.

Maslach, C. (1982). *Burnout: the cost of caring*. Englewood Cliffs, New Jersey, Prentice-Hall.

Maslach, C. (1993). Burnout: a multidimensional perspective. In W. B. Schaufeli, C. Maslach and T. Marek (eds), *Professional Burnout: recent developments in theory and research*, pp. 19–32, London, Taylor and Francis.

Maslach, C. and Jackson, S. E. (1981). *The Maslach Burnout Inventory: research edition*. Palo Alto, California, Consulting Psychologists Press.

Mason, K. (1998). *Mothers in God: a Catholic perspective on women as bishops*. Edinburgh Movement for Whole Ministry, Occasional Publications, 10.

Merton, R. K. (ed.) (1957). *The Student Physician*. Cambridge, Massachusetts, Harvard University Press.

Mills, E. W. and Koval, J. P. (1971). *Stress in Ministry*. Washington, DC, Ministry Studies Board.

Murray, J. B. and Connolly, F. (1966). Follow-up of personality scores of seminarians: seven years later. *Catholic Psychological Record*, 4, 10–19.

Musson, D. J. (2001). Male and female Anglican clergy: gender reversal on the 16PF5? *Review of Religious Research*, 43, 175–83.

Musson, D. J. (2002). Personality of male Anglican clergy in England: revisited using the 16PF5. *Mental Health, Religion and Culture*, 5, 195–206.

Musson, D. J. and Francis, L. J. (2002). A comparison of the psychometric properties of the 16PF4 and 16PF5 among male Anglican clergy. *Pastoral Psychology*, 50, 281–9.

Myers, I. B. and McCaulley, M. H. (1985). *Manual: a guide to the development and use of the Myers-Briggs Type Indicator*. Palo Alto, California, Consulting Psychologists Press.

National Conference of Catholic Bishops (1985). *The Health of American Catholic Priests*. Washington, DC, United States Catholic Conference.

Nesbitt, P. D. (1997). *Feminization of the Clergy in America: occupational and organizational perspectives*. New York, Oxford University Press.

Noworol, C., Zarczynski, Z., Fafrowicz, M. and Marek, T. (1993). Impact of professional burnout on creativity and innovation. In W. B. Schaufeli, C. Maslach and T. Marek (eds), *Professional Burnout*, pp. 163–75, London, Taylor and Francis.

Office of Population Censuses and Surveys (1980). *Classification of Occupations 1980*. London, Her Majesty's Stationery Office.

O'Keefe, M. (1990). *What are They Saying about Social Sin?* Mahwah, New Jersey, Paulist Press.

Otto, R. (1923). *The Idea of the Holy (Das Heilige)*. New York, Oxford University Press.

Philpot, A. (1998). *Priesthood in Reality*. Buxhall, Kevin Mayhew.

Bibliography

Pines, A. M. (1993a). Burnout: an existential perspective. In W. B. Schaufeli, C. Maslach and T. Marek (eds), *Professional Burnout: recent developments in theory and research*, pp. 33–51. London, Taylor and Francis.

Pines, A. M. (1993b). Burnout. In L. Goldberger and S. Breznitz (eds), *Handbook of Stress: theoretical and clinical aspects*, pp. 386–402. New York, The Free Press.

Pines, A. M. and Caspi, A. (1993). Burnout in organizational consultation. In R. Golembiewski (ed.), *Handbook of Organizational Consultation*, pp. 615–19. New York, Marcel Dekker.

Plante, T. G., Manuel, G. and Tandez, J. (1996). Personality characteristics of successful applicants to the priesthood. *Pastoral Psychology*, 45, 29–40.

Ranson, S., Bryman, A. and Hinings, B. (1977). *Clergy, Ministers and Priests*. London, Routledge and Kegan Paul.

Rausch, T. P. (1982). The image of Mary: a Catholic response. *America*, 146, 231–4.

Robbins, M. (1998). A different voice: a different view. *Review of Religious Research*, 40, 75–80.

Robbins, M. (2001). Clergywomen in the Church of England and the gender inclusive language debate. *Review of Religious Research*, 42, 405–14.

Robbins, M., Francis, L. J., Haley, J. M. and Kay, W. K. (2001). The personality characteristics of Methodist ministers: feminine men and masculine women? *Journal for the Scientific Study of Religion*, 40, 123–8.

Robinson, E. (1987). *The Language of Mystery*. London, SCM Press.

Rossetti, S. J. (1997). The effects of priest-perpetration of child sexual abuse on the trust of Catholics in priesthood, Church and God. *Journal of Psychology and Christianity*, 16, 197–209.

Rovers, M. W. (1995). Personal authority in Roman Catholic seminarians in Canada: a national survey. Unpublished PhD dissertation, Department of Educational Psychology, University of Alberta, Edmonton, Alberta.

Royce, J. E. (1987). Alcohol and other drugs in spiritual formation. *Studies in Formative Spirituality*, 8, 211–22.

Ryan, P. (1993). Alcohol programs for Catholic clergy in Florida. *Journal of Alcohol and Drug Education*, 38, 41–9.

Schaufeli, W. B. and Van Dierendonck, D. (1993). The construct validity of two burnout measures. *Journal of Organisational Behaviour*, 14, 631–47.

Schillebeeckx, E. (1981). *Ministry: leadership in the community of Jesus Christ*. New York, Crossroad.

Schillebeeckx, E. (1985). *The Church with a Human Face*. London, SCM Press.

Schoenherr, R. A. and Greeley, A. M. (1974). Role commitment processes and the American Catholic priesthood. *American Sociological Review*, 39, 407–26.

Schoenherr, R. A. and Young, L. A. (1993). *Full Pews and Empty Altars: demographics of the priest shortage in United States dioceses*. Madison, Wisconsin, University of Wisconsin Press.

Schuth, K. (1999). *Seminaries, Theologates, and the Future of Church Ministry*. Collegeville, Minnesota, The Liturgical Press.

Scordato, A. J. (1975). A comparison of interest, personality and biographical characteristics of seminary persisters and non-persisters from St Pius X preparatory seminary. Unpublished PhD dissertation, Department of Guidance and Counselor Education.

Seidler, J. (1979). Priest resignations in a lazy monopoly. *American Sociological Review*, 44, 763–83.

Sipe, R. A. W. (1990). *A Secret World: sexuality and a search for celibacy*. New York, Brunner/Masel.

Sipe, R. A. W. (1992). A House built on sand. *The Tablet*, 12 September, 1118.

Smith, D. M. (1993). Why are so few entering priesthood or male religious life? Paper presented to the Bishops' Conference of England and Wales, Low Week 1994 Meeting.

Smith, M. J. (1996). The priest's life: a survey of training and other factors contributing to the well-being of Catholic priests. Unpublished MPhil dissertation, University of Birmingham.

Smith, W. L. (2000). Contemporary Irish priests in America. *Research in the Social Scientific Study of Religion*, 11, 193–207.

Sorensen, A. A. (1976). *Alcoholic priests: a sociological study*. New York, Seabury.

Stecher, R. (1997). Challenge to the church. *The Tablet*, 20–27 December, 1668.

Stewart, J. H. (1969). The changing role of the Catholic priest and his ministry in an inner city context: a study in role change. *Sociological Analysis*, 30, 81–90.

Struzzo, J. A. (1970). Professionalism and the resolution of authority conflicts among the Catholic clergy. *Sociological Analysis*, 31, 92–106.

Swenson, D. (1998). Religious differences between married and celibate clergy: does celibacy make a difference? *Sociology of Religion*, 59, 37–43.

Tapia, M. del Carmen (1998). *Beyond the threshold: a life in Opus Dei*. New York, Continuum.

Tauer, C. A. (1988). The traditional probabilism and the moral status of the early embryo. In P. B. Jung and T. A. Shannon (eds), *Abortion and Catholicism: the American debate*, pp. 54–84. New York, Crossroad.

Torjiesen, K. J. (1993). *When Women were Priests*. New York, Harper San Francisco.

Turton, D. and Francis, L. J. (2002). Assessing ministerial job satisfaction: the reliability of the revised MJSS among male Anglican clergy. *Review of Religious Research* (in press).

Tyrrell, G. (1994). *Medievalism*. Tunbridge Wells, Burns and Oates. (First published by Longmans, Green and Co., London, 1908. This edition, with a foreword by Gabriel Daly, OSA, reprinted from the third impression, with additions, 1909.)

Unsworth, T. (1993). *The Last Priests in America: conversations with remarkable men*. New York, Crossroad.

Ventimiglia, J. C. (1978). Significant others in the professional socialization of Catholic seminarians. *Journal of the Scientific Study of religion*, 17, 43–52.

Verdieck, M. J., Shields, J. J. and Hoge, D. R. (1988). Role commitment processes revisited: American Catholic priests 1970–85. *Journal for the Scientific Study of Religion*, 27, 524–35.

Walker, A. (1983). *The Colour Purple*. London, The Women's Press.

Wallace, R. A. (1993). The social construction of a new leadership role: Catholic women pastors. *Sociology of Religion*, 54, 31–42.

Wilkinson, A. (1978). *The Church of England and the First World War*. London, SPCK.

Wills, G. (2000). *Papal Sin: structures of deceit*. London, Darton, Longman & Todd.

Wilson, R. M. (1974). Persistence and change in the priestly role in relation to role satisfaction: a study of R.C. priests and ex-priests. Unpublished PhD dissertation, New York University, DAI 35: 4267A.

Winter, M. (1985). *What Ever happened to Vatican II?* London, Sheed and Ward.

Wittberg, P. (1993). Job satisfaction among lay, clergy and religious order workers for the Catholic Church: a preliminary investigation. *Review of Religious Research*, 35, 19–33.

Wolf, J. G. (ed.) (1989). *Gay Priests*. New York, HarperCollins.

Wynn, W. (1988). *Keepers of the Keys*. New York, Random House.

Young, L. A. and Schoenherr, R. A. (1992). The changing age distribution and theological attitudes of Catholic priests revisited. *Sociological Analysis*, 53, 73–87.

Zeldin, T. (1994). *An Intimate History of Humanity*. London, Minerva.

Zimbardo, P. G. (1970). The human choice: individuation, reason and order versus deindividuation, impulse, and chaos. In W. J. Arnold and D. Levine (eds), *Nebraska Symposium on Motivation 1969*, pp. 237–307. Lincoln, Nebraska, University of Nebraska Press.

Index of Subjects

227

Index of Names